Christina Pabst

DISCARD

About the Author

DWAYNE RAYMOND worked with Norman Mailer from April 2003 until Mailer's death in November 2007. He provided editorial assistance on Mailer's final four books: *Modest Gifts, The Big Empty, The Castle in the Forest,* and *On God: An Uncommon Conversation.* Raymond contributes regularly to the Huffington Post and has written for *The New York Times Brief Guide to Essential Knowledge, The Mirror, In Newsweekly,* and *The Boston Reader.* He was a writer and producer for the NBC daytime news magazine show *Real Life* and served as associate producer for MTV's *Real World Boston.* He lives in Provincetown, Massachusetts.

MORNINGS
WITH
MAILER

MORNINGS
WITH
MAILER

A Recollection of Friendship

Dwayne Raymond

HARPER PERENNIAL

NEW YORK • LONDON • TORONTO • SYDNEY • NEW DELHI • AUCKLAND

HARPER ● PERENNIAL

HarperCollins books may be purchased for educational, business, or sales promotional use. For information, please write: Special Markets Department, HarperCollins Publishers, 10 East 53rd Street, New York, NY 10022.

FIRST EDITION

Designed by Justin Dodd

Library of Congress Cataloging-in-Publication Data is available upon request.

ISBN 978-0-06-173359-8

10 11 12 13 14   OV/RRD   10 9 8 7 6 5 4 3 2

For my mother, Joann LaVallee . . .
. . . and for Astrid, of course.

CONTENTS

First Sight

As a boy of fourteen in 1977, I sat with my mother in our living room at home in Oregon to watch the Academy Awards. The show was a tradition we looked forward to each year, but this particular broadcast was special. The newspaper had said that my hero, my favorite writer, would appear that evening to present the Best Documentary award. I could narrowly manage my excitement about seeing Lillian Hellman on television for the first time.

Just before Christmas the previous winter I'd borrowed my mother's copy of Hellman's autobiographical book *Penti-*

mento. Upon reading the last line of her opening paragraph—"I wanted to see what was there for me once, what is there for me now"—I was hooked. My mind was too young to grasp the complexity of reflection through the tortures of time, but that was not essential. What *was* relevant was that I had, for the first time, been seduced by words that were at once severe and tenderly measured. By springtime, I was almost obsessed with the woman's writing and I needed to see how she carried herself on television. Did she move her hands when she spoke? Would her voice be as riveting to my ears as her written words were to my eyes? By seeing her, might I better understand why her prose penetrated me so deeply, tormented me like a secret lust? I had pledged loyalty to a writer for the first time.

Then, onto the TV screen walked an unusual looking but finely dressed man with a scrunch of graying hair and electric, all-consuming eyes. In an exceptionally urgent tone, he began to address the millions who were watching, prior to presenting an award for screenwriting, but I had a hard time processing all he was saying. It struck me that he could not *possibly* be as remarkable as he presented himself to be, with his hurried speech and cultured coolness. There is no doubt that I was cynical toward him then, but I couldn't stop watching.

"Who *is* that?" I asked my mother.

"That's Norman Mailer," she said. "He wrote *The Naked and the Dead.* You should read it."

Without a doubt, the name of Norman Mailer's book was stimulating. It excited me while sparking an unexpected embarrassment. The words had sprung without hesitance from my mother's lips: *The NAKED and the DEAD.* That title kicked up a whole host of primitive sensations in me. The words twisted me up and forced me down an avenue of thought more dangerous than the obscure title *Pentimento* ever could.

Lillian Hellman's work captivated me, but held me in an unruffled shelter. Her writing had become like an addiction for me, so this unfamiliar author on the television, and his suggestively titled book, would have to get in line. I remained faithful to Hellman's works for several years after that. Then, after my reading of her was complete, *The Naked and the Dead* arose again. That was the year I graduated from high school.

I heard an utterly scoundrel voice when I read Norman Mailer's war book, a complex novel he'd written at age twenty-five, seven years older than I was when I finally gave it a chance. While reading it, I realized the extent to which involved, fractured prose could also be seductive—and maddening! I didn't finish it until years later, and well after devouring the works of Dashiell Hammett, Ernest Hemingway, Irving Stone, and several others. But *The Naked and the Dead* and the man who wrote it lingered—smoldered, even—in the dark of my mind.

I have no vivid recollection of seeing Lillian Hellman on television that night. Whom I *do* recall clearly is Norman Mailer—the novelist who spoke fast and wrote a tough book. And as decades passed after encountering him that first time, I could not know that I would ultimately develop what can only be described as a paternal affection for the man. Worse, when I did give in to that fondness, I was privately riddled with silly guilt that I had never forgiven him for being so difficult to read in my youth. To me it seemed his book *should* have been easier since he was absurdly young when he wrote it. Rules, however, are not rational when it comes to relationships between writers and their readers. For me to digest that notion would require an unusual course of study—throughout which I would know him finally, and multifariously, as Norman.

ONE

An Agreeable Proposal

I encountered him at dusk, near a heap of bananas. To be precise, however, our first real introduction occurred on a bitter spring night three years earlier in 2000, when I worked as a waiter at a small Cape Cod restaurant called the Commons. Norman Mailer, his wife, and two guests had come in to dine. It was the end of April, the last lingering period of our winter season, a sluggish and difficult time for business in Provincetown, which is mainly a summer destination. The town sits isolated at the tip of the Cape, bordered by beaches that are inviting in temperate months and merciless the remainder of the year. In gray, squally periods the seclusion can be brutal; trophy houses sit vacant, narrow streets are deserted, and the three thousand folks who tough winter out adjust their lives accordingly as the economy dwindles amid shortening days. For those who live and work here, the shift in seasons requires a sturdy disposition. Often residents invent private rules for survival by weighing financial gain against how much work is required to accomplish a task; time becomes precious as the urge to return home to hibernate the winter out takes hold.

The evening Mr. Mailer's party came to eat, the buzz around the waiters' station was that no one wanted any more customers. It had been yet another unprofitable wait shift, and the Mailers might stay well after closing. At best, the table would be worth a twenty for the extra hours. A fellow waiter, Margaret, a small woman with a large mouth, popped off, "Besides, everyone knows Mailer is difficult!"

I had no basis for what to think about Norman Mailer. I knew he lived in town, but I'd never seen him and knew nothing about how he lived. I figured if he was crazy enough to stay here all winter long, he was probably a fairly regular guy. There were the few stories I'd heard about him shopping at the A&P or chatting in line at the post office with townies. That information didn't exactly inspire images of abstract fame or swollen ego that one often attaches to celebrity, but what did I know? Margaret said he was difficult, and since she was more or less a dependable busybody there must be some nugget of truth to it.

As I watched Mr. Mailer plot his way to the table nearest the window with the aid of two canes, it seemed to me that this elderly man with white hair, stout mass, and wide smile could not possibly be a tricky customer. I was impressed by the way he gestured for his wife to sit first and then inquired about the comfort of the others before he took his own seat. Mr. Mailer seemed refined and generous, and his well-mannered disposition was unmistakable.

The memory of seeing him on television when I was a boy came flooding back as I watched from a distance. I could scarcely equate him now to the quick-tongued man who remained as a shadow on my brain. I'd read some of his other works in the years between then and now, and I was inclined to distrust the accounts I'd also read about his supposed antics. I was aware that much of what is written about famous people is often completely made up or an exaggerated version of a cluttered truth. Considering that, I trusted my gut.

I had a tendency to respect writers more than most artists, because I knew, in a small way, how difficult the business was. I'd worked as a writer in several careers by then, scripting copy for a television show and stinting as an assistant managing editor for a small Boston newspaper, to mention two. I admired anybody who wrote for a living (not to mention a solid living). Lastly, I held an express appreciation for Norman Mailer's work. Perhaps chance or enigmatic design had entered the picture, but on the evening Mr. Mailer entered my restaurant, *The Gospel According to the Son* sat three-quarters finished on my bedside table. A friend, a particularly pleasant woman who was not outwardly devout but nonetheless obdurate in her Catholic faith, had loaned it to me. "It touched me," she said when she passed it on. "But I'm not sure I understand it all."

That comment —"I'm not sure I understand it all"—was a familiar remark one encountered when Norman Mailer's books came up for discussion. To be honest, the phrase had tumbled from my own mouth more than once.

Now there he was in front of me, the Author whose work three generations could not always wholly grasp, waiting to be fed. Brash naïveté told me I was up for the challenge. I informed the other waiters that I would take the table and they could start shutting down for the night. After all, how long could the job of caring for Mailer possibly go on?

I approached and introduced myself.

Mr. Mailer looked up at me. A grin that had not left his face since he walked in the doorway now widened to a full smile. Behind his gemstone-blue eyes I saw the grand instrument that was his brain fire to life for the first time.

"Dwayne. You must be from the South," he said. His voice was quick, his tone sharply amusing. It was not so much a question as a declaration. He was positive he had pegged my birthplace merely by geographical association.

On my end, I was ensnared in an awkward position: The author was wrong. I took a moment to answer.

"No," I said tentatively. "I'm actually from the Northwest. Oregon. I've never really been to the South."

That wasn't entirely accurate. I'd been to Florida twice, on disastrous attempts to escape Provincetown's sanity-sucking winters, but those occasions had only reaffirmed my affection for Cape Cod as home. No matter how isolating it could be, I was, at the very least, comfortable with Provincetown's unique wintertime peculiarities. The South's balmy lure seemed false and frivolous to me, and I had resolved to avoid it in the future.

Upon hearing he was off the mark, Mr. Mailer's grin abated slightly but didn't leave his face completely. "So, where does the 'Dwayne' come from?"

Apparently, he required an answer. If his initial conclusion had been wrong, then he needed to know precisely why. This was also my first brush with his ardent thirst for accuracy. I told him my name was my dad's idea. My father wanted to name me for his best friend, but my mother wrote it incorrectly on my birth certificate. This admission that my existence was first noted with a spelling error was a true but pointless comment spawned by a sudden bloat of nerves.

"I was supposed to be a *D-U-A-N-E*." I stammered, "My dad wasn't thrilled about it."

I realized that somehow I'd slipped into an area just shy of incoherent. Although I have never been inclined toward celebrity awe, meeting Norman Mailer was causing a decidedly abject effect. Mr. Mailer was not only one of the world's greatest writers and foremost political thinkers, but also ridiculously famous. The rush of adrenaline triggered by my proximity *to* him, combined with the oddity of being quizzed *by* him, was suddenly at full charge. Surely my befuddlement was painted on my face like a clown's mask. Norris, his stunning wife of twenty-eight years, tossed me a life jacket in the form of reprimand to her husband.

"Oh Norman, just because someone is named 'Dwayne' doesn't mean they *always* have to be from the South," she said, smiling up at me.

Norris Church Mailer *was* from the South, and all of the most favorable traits this suggests sprang elegantly from her through a masterfully applied layer of luxurious New York polish. Mr. Mailer accepted his wife's verbal punch and the reality of my origins. He returned his attention to me and ordered a whiskey sour with extra fruit.

The remainder of the evening went smoothly, and at appropriate times Mr. Mailer and I shared a good deal of conversation. I don't recall everything we discussed, but at one point I mentioned that I wrote.

Perhaps it was bold of me to divulge this to the man who had written forty books and founded *The Village Voice*, but what I had sensed from Mr. Mailer was a desire for truth from whomever he was talking to. Even though I was just a waiter, I was no exception. It didn't matter to him that I'd barely been published—a few articles and some TV news writing. The point was that I cared about my work, and as a result, he did, too. I came to understand over the years that Norman Mailer never took his own rocket blast of success as typical, as some who find great notoriety at the whim of the universe often did. He knew that his achievements were statistically exceptional and he once declared that he felt as if he had, perhaps, "arrived at the bullfight too early." That modest acknowledgment usually kept him from waving the flag of superiority in anyone's face.

Over the following three years, I encountered both Mr. and Mrs. Mailer on occasion. They sometimes ate at whatever restaurant I happened to be working in for a season, or, now and then, I would bump into him at the post office. Several times I met him on the street while he was taking a walk. He was always generous with good words and he never avoided conversation by pretending to be in a rush. As we'd chat, his questions often revolved around what it was like for *me* to live and work in Provincetown now. When he had come to town many decades before, Ptown, as it is affectionately known by many, was an entirely different environment. In his day, it swarmed with artists and mislaid souls who drank with brawny fishermen who wrangled with weekend bikers who roared through town in packs. The result was a population that was up to no good and constantly on the hunt for fun. He made the remark often in interviews that Provincetown was perhaps "the freest town in America." Looking back on our spontaneous discussions, I wonder if possibly he was trying to determine if this was still accurate. As he was elderly now, and spent most of his time in the tranquil East End of town, he was not as familiar with the fabric that made up Ptown as he once had been.

Encountering him was something I looked forward to, as our chats were happy accidents seasoned with significance. I never knew when I'd bump into him, and I never sought him out directly. There was one August evening, however, while riding my bike through his end of town, when I considered stopping to visit him. The sun was setting and the water in the harbor behind the houses along the street was splintered with the unusual blue that sundown in Provincetown generates. I was near his old red brick home and I recall thinking that the house was set perfectly against the shore. Yes, many others lined the beach, but none seemed to have the same magnetism that this one did. The ivy-covered walls of the Mailer house appeared to meld fluidly into the lawn surrounding them. I imagined the house hid old mysteries and the faded echoes of laughing children. Also, it seemed entirely out of place among the other wooden homes on the street because it looked more like a private Victorian library than a house.

For a few moments as I paused on the street I thought about knocking on the door. I believed I knew the Mailers well enough to do it, but I feared the act would appear impetuous. What, exactly, would I say? I got off my bike and sat near a row of boxwoods across the road and spent several minutes debating the idea. I wondered what it must be like to live there, in that big house with all that room. I was not awestruck by the size of the house; I just thought it must be a fine place for a writer to work. I knew from years of practice that good writing did not come easily when you lived in mediocre surroundings.

I did not knock on his door to say hello that night. I skipped the idea and instead pedaled out to Beach Point for a walk on the sand. Taking an evening wade was the easier choice.

Two summers passed, and I tolerated a thousand nights of serving strangers food and as many days of unbalanced direction. I also perfected the act of turning my head from tough decisions. My days established themselves as comfortable, if not tediously unsettled. Then I ran into Norman Mailer one more time, just near a barrel of half-ripe bananas.

I went to the grocery store in the early evening of April 1, 2003. That Tuesday offered yet another freezing spring night, and piles of hard, ugly snow still dotted the town, making it look even more dismal. I had already shopped once that day, and my partner, Thomas, quizzed me about why I needed to go again as I dropped him at our home. "It's starting to snow," he said. "What the hell do we need?"

"I have no idea" I said, "But I'll be back in a while."

We had just returned home from a late afternoon drink at the Little Bar, our regular haunt, complete with an ancient granite fireplace and familiar faces. The Little Bar, as its name suggests, is a small offshoot of a larger establishment, the Atlantic House, which was built in 1798. The watering hole had, throughout the years, etched itself into history as some businesses can. Eugene O'Neill and Tennessee Williams, to name just two long-ago patrons, spent more than a little time there. O'Neill once lived and wrote in a room above it, and Williams was known to drink and hold court among the young men he was half afraid of. As you sit in front of the fireplace after a long workday, you can almost sense his ghost trolling furtively among the men of this new century who gather there. I found the old tavern to be practically a temple because of its peculiar gravitational pull for writers. I knew of several less prominent authors than Williams and O'Neill, and not a few poets and essayists, who used the place, for better or worse, as a church.

The crooked slabs of rough slate that comprise the bar's floor make no distinction about who walks on top of them; affluent or broke, you are bound to stumble after drink three, so you buy your communion of choice and hope for the best. Generally, one's harshest worries are relaxed in the air of the place, air tinged with the odor of evaporated liquor and low-wage sweat.

Black-and-white photographs of former patrons and well-known drinkers who have passed through the place over the years ornament the walls. Several arbitrarily grace one side of the narrow room, and still others are staggered behind the bar—some tacked up, some only taped. A framed picture of Norman Mailer is nailed solidly above the cheap bottles and just to the left of the coffee pot. In the photograph, which was shot by Annie Leibovitz in 1976, he is dressed in a white suit with wide lapels. He's got his right hand nonchalantly buried in his pants pocket, and the look on his face is one of complete possession and charge of his celebrity. I always liked the picture but recognized only a fraction of the image of the much older man in it who ambled with common intentions around our town now. I was not familiar with the supremely confident attitude captured in that moment, which seemed as dated as the clothes he wore.

Thomas had been correct: I didn't have a reason for going shopping again. All I knew was that I felt compelled to go. It made no sense, but one principle I give credit to is never to ignore intuition. I shoved the Volvo gearshift into reverse, backed from our driveway, and headed to the store. The snow increased, and I recall sinking into a state that was not unlike being on autopilot as I drove. Once at the market, I found a basket and roamed the aisles without purpose until I found myself coming to life in the vegetable section. Twenty feet away from me was Mr. Mailer. True to the ways of town and far removed from the swaggering figure in the photograph at the Little Bar, he looked like any other elderly gentleman doing the evening's shopping. He was examining a mountain of bananas in a green plywood bin, considering each cluster as if one would stand out markedly from the others. His glance up to me a few moments later was accompanied by a wave, and so I went over.

"How are you, Mr. Mailer?"

His mismatched canes were hanging from the plastic handle of his shopping cart and he leaned on the edge of the bin with one hand as the other held his carefully chosen bouquet. He placed his bananas into the child's seat of the cart, met my handshake, and said he was fine, just fine.

We exchanged small talk about the bad weather and the Little Bar, where I'd just come from, a place he said he hadn't set foot in since directing his movie *Tough Guys Don't Dance* back in 1986. He then remarked that it was intriguing that we'd run into each other, because I had been the subject of a discussion between him and Norris an hour or so before. Neither of them knew my phone number or recalled my last name, to look me up in the book. I'd long since moved on from the Commons, and the person they had spoken to on the phone there didn't know where I now worked. They were at a loss as to how to get hold of me.

"I'm into a project and I want to talk to you about it," he said. "Are you still writing?"

I told him I was but not as much as I would like. He nodded his head in understanding and then asked if I could make it over to his house the next afternoon at three to talk. As he said this, he shot a glance down into my shopping basket.

When someone peers at your groceries in the market they are, in a way, sneaking a look at a part of your personality you normally keep hidden behind cupboard doors. The recipient can feel exposed to some degree, not unlike how you feel when you discover that your diary has been read. Mr. Mailer's eyes lingered on my basket for what I considered to be a moment too long. I had mushrooms, a bottle of tonic water, some garlic, balsamic vinegar, and a stalk of fennel. He looked back up at me, right in the eye. He always looked you straight on when addressing you, and you rarely felt uncomfortable unless your discomfort was his intent. Then, all of a sudden, his gaze drifted off toward something else, and so did his desire to chat further.

I did not feel so much uncomfortable as I did puzzled. Clearly, his mind had become occupied by another issue. We'd been chatting along just fine until his look landed on my groceries. I assumed I would never know what thoughts went plowing through his head. Surely, they had nothing to do with me or the contents of my basket.

"Yes," he finally said after a second or two of silence, "come by at three. We'll have a good talk then." With that, he said goodbye, smiled, and pushed his shopping cart with his carefully picked bananas and other items gradually toward the checkout line, his canes still dangling from the handle that served as his mobile support.

I left the store and drove aimlessly around town, all the while replaying the meeting in my head. I didn't know what to make of our encounter. I decided to park my car for a while in the West End, near the town boat launch, one of my favorite spots to think. The tide was high and the waves were creeping up the trailer ramp. Even though the night was cold and snowy, I had the window down an inch or two, to better hear the ocean and to taste its spray. Anyone who lives by the sea knows that mist blowing off the water is like Valium to an uneasy mind. I breathed it in. My chance encounter with Mr. Mailer had spawned scores of questions.

The hours I'd spent working as a waiter through the years had driven me to nearly detest their every moment. I had become consumed by a growing dislike of strangers and an even deeper revulsion at taking their food orders. I was weary with pretending to care if they liked their dinner or not. This surprise invitation from Mr. Mailer might, I thought, turn out to be a significant avenue away from it all. Then again, maybe I would end up helping him out with whatever it was he wanted and that would be that. Odds were I would have to continue plopping lobsters in front of tourists with bogus enthusiasm— at least on weekends. After Mr. Mailer was done with me, the project, or both, I'd then likely return to the dull existence of waiting on tables full time. That thought heaved up even more open-ended questions about where my life was going.

I had forgotten most of the reasons I'd moved to Province-town by squandering away the core of them over years of menial jobs taken merely to stay afloat. My idea to settle firmly into the life of a writer had eroded, and the only true bright spot was my relationship with Thomas. Thomas was a sensitive carpenter who brought out the best in me without even trying. He'd come to live with me recently after decades of struggle to find his own center, which often still seemed out of reach and sometimes ambiguous. Overall, we found ease at being together even while navigating our new familiarity. All other aspects of my life were unremark-able and rooted in a daily grind of repetition and fractured aspi-rations. Now, perhaps, a new door was opening; one that offered a revival of my interests and one that would teach me to think again while stilling my downward-spiraling stagnancy.

I returned home to tell Thomas about my encounter; he was usually the patient sounding board for my mental meanderings. He was slightly unclear as to exactly who Norman Mailer was, although he was familiar with the name and knew that he lived in Provincetown. Thomas and I were both children of the sev-enties, and as with almost everyone who came of age in America in that period, the name Norman Mailer was as recognizable to us as the term *Watergate* or the music of Pink Floyd. I repeated what I knew about *The Naked and the Dead*, *The Executioner's Song*, the countless *Playboy* articles, and the Marilyn Monroe connec-tion Mailer was weirdly famous for.

"So let me get this right. He's famous for a book he wrote about World War Two, another about a murderer, and he's con-nected somehow to Marilyn Monroe?" Thomas asked.

"Yes."

"So what does he want to talk to *you* about?"

"He mentioned a project," I said. "Other than that, I honestly have no clue."

The next day at two thirty I started my walk to Norman Mailer's house through yet another light snowfall. Commercial Street is the name of the main road that cuts a twenty-two-foot-wide swath through Provincetown. It is buffered from the beach by close-set old wooden homes, some sparkling, some ramshackle. It is the street on which both Mr. Mailer and I lived—albeit at opposite ends. It twists and turns at the whim of the shoreline, and the gaps between the houses allow the wind to cut through to assault passersby at irregular intervals. My walk was not a very long one, but it was a very cold one, as this April day was more obedient to the callous normalcy of February.

When I was four blocks away from Mr. Mailer's house, I ducked into a restaurant to have coffee. I needed it to warm myself and quell my nerves. A well of apprehension had opened and begun to churn my insides over the previous ten hours, and with that jumble, my self-esteem plunged. I needed this break to relocate some balance. I considered ordering a stiff drink instead of coffee, but I knew that would be an altogether unintelligent decision. I was certain that this was not the time to bow to bottled bravery, no matter how happy the thought. I stuck to caffeine.

When I finally made it to the large three-story brick house I rang the bell with a small but lingering hesitance. I didn't know what I was facing or the direction our talk would go, but I intuitively knew that whatever happened in this next hour would involve a shift to my life. Then again, there was the considerable chance that there would be no budge, no racket of change, and I would move on, left with only an anecdote to offer up to enliven future dull conversations.

A minute passed before he opened the door. That delay picked at my anxiety even more, until I reasoned that it was likely a struggle for Mr. Mailer to answer the door at *any* speed—if indeed he even answered his own door. Finally, it swung wide open to reveal him wearing what I would come to know as the first of two uniforms: khaki pants and a denim blue work shirt. He invited me in.

"Hello, Mr. Mailer," I said.

"You should call me Norman," he declared as he closed the door. I always did after that.

He led me into the living room, where Norris was sitting in one of two large wicker chairs on the far side of the room. She was dressed warmly in what appeared to be a heavy robe and looked more tired than I had ever seen her before. She managed to muster a smile for me, however, and her beauty radiated. I knew she had endured some tough medical difficulties, and I was unsure about what to say or how to react now that I was in the same room with her. Her eighty-two-year-old mother, Mrs. Davis, had come to stay with them, and she was seated near her daughter.

Their white chairs were positioned at a slight angle just in front of two large picture windows that reached from floor to ceiling and nearly wall to wall. Through them, behind the women, Provincetown Harbor was splayed out like I'd never seen it from another home in town. Many people had nice views of the harbor from their living rooms—I'd been in many with windows facing the water—but this was the first time I'd seen a view that was so startlingly frank. Clearly, the ocean was the central draw.

Norris Mailer had inherited the most valuable of her mother's features. She had modeled in the years after moving to New York to be with Norman and had continued with that career on and off well into her mid-forties. Her brown eyes flecked with grains of hazel struck me as intelligent. Her complexion, even in the midst of her difficult health struggles, was the most captivating element of her beauty; it spoke of porcelain and cream and fine Khmer silk. I noticed that her red hair was being tenderly and faultlessly stroked by the afternoon's dimming rays. I bent to offer Norris a gentle hug at her urging. I hadn't seen her in nearly half a year, and the rough months between then and now were evident, though the hard days had not chipped away at her beauty.

In the years since that first meeting at the restaurant, Norris and I had met each other several times socially. In Provincetown—in winter, particularly—the term *socially* can mean anything from sharing a drink at a cocktail party to bumping into somebody at the hardware store.

Now we exchanged a few words to catch up, and she introduced me to her mother, Gaynell. I shook the elderly woman's hand and was reminded of my grandmother's hands as she would walk me through my father's gardens when I was six: strong but swathed in fragile paper lace. Gaynell said a gracious "Hello" with an inflection that placed her clearly from the heart of Arkansas, and I was instantly taken in by her Southern way. Norman, witnessing all of this stone-faced, turned and walked toward the dining room without speaking. His single cane—he always used only one while in the house—clunked on the shiny hardwood floor as he left me with the women. A moment later he urged me to join him with a controlled call. He had already taken his seat.

Norman always sat at the side of the table because it did not face the bay window that capped the south-facing room. The dining room window, with its sprawling ledge, was only one quarter the size of the ones in the living room, but it offered the same extensive panorama of our harbor and Long Point, the final curling finger of Cape Cod. He told me his eyes had become sensitive to sunlight in recent years and logic dictated he sit facing the wall.

"Except for dinner. I sit there at dinner," he said, nodding his head toward my chair, at the head of the long table, just to his left.

Norman brought our talk right to the point. His purpose in asking me over was that he wanted me to assist him with research on a "project." Again, that word. I figured the "project" he was talking about must be a book. Considering the largeness of that, I was intimidated, intrigued, and petrified all at once. What the hell, I wondered, could I possibly do to assist Norman Mailer on a book? I did my best to conceal the curiosities that were holding a boxing match in my stomach from climbing to my face.

He soon answered my questions. My tasks would vary from light "secretarial" work—Xeroxing pages from books he'd read and keeping them in good order and sorting through his mail—to more demanding things. He said he would ask me to familiarize myself with a host of assorted subjects in order to be closer to the track of his work. "Later," he said, "I'll tell you more about what I could be needing."

Then he brought up the prospect that I could perhaps assist him in other areas. He mentioned the *possibility* of driving him to appointments, *conceivably* making travel plans, and, "You never know, *maybe* speaking to reporters." Again, he listed no rigid specifics.

"Oh, about the appointments. You do drive, don't you?" he asked.

"I have a crappy old Volvo," I said. "Yes."

"And I'm correct that you've done a fair amount of research work in the past? You said you worked at a newspaper, didn't you?"

"Until it went out of business," I said. "Then I got a job working in television. As far as I know, they're still in business."

"Too bad," he said. "Of the two, I would have hoped for a different outcome."

I would, in later days of course, hear many rants from him about his loathing of television. It first struck me as outlandish, since I knew that Norman was among the first writers in America to meticulously exploit the medium to elevate his status to the level of Literary Rock Star. Truman Capote and Gore Vidal had used TV also, but Norman Mailer perfected the game. I came to appreciate his altered opinion over time, though. Television, he said, had atrophied into a series of vile interruptions to the "maturity of concentration." Corporate broadcasts eviscerated the minds of children and adults even as they alleged to inform or entertain. In Norman's view, television's principal god was commerce, hence its rabid selling of soap or cars every nine minutes with false promises rhymed in soulless drivel. Like every cultural element he commented on, he had studied television methodically before coming to his conclusion. In 2006, when we were researching a piece for *Parade* magazine concerning children and education, he told me about a stretch of months many years before when he was at a crossroads in his own life. During that period, he devoured television, absorbing all it had to offer. "The only valuable knowledge I brought from that experience was that I learned I should have shut it off sooner," he told me.

"So, does this proposal sound like something that might be agreeable to you?" he asked, despite my confession about working for the tube.

If this was an interview, it was unlike any other I had experienced. No one had ever asked me if the potentials of a job were "agreeable."

Nonetheless, while assessing Norman's calm enthusiasm as he listed the possibilities, there appeared to be no doubt in his mind that I would be "agreeable" without reservation. He seemed confident that I would want to assist him with the "project" and, apparently, any number of other things. He went on to inform me in a surprisingly temperate manner that as his writing progressed, I would be "of great use" to him.

"You may find yourself with lots of reading to do, a good amount of filing to take care of, certain errands in need of attention, and sometimes getting my desk back in order. I can be terrible about doing it myself. Your responsibilities could be varied," he said.

Sitting in front of him, listening to him recite this laundry list of potential duties, the main character of Herman Melville's tale *Bartleby the Scrivener* suddenly popped into my mind. Bartleby, who after being hired by a man of distinction, soon finds himself paralyzed, able to answers his employer's requests only with the simple statement "I would prefer not to." I prayed I wouldn't become similarly ensnared weeks or months down the road.

Further doubts: What if Norman asked me to do things that were far beyond my abilities? The man had two Pulitzers, the National Book Award, and forty books to his name. How the hell would I get myself out of that embarrassing quagmire? Nevertheless, I had to admit I was intrigued at the prospect of working with him on his "project," even if I seemed to be—to myself, at least—less than the ideal candidate for the job. I knew I was far from stupid, but I wasn't exceptionally well educated, either. At the time I was merely a competent waiter with hip-high aspirations living in a community that harbored only a few disciples of ordinary success. I had relocated to Province-town after the age of thirty to avoid all of those normal expectations, finding it easier to simply obstain from the game. One could hunker down in this abnormally tolerant place and spin one's wheels in idyllic limbo without having to prove anything to anyone—including oneself. Nevertheless, I had to admit I was intrigued at the prospect of working with the man who single-handedly elevated, among other things, writing about boxing to the ranks of high art, and who had once sparred with Joe Frazier. When we spoke, Norman knew nothing of the bumpy road that had led me to his dining room table. He wasn't privy to my personal failure to discover worth or reason in past employment. He also didn't know how I'd shunned the usual track to adulthood by bolting from college and squandering myself for months in Europe to "find myself." This deficit was a potentially large problem.

Only after I got close to him did I figure out that Norman had known all along that I was craving consistency. My life to that point had been an experiment in freedom—or that's how I described it—but the truth was I had not found anything to care enough about to allow myself to take root. Somewhere along the way I had crossed the line from being fashionably bohemian to terrified of responsibility. That in itself was not unique, but I had also mastered the ability to fritter away days into forgettable years without deference to growth or accountability. It could be said that the last train of my youth was pulling from the station and I was finally hearing a piercing whistle that sounded a lot like "Maaaiiiilerrrrrrrr." Until then,

I had insulated myself from all alarms with old daydreams and immediate escapism.

When we first sat at his dining room table together, Norman was three months into his eightieth year. The physical evidence of that was that he was stooped slightly and his face was furrowed with the normal allocations of time. His canes had become celebrated accessories, and with them he was anything but swift. Old age, however, was in no way apparent in his vigorous voice or refined thinking. He was stunningly alert and dead-on precise. His years were only noteworthy when he cocked the right side of his head slightly toward you to ask, "What?" He was half deaf, and it would be about a year and a half before he used his hearing aids regularly and without debate. His age was apparent also when he switched glasses from reading to distance, and exhibited bewilderment as to which pair was which if he happened to pause in the act for a moment. In the years to come, I always forgot Norman was eighty years old until he got up to meander to the bathroom at a snail's pace or mistakenly answered the wrong phone line and blamed the mix-up on the device itself. ("If we have two goddamn lines, then why are the rings exactly the same?" They were not, but to his fatigued ears perhaps they did sound similar.)

Norman was gracious toward me on that first meeting, which lasted about an hour, and almost always thereafter. At the end of the conversation we both seemed reasonably content with where we stood. To me, *where we stood* was that I should be open to any number of surprises from then on, and the ambiguity of that seemed curiously comfortable. In Norman's mind we had agreed that I would show up each weekday to help him with whatever he thought needed attention. We'd refine the details as the days went. For him, allowing an association to develop organically meant both parties would "learn on the curve." Despite my reservations and insecurities, I had no choice but to agree with his proposal.

I began to start my goodbye, but before I could stand, he hastily said, "You're fond of cooking, aren't you."

Once again, what he said was not so much a question as a declaration. He was redirecting our conversation and hinting at what would become a principle function of my tenure with him. The recollection of him scoping out my shopping basket the night before returned, and I realized that right there by the banana bin he had recognized that not only could he get a literary assistant but he could also finagle himself a cook. I settled back into my chair.

"Yes, I like to cook very much," I said. While I had never cooked professionally (my work in restaurants had always been limited to the front of the house), I was skilled, and always cooked at home for friends and devoured cookbooks like they were pulp novels. Cooking was a knack I had acquired as a kid and developed a small talent for as an adult. Somehow Norman had sensed this, and he'd set out to lasso it along with my other skills.

"I was hoping that you might consider doing the cooking a few nights a week," he said. "Norris is on the mend, and it would be a great help to all of us around here. As you can imagine, her mother is not much help. Keep in mind this wouldn't be always, just sometimes." There he was, greasing the road. I had to love it.

When he asked me this, I didn't know Norman loved food and thought himself a fine cook (he wasn't, generally). He was inventive when it came to theories about flavors and combinations, and over time I became the ideal collaborator.

I agreed to this latest addition to his proposition not because I sensed that to decline would have been a deal breaker, but because it would have violated the optimistic air of our meeting up to that point. Besides, the large kitchen behind me, with its six-burner stove, dual ovens, and black granite prep island, was a small apartment dweller's dream. I told him I'd be happy to give the cooking a shot.

"I know you're a good cook," he said with a smile. "I was a cook when I was in the army. Remind me to tell you about it sometime." I never did ask him directly to tell me about it, but I heard scraps of the tale countless times over the next five years.

As I finally stood, he swiveled slightly in his straight-backed chair. "Barbara?" he shouted. He always called Norris by her birth name, Barbara, unless he was referring to her in conversation, a habit that also slipped into my ways after years of tenderness between us.

Norris hollered back from the living room: "What?"

"Darling, where are the books?" The books he was asking about were copies of his latest hardcover, *The Spooky Art: Thoughts on Writing*, which had been released earlier that year. Norris said they were in the bar, which was just off the dining room.

Norman asked me to go in there and grab a copy for him. I did, and with a black Pilot pen, he wrote in it and handed it to me. Instead of cracking it open in front of him to read the inscription, I decided to hold on to it to read later. I didn't know if there was a standard etiquette when an author handed you an inscribed copy of his work. I still don't. I suppose it depends if you like the author or like his book. In this case I liked both, but it was the first time a writer had given me a book in person. To be safe, I squirreled it under my arm and timidly said, "Thank you. You know, Matt Lauer recommended this several weeks ago."

"Who?" Norman asked.

So went my introduction to Norman Mailer's selective lack of familiarity with popular culture, and television personalities in particular. I might as well have plucked a random name from the phone book for all the relevance "Lauer" held for Mailer. Norman was so unschooled in the TV viewing habits of America that when I mentioned Jerry Seinfeld's show, after it had been off the air for more than six years, Norman said, "Yes, I know his show. He is not funny. I can't believe it's been on this long."

On the way home I stopped again in the restaurant up the street to have a drink, at long last, and consider the previous hour. I was to begin working with Norman Mailer and had no idea what his book was going to be about or where the journey would end. What I did have was a sense that I'd landed on something resembling solid ground. I saw a potential end to my days of restlessness and realized that this work would demand effort that I had seldom tapped before. I also had the feeling that this association would be one of equal exchange. I would help Norman Mailer with whatever he wanted, and he would in turn clarify some of the large questions we all grapple with and that I did not understand at all. That may sound like a broad assumption, but I instinctively knew that being around him and listening to his words was not the same as being in the company of any other people I'd ever known. Certainly I would learn a great deal from him through the work, but more indefinable lessons would undoubtedly be illuminated simply by being around his astonishing intellect. When you found yourself close to Norman, you had no choice but to be a sponge to his authority and advanced knowledge about issues. I didn't know this conclusively as I left his home that first day, but I held tight to the suspicion. Certainly, I knew, I was entering into an uncommon situation.

I ordered an Irish coffee and opened the book he had signed. Scrawled on the title page in a difficult-to-decipher script were the first ten of the countless words Norman would write to me over the years. Those words would comprise notes, directions, ideas, suggestions, criticisms, subjects to research, vitamins to find out about, doctors to investigate, books to order, and gracious inscriptions within the covers of three of the four books I would assist him on. The inscription read:

To Dwayne
for the kickoff
Cheers
Norman
April, 03

TWO

A Modest Interruption

As the days after our meeting at the dining room table rolled by, an easy routine developed. I relinquished my evening restaurant shifts after a few weeks in order to go over to Norman's house each morning with a fresher head. I would often enter to find him on the phone or deep into a game of solitaire. He played a convoluted version of the game, one that he'd mastered decades before, which involved memory and skill over luck, and it was one of the tools he used to prepare for work. The cards cleared his mind while his other device, the *Boston Globe* crossword, "combed his brain." He rarely attempted the more difficult *New York Times* puzzle, because he was aware that his skills were not committed enough to master it beyond Wednesday or Thursday. (As he taught me, the puzzles become more complex as the week progresses.)

"I have no intention of adjusting myself in order to beat the *Times*," he said. "I sacrifice too much of my day to this as it is.".

After finishing the crossword (and often slyly fixing a few empty blanks from the answer key), he would grab the dog-eared stack of cards that lived in the middle of the table near his vitamins, letter opener, spare pens, notepad, and magnifying glass. Later, after some weeks, I would take his daily mutter of "Okay, just one more game" to signal that he would indulge in at least four more rounds before beginning work. I would fill the time with sorting the mail on the bay window ledge or talking with Norris in her upstairs study. Often an hour would pass before he made his labored ascent to the attic. In the early days, however, Norman would always stop his game as soon as I arrived, to talk with me without distraction.

From the onset he demonstrated a measure of trust toward me that I had never experienced—not from friends or family or certainly previous work relationships. We discussed the offers from any number of magazines that were continually asking him to write articles. A yes or no answer was rarely swayed by money, and he explained his philosophy for that. "In my position it's about weighing the effort required. Money is just money. It's like cabbage," he said. He would ask me what I thought about a proposal and listen politely to my opinion.

Then, he would do exactly what he had already decided, but at least he brought me into the fold of the discussion. It was natural for him to at least talk about options with me, because he knew that any new diversion would impact the work and therefore affect my day.

Although his secretary, Judith McNally, who lived in Brooklyn and had been with him for over twenty-five years, did the bulk of the transcription of his longhand at that time, I did much of the research to corroborate his work. Norman would write a draft, I would fax it to Judith, and she would then email it back typed in fourteen-point font and triple-spaced for easy editing. For the first two weeks I worked with Norman, however, he more or less hid Judith's existence from me. This was not his finest scheme.

Nearly every morning when I arrived, he was on the phone with someone whom he had a tendency to call "Dear." At first I thought nothing of it, but later, when I asked who he was speaking to, he simply said, "Oh, that was Judith," as if I knew who she was or what role she played or that she even *existed*. He left out the little detail that she had been his primary aide for over twenty five years. At the end of the second week, she happened to call while Norman was upstairs working. I picked up the phone in the bar downstairs.

"Oh, good. There you are!" Judith said with a cheerful yet utterly unique voice that sounded like a bag of gravel being dragged across a cracked blackboard during an earthquake. "He said he had a man there. Nice to meet you. Finally."

She then told me how Norman had "mentioned out of the

blue last week" that he'd hired someone to help with "things around the house." He had not elaborated further, and she hadn't pressed him. He had not mentioned me since, she told me. As I had heard her name only once or twice, it never occurred to me to question who she was or what she did. As far as Norman would have me know at that point, I was the only real help he had when it came to the book work or his other endeavors. Immediately after hanging up the phone, I went upstairs to tell him Judith had called. He was sitting at the window by the fax table, not at his desk, and I pulled up a chair.

"What's up?" he asked.

"I just got off the phone with Judith. She said you mentioned me," I said. "What's the deal? I didn't know you had a secretary." I crossed my arms, waiting.

His reticence at my remark was my introduction to his irksome manner of dismissing situations as irrelevant merely because *he* deemed them so. I was ignorant about his system of diversion at that point, and confusion was fixed on my face. When I didn't respond and continued to look bewildered, he then tried to explicate his reasoning for keeping me and Judith relatively separate.

"Listen, Judith is a proud woman, and I don't want her thinking that I'm infringing on her area by having you here," he said. "I never know how she might react to someone new close by. She doesn't suffer fools lightly."

"Well, she seemed pleased I'm here," I said, tentatively accepting his rationale and relaxing.

Judith and I had talked that first day for well over fifteen minutes. I liked her right off, and over time I discovered that she was smarter and tougher than I could ever dream of being. In my determination, she had all the traits of a ruthless union boss combined with those of a cultured charm school matron. Later I learned how she could tell someone with a chill that penetrated the phone that she would feed their remains to a pack of vicious dogs if they did not abide by her rules for engaging with Mr. Mailer. Her nature also dictated that she finish the pledge with ". . . and kindly pass my sincere regrets to your wife and infants from me for having to do this?" From my angle, she was the best possible protector Norman could ever have and certainly someone high on my list to keep on the better side of. As it turned out, I didn't have to work hard at that. Judith and I became friends immediately, and she was the guiding force for me finding my own inner union boss/charm school matron. She and I spoke daily for the next twenty-two months, until her calls abruptly ceased and an unfillable void appeared in our small unit.

Norman was truly open in all areas of our relationship after owning up to Judith. If he was having some conflict in his schedule or if a call came from someone he didn't wish to speak to that had managed to slip past Judith's barrier, he would probe me for options or my opinion. Where many people who have assistants might shield them from certain aspects of their private life, Norman never hid anything personal from me—even when I expressed that my having knowledge of some dealings was not essential. He would discuss money or family struggles in front of me with no reservation whatsoever.

"You don't need to leave the room when I'm on the phone with my agent or the kids or anybody else," he would say. "I'll let you know if I need privacy." In our entire time together there was not one occasion when he asked me to leave him, although I did take it upon myself to scoot out the door when I felt uncomfortable as he offered advice or admonishment to one of his children or to Norris. I realized over time that his notion of complete disclosure was the glue he used to create a bond that I thoroughly respected.

All of my friends knew I was working with Norman Mailer, and naturally they were curious about it. Because there was an unspoken understanding between Norman and me that I would reveal little about our work together, I rarely shared anything with them beyond the rudimentary. I developed a powerful sense of allegiance to Norman. My self-censorship was a point of practicality for me: to disclose details of our work would have been equivalent to deceit in my mind, and therefore an impractical act. Norman recognized that feature in me before I ever did, and depended on it. I began to consider his approach to ethics as a tutorial on how to better navigate the difficulties of my outside life; I began to assess choices for repairing flawed facets of my timorous character.

Norman waited until the second day of our collaboration to take me up to the third floor, where he worked. He had not yet divulged the subject or title of the "project" to me, and I was beginning to wonder if he'd changed his mind about letting me in on it. When he finally asked me to join him upstairs, I was relieved. The route up involved climbing three flights of stairs—two carpeted and the last one wooden, steep, and creaky. Norman accomplished the climb slowly, holding fast to the banister as his single cane methodically thudded its way up with him.

His part of the long attic room spanned two thirds the length of the house. The ceiling was slanted upward from the right side of the wide floor, like the walls of an angular cave. The area where a small table and fax machine stood was dormered out, and its sharp edges seemed to leap at your temples as you passed it. Norman would forever remind me, "Watch your head!" I was six feet tall to his five six, and he was almost comically considerate of that difference. I soon acquired the custom of walking with a pronounced slouch when I was in the attic.

Norris's much smaller studio was up on that third floor also, and one entered it by turning right instead of left and passing through a low doorway that always made me think of the entrance to a child's hideaway—Christopher Robin's den of imagination. That doorway was also ripe for head-banging. All of us, Norman included, dented our foreheads repeatedly while passing in and out of it over the years, until Norris, after knocking herself senseless one day and bellowing out an uncharacteristic "Fuck!" had Thomas make the entrance bigger. "I don't know why I didn't have this done years ago," she said.

Norman's office was filled with bookcases of different sizes and heights, and all of them overflowed. In the center of the room near a high white shelving unit stood a massive weight machine. I don't know whom he had hired to install the gigantic gym in that awkwardly shaped room, but it resided near him like an obedient monster. I was jolted aware many times while quietly working two floors below by the *klunk* of its weights repetitively colliding as he worked the pain from his arthritic knees. His habit was to cease working every two hours or so to exercise his legs—positive that movement staved off inevitable deterioration. As the weights crashed and rose in bursts, the shelves around him shook in sympathy.

He had yet to tell me the subject of his novel as we stood at the top of the stairs and surveyed the room on that April day, but as I moved in I began to note the titles of the books on the shelves and the labels of the file folders. All were marked "Germany" or some derivation thereof, and the name Hitler haunted the room like an impertinent echo. The answer to my question about his book's subject began to announce itself.

"I want to do three volumes," he said as I studied the stacks and rows of books and the hand-scrawled headings on the files. "The job will take about eleven years." He then confirmed what I already suspected: the novel was to be about Adolf Hitler.

Norman's book would be a fictionalized biography of Hitler's childhood. He was looking to define the man who became the twentieth century's symbol of genocide and option his unique explanation as to how such a fiend had spawned from peasant stock. He told me about his omniscient narrator and core character, D.T., an inquisitive, top protégé of *der Teufel*—the Devil.

"I'm calling it *The Castle in the Forest*," he said, with no explanation of the title. "But I will change that, I'm certain."

I thought about his declaration that the work would take eleven years and I tried not to react with the skepticism that would be natural at hearing such a statement from a man who would be ninety-one if he accomplished his goal.

We moved in toward his old wood desk, which sat flush at the end of the room, against three large, cloaked windows. Through breaks in the hangings I could make out slivers of Provincetown and the harbor, which spread far away south and west into the horizon. Our town is rare. We sit far out into the Atlantic at the narrow end of what looks on a map to be a crumpled cornucopia, a twisted horn of plenty that curves up and forlornly out into the ocean. The craggy tip appears to have suffered the worst damage, but in that dilapidated end curl hides the jewel of Cape Cod that is Provincetown. Overseeing the spread of houses of our town and the sea that surrounds it is a 252-foot-tall granite monument erected in 1910 to honor the *Mayflower* Pilgrims. It is imposing and blunt and dominates our skyline like an exclamation mark. Sailors have, for a hundred years, used it to guide their boats safely to our port. From Norman's study that day, the tower looked stoic and the sun sparked up at us, reflected off the bay with abstract abandon.

In better days, the brightness did not interfere with Norman's vision. He told me that when he was writing *Tough Guys Don't Dance* he spent hours gazing out at the view, ruminating about the town that would itself emerge as a central character in that novel. Unfortunately, Norman now had to curtain the splendid view, but he liked knowing the panorama was there.

We stood together in the dim room until he hung his cane on a handle of the workout machine and switched on the brass floor lamp near his chair.

"All these books are for research," he said, indicating the hundreds of volumes that surrounded us. "I'd like you to familiarize yourself with them and everything else in the room. Spend time here as you like, and read whatever you want. I'm just reading these days, myself, and will be for some months. Mainly, you'll be Xeroxing books on the machine back there."

He pointed toward the stairs we'd just climbed, where a copy machine sat nearby on a cabinet—the ceiling just two feet above it. I wondered how I'd fit myself into the nook to work.

"Take a good look at what's been done so far and you'll get an idea of what I'm doing," he said, sitting down at his desk.

What was "done so far" were fifty or sixty manila files heaving with thousands of copied pages. They had been prepared by someone else and indiscriminately stacked together. I was to add to and organize the mess.

"I'm reading Heiden now," he said, as if I knew what or who Heiden was. "I'm just about done with him. When I am, you'll go through the book and copy the pages I've indicated. You'll soon get the hang of it."

I looked down at the book on his desk, the one he was talking about. The page where he'd stopped reading was sloppily folded in half to mark the spot. That day was when I first noticed his habit of not merely bending a small corner, as others might do, but mangling an entire page to make a hefty crack in the book. It was a practice that would forever irritate me and that he never ceased. He swiveled close to his desk in an ancient wooden chair that was padded with two pillows. The chair looked as if it had been kicked down a flight of stairs at least once—and likely had been. He then opened "Heiden" and showed it to me.

The book was Konrad Heiden's *Der Fuehrer,* a dry but scrupulous account of Hitler's life, and it was thick—over seven hundred pages. As he thumbed at it, I could see that nearly every page had marks, notes, and dates scribbled on it. If he wanted me to photocopy everything he'd marked, it would take days! Looking around at the hundreds of other books in the room, I wondered if they also were waiting for me. My glance returned to the Heiden book that was now splayed open on the desk.

Norman's desk was a mess. Three coffee cans were crammed with what appeared to be every kind of pen, pencil, or felt tip marker created (yet he always picked at his shirt pocket to find his favorite Pilot). He rummaged like a madman through the stacks of papers, mail, clippings, notes, three-by-five index cards, pens, quirky knickknacks, two alarm clocks, a dog skull, and bent paper clips on his desk. His legs might have been slow and measured, but his arms moved like wind machines. He pushed aside a heap of a manuscript that was carelessly unclipped. The pages fanned out into a messy spread.

"Have you thought about getting some trays for all those papers?" I asked him.

"Yes, I have, and that's a fine idea," he said. "Why don't you take a drive and see what you can locate. Do they have them here in town do you think?"

It is always a question whether one can find an item reasonably easy in Provincetown. As our town is a long way away from what one could arguably call a normal municipality, his inquiry didn't strike me as odd. I assured Norman I would try.

Half an hour later, at the hardware store, with his credit card stuffed in my back pocket, I stood in front of a stack of trays. Surprisingly, they had three types. I surveyed them all and chose ten black plastic trays because they looked as sturdy as the wooden ones but half the price.

I was slightly aware of Norman's aversion to plastic, but I figured that small detail would pale next to my economical decision. I would surely score high points by purchasing double the goods for half his money. Norman was not as wealthy as many people assumed, and the truth was that 627 Commercial Street was a working man's address. By saving him some cash, I was confident that my choice was the correct one.

I returned to the attic later with two large bags bulging with ten plastic trays. I was ready to get him organized, and I'd begun the process wisely. I stood next to him at the desk, proudly showing him the reasonably priced solid plastic trays. He furrowed his brow and shot me a look as if I'd showed him ten atrocities against humanity.

"Didn't they have any wood ones, for Christ sake?"

My dread of being permanently chained to the Xerox machine became a reality, but I discovered a kind of solace in the monotonous work, because I knew I was performing a valuable service for the author at the opposite end of the room.

Though that notion may sound trite, the truth was that even basic work made me feel as if I were part of something worthwhile, which offered a sense of satisfaction that had not stirred in me for a long time—perhaps ever. Norman worked every day, hours on end, soaking up Hitler's story and constructing his own version. Seeing him accomplish that as I depleted the copy machine of ink taught me what dedication to work meant. Books did not appear out of a mere effortless longing to tell a story, as many people assumed. Writing a novel involves endless study and sacrifice. I began to understand that I was witness to something exceptional. (No one was allowed into the attic. Even his children, although not banned from doing so, rarely climbed to their father's study.)

I was becoming keenly aware of Norman's high standards, and occasionally I would suffer an irrational fear that perhaps I wasn't doing the copy work correctly. He made no remark to that effect, however, and *Herr* Heiden's folder continued to expand, as did my belief that Norman's confidence in me was wholehearted.

At some point each afternoon I would stop photocopying and head to the market to shop for dinner. It had become my habit to talk with Norman and Norris each day about what they might like to eat that night. The cooking was becoming important to all of us; I loved the division of work, and they seemed to enjoy what I came up with after we had all agreed on the base ingredient. Norris was still on the mend, and that I had, more or less, taken over the kitchen allowed her ample time to focus on getting better.

Each day, I would wander to Norman's desk to let him know I was going out. Generally my bending down to interrupt him never bothered him. He had come to expect it at a certain time each afternoon. We would discuss that night's meal or chew over a new idea for a recipe that had occurred to him out of the blue. I was beginning to understand that Norman thought about food as often as he contemplated man's reason for existence—which was all the time. He forever enjoyed talking about a meal.

Early on, I was hesitant about disrupting him when he was engrossed, but he cleared up my confusion almost immediately. "It's okay to interrupt me," he told me, "I'm just reading. But keep in mind that when I start writing I can become irritable." Some months later he would live up to that.

Three weeks into our routine I approached to tell him I was headed home for the day. Glancing at his hands, I noticed he was not reading a Hitler book but a dilapidated, marked-up copy of one of his own books, one I'd never heard of, entitled *Deaths for the Ladies (and other disasters)*.

The book was an anthology of poems he had published in 1962 that swiftly fell into a literary abyss as black as the cover that bound it. He stopped reading and began to tell me about the book, how it had been an experiment for him. He had written it during a period wherein he was smoking pot, drinking more than he should, and jotting down poems on cocktail napkins while trolling the night fissures of Manhattan.

"It was not unusual for me to squander mornings decoding what I found in my pocket from the night before. A good bit was lost to illegibility," he said.

To me his poems were like none I had read before. They were disjointed and sharp like shards of a broken mirror flung at your eyes. The lines were uncomfortable, and they chipped away at my ideas of what I believed to be the elegance of poetry. Almost no one back then had the brazenness to write and publish such poems, especially a famous novelist. The book was a public admission of his skewed normalcy, so there was little surprise that it failed to sell. I wondered if people really wanted to read pages of prattle teetering on the periphery of reason—no matter how well written. Such works are unsettling, especially to the sensibilities of the sheltered, pill-box culture of 1962. After reading a smattering of them, my impression was that they were one popped brain corpuscle away from insanity—but ordinary insanity. What they also were, however, was funny.

Norman had actually written one poem about a drunkard vomiting in the foyer of a society lady's home. I decided the poem was commentary on the behavior Norman was often accused of exhibiting at those overmythologized, gin-soaked literary parties of the late 1950s. That poem, and the hundred or so others that accompanied it, was a running observation on immodesty published far ahead of its time. Pseudo-virtuous public confession had yet to become accepted atonement.

Some days later, I happened across a folder full of his drawings, or "droons and doodles" as he called them. They were line scribbles of faces or characters often frozen in abstract peril. Beneath most of the drawings he'd written a line or two of ironic remarks. The cartoons in no way purported to be anything more than what they were, but there was no denying that they contained humor.

When I asked him what they were all about, he simply said, "I've been doing them for years."

He then pointed out a larger stack of folders on the cluttered table to the left of his desk, which he always referred to as the "Ping-Pong table," but didn't look like one I'd ever seen. I got them for him, and he began to shuffle through them, telling me about each one. There were many, and they were all amusing or satirical or both, and we spent more than an hour discussing them. As he turned the pages with his ever-present pen in hand, he occasionally made a small change or completely crossed out the text only to scrawl another entirely fresh idea. For Norman, a work was always in progress until printed, bound, and stamped with a price tag. Even then he was tempted to make changes. I once saw him attack a paperback copy of his novel *Ancient Evenings*—twenty years after it was published.

"What are you going to do with all the drawings?" I asked him. "Have you ever published them?"

"I've considered it, but maybe not enough," he said with a sliver of melancholy in his rasping voice.

"Well, what about pairing them with the poems? You know, a book of the funnier poems mixed with these? It could be a good idea." I opened *Deaths for the Ladies*, which was still sitting on the right side of his desk.

He immediately shot the idea down as being too time-consuming. He *had* considered just that idea, but he never pursued it seriously. Furthermore, he informed me that his publisher wouldn't want such an insubstantial book from him just now.

"They expect a novel out of me, not a small book." He turned again to the drawings, and for a few moments I could almost hear the gears of his mind churning as the day's last rays seeped in from between the heavy curtains. I'd kneel down next to him, on the right, where I often crouched when we spoke at his desk. Soon he said, "No, I don't think so. Not now." Then he picked up the German book he was reading, and I rose to go, slightly dashed that my idea had fallen on deaf ears.

As I turned to descend the stairs and hollered a goodbye to Norris in her study, my last sight of Norman was of him putting aside the Nazi book and picking up his drawings. The disheveled copy of *Deaths for the Ladies* remained open and near him where I'd left it.

On an afternoon nearly two weeks later he called me to his desk in a rather contented voice and stated: "I'm going to do another book. I think you'll find the work interesting." His face was wrapped with the inane grin that only he could muster when giddy to tell me about his latest plan.

The next morning all research pertaining to Hitler came to a halt. Norman immediately redirected his energies to the little project that would grow up to be his remarkably delightful paperback *Modest Gifts*.

For necessary space, and much to Norris's annoyance, we set up shop in the dining room for the next several weeks to assemble *Modest Gifts*. I spent hours upstairs fishing through hundreds of drawings he'd created over the years. I made numerous copies of them while cataloguing new folders and stacking them on the far end of the long table. Norman spent days poring over *Deaths for the Ladies* and *Cannibals and Christians*, another anthology that contained his poetry and which I was also unfamiliar with until then, marking selections. I then copied them so they were easier for him to read, and he edited each one, sometimes heavily, other times revising only a word or two. He changed the language in several of the poems so they didn't drown in the fashion of the time in which they were initially written. I keyed all of them into my computer in order to print versions that he could more easily work with. Then he set out to couple poems with drawings.

I had made twenty copies of each sketch, but frequently that was not enough. I got a fair amount of exercise racing up and down the stairs to the attic copy machine to make more. Norman edited furiously, always demanding the perfect shade or most significant word. Days of this went by: edit, copy, pair poem with doodle, toss it out, reconsider the whole concept, dig into the trash to retrieve the one tossed away in frustration to reedit it yet again with a new idea. Each day was like a tornado of originality and, for me, a tempest-like course on how to think.

In time, Norman began to construct the book. He didn't know precisely how he wanted it to look, so he produced about six different versions. His intention was to create a narrative with each chapter, in some cases logical; in others, bordering on the peculiar. One segment in particular contained a series of drawings depicting what he drolly called his whores. The whores in question were fifteen or twenty doodles of women, all with curious expressions or inferred moods, ranging from the complex to the comically vapid. After putting the section together and goading me for a half hour to assist him in coming up with as many synonyms for *prostitute* as we could, he decided he really only liked about half the drawings. The idea for the segment was scrapped, but he still wanted to put his favorite hooker doodles somewhere in the book. Indeed, six did find their way into the chapter titled *Levels of Procurement*, and one, his favorite, is the opening drawing for the chapter, "A One Night Stand." She is insolent and has turned her back on her artist, as if to say, "Go now. I'm bored with you."

When I began to see a light at the end of this eccentric tunnel, we had seven versions from which to choose the final draft. Norman considered all of the variations and borrowed sections from each to fashion his definitive edit.

"This is the more like directing a film than making a book," he told me, munching away at his favorite lunch dish, the Berry Trio.

As our work on *Modest Gifts* mostly occurred in the dining room, Norman embraced the concept of the working lunch. One afternoon he invented what would prove to be the first in a series of long-standing menus for his midday meal. My job as number one typist and graphic apprentice quickly expanded into number one lunch maker. Norman found the proximity of the kitchen to be a happy perk where work was concerned; I could make his lunch and assemble his book without having to move more than fifteen feet between one work station and the other.

I never knew where his idea for the Berry Trio came from, but he was unyielding that it be prepared with precision. The details about how to attain that precision, however, defied his exact explanation. He merely told me what he wanted, that he remembered how it looked and its "consummate essence," and that he liked it very much. He then asked if I could re-create it. I have a suspicion that the concoction was sparked by a memory of a *petit déjeuner* he once enjoyed in France, but I have no solid evidence to back that up. What he wanted, nonetheless, was a mixture of raspberries, blueberries, and chopped strawberries mixed into a sauce of clover honey and the juice from half a lemon. While mixed berries are nothing new, his notion that the mixture had to be precise was.

"I suspect it's good for the brain," he told me, "The balance of sweet and tart sits well with me."

The problem with mixing honey and lemon is that the two liquids don't much like each other. The first couple of times I prepared the dish, it was marred by clumps of sugary-sweet goo that did not bode well with the author's half-memory.

"We've got to get these two elements to go together better," Norman finally said, stirring the berries with his spoon. That June was hot, and my mind was otherwise occupied with trying to get the *other* elements, the drawings and the poetry, to meld effortlessly. He constantly wanted me to suggest options for pairing the pictures and poems, and now he was pressing me to marry two angry liquids to please his whim. I was becoming somewhat annoyed with all of the mixing and matching.

"I don't know what to do," I said. "It's just too damn hot for me to think straight."

"Maybe if we try heat," he said. "Perhaps warming the honey might coax it into accommodating the lemon juice better?"

He was right. The key was to warm the tough honey slightly in a pan over a low burner before it would accept the acidic juice. I tried his idea and it worked. Almost.

"The whole dish is slightly tepid now," he said. "How do you propose we fix that?"

I picked up his bowl of perfectly mixed yet slightly warm berries, honey, and lemon juice and went to the freezer to get two fat ice cubes. I put them in the bowl, mixed them around for about a minute to radiate their chill, plucked out what remained of the ice, and plopped the brain-berries back in front of him. He took another bite.

"Great!" he said with a smile. "Now where are the whores?"

The process of constructing *Modest Gifts* took three months. As he doodled away, I would retype each poem, with his direction as to how he thought it should look on the page. While doing this I received a piercing lesson about Norman's hatred of technology and, more specifically, computers.

As I keyed in the new structures of the poems on my laptop, he decided he wanted to see what they looked like *as* I was doing it. I brought my computer around to his side of the table to show him. Norman had impeccably groomed fingernails that were short but sharp, and as I showed him the text I was retooling on the screen, he began poking at the display and asking if

I could "move *this* to *there* and *that* line down *here* and *that* stanza a little more to the right."

I shifted into panic mode. If he continued doing this, he was going to rupture the monitor. I gently urged him to stop jabbing the screen.

"What?" He had no idea what I was agitated by.

I explained that while the screen might *look* like a TV, it was not made of glass. "It's a thin plastic film, and if you puncture it we'll have to buy a new one."

"Well, that doesn't seem to be a very good design at all," he said. "How the hell is anybody supposed to do work on such a thing?"

"Because people don't normally poke the screen with their finger, that's how," I said, moving the laptop away from him a bit. "Just let me print the pages out and then you can tell me what changes you want to make."

"But that will take too damn long," he said. His voice was getting stern. And loud.

"Well, we have to do it that way, because I don't know what the hell you want. I'm not in your head!" My volume had increased too.

"You'd be the first if you were," he shot back.

And thus I fell into my first tutorial on Norman's eternal distrust of technology and his near mania concerning wasted time. Anything that stood in the way of his rapid-fire mind was a hindrance, and he often adopted a tone that suggested someone had erected a barrier on purpose. If it took two minutes to print a section of text, then that was two minutes too long. It irritated him to no end. He was unwavering in his hatred of technology and had been harping and writing about it since before I was even born. To Norman, technology was vile, overglorified, and wholly overdepended upon. I wanted to bark at him that while he was riling against "new age machinery," he was utterly ignoring the reality that without the computer it would take two *weeks* to do what we could now accomplish in two hours. Instead, I attempted to calmly explain that as many times as he would like to alter a text, that's exactly how many times an *entirely new draft* would have to be typed. That, I told him, would piss him off even more. So, like it or not, we needed the computer.

Even though Norman was safely enclosed in a womb of technology (with me or Judith using it at his direction), he refused to alter his opinion that computers were essentially trouble. I finally gave up and moved the laptop back in front of him

"Okay, then we'll do it your way," I said. "But please don't poke the screen."

I moved my chair close to his and we both stared into the monitor. Neither of us spoke for a couple of minutes.

Clocks ticked.

We'd had our first run-in, albeit a minor one. He continued to peer at the computer, and I sensed it was all he could do to resist jabbing at it again. He did not turn to face me. Our impasse was not so much a collision of wills as a difference of ways.

"Fuck," he said, still looking at the glowing enemy. "I can't see this damn thing clearly anyway. The light is unnatural! Go ahead and print it out, and I'll go over it later."

With that he grabbed the sports section of the paper and meandered to his bathroom to stay dormant for a while and bone up on baseball scores. Over the years I would come to call his downstairs bathroom the Second Office; his favored destination in which to consider "highly significant statistics about football or the latest idiocy of the Red Sox."

I went upstairs with the disk containing the poems to ask Norris to print them out, as I didn't yet have a printer available downstairs. She was at her desk working hard on what would turn out to be her second novel.

Norris's studio was cheerfully appointed with antique dolls, soft colors, and elegant art books. Unlike at Norman's end of the attic, the shifting Cape light was allowed in through diaphanous white curtains. Norris was a talented artist and there was a pleasing aroma of long-ago dried oil paints faintly lingering in her studio, even though she had not painted regularly for some years. I met her up there in the mornings while Norman decluttered his mind with solitaire downstairs. After a period, Norris and I discussed most everything with each other: Norman, her mother, my partner, dinner, the bills, the house, kids, the ex-wives whom she still wrote alimony checks to, her longing for her old life in New York, and, often, her health. There was no shortage of topics for us, and frequently I would look at the clock to find that we'd spent nearly an hour chatting. Our morning meeting became a two-way therapy session that both of us came to count on through the years.

"What were you two fighting about down there?" she asked. I sat down where I normally did, just to the left of her desk.

Apparently the volume of mine and Norman's squabble about method had carried up the stairs. I was slightly embarrassed that she'd heard Norman and me going at each other. It's in my nature to feel awkward about run-ins with people, especially those I care for deeply, and Norris knew that. I tend to feel vulnerable even if I believe I'm correct. I told her how he'd poked his finger repeatedly at the computer screen and that I was afraid he was going to ruin it.

"He wouldn't stop jabbing at it!" I said. "And when I told him to knock it off, he got annoyed."

"He *can* be difficult," she said. Clearly she was amused. Our disagreement was indication to her that another wall had toppled. Norman had showed me his famous gruff side.

"Well, it's going to take forever to get this done if he won't at least cooperate a little with me," I said. Norris stopped typing, leaned back in her chair, and turned with a sigh.

"Well, sweetie, as far as I'm concerned, anything that keeps him from writing the *other* book is just fine with me," she said.

Up to then I was not directly clued in that Norris didn't like the idea of Norman writing a book about Adolf Hitler one bit—although I had suspected it. The subject was dark, and Norman's necessary immersion in it had consumed him. This is not to say that his general good disposition had gone caustic—not in the least—but considering Norris's serious health problems and her mother's and Norman's advancing age, any further dismal ingredient was considered an unwanted addition to the already overflowing stew of her life. What's more, the entire top floor of her house now resembled a Nazi propaganda vault. Her feeling was that any subject floating around in the house that was so inherently evil could not be good.

"We fight about it all the time at night," she said. "I told him I won't read a word of it until it's done. Maybe not even then." She admitted this to me like she'd been dying to get it out.

Most of her old and dear friends were in New York and few if any people she confided in lived in Provincetown. Norris had been coming to the Cape as long as she'd known Norman, but as circumstance sometimes happens, the bond of deep, everyday alliances never fully developed here. This is not to say that she had no friends on the Cape—certainly not. I was merely closer, and around all the time, so it was natural that we'd form a tight friendship. Also, we had a common need to vent about His Highness (a name we called Norman with equal parts love and irritation).

Because I spent a large amount of time in the house, I couldn't help but witness their arguments and, more often, their profound tenderness toward each other. Neither she nor Norman ever tried to shield me from anything. The home was big, but not that big, and voices carried easily from one room or floor to the next. Any attempt to raise a wall of privacy on my part would have resulted in me holding my hands over my ears or eyes for too much of the day. Consequently, I joined Norris in the exclusive Daily Dose of Norman Mailer Club. As select as that club was, it demanded trust. This was easy for

us to find in each other because our early lives had been similar. We'd both grown up in small towns, dreamed of getting
out and away, but still understood the necessity of kinship and
family. Norris and I found comfort with each other that grew
like ragweed over time.

It took Norman and me the better part of three months to
get *Modest Gifts* ready for Random House, which had, much
to Norman's pleasure, enthusiastically agreed to publish it. He
at first assumed they would pass (even though they had never
chosen to pass on his work before) and that we would then option it to another, smaller publisher. Norman was determined
to get the book out no matter what, now that he'd put it together.

Norman loved the *idea* of poetry more than poetry itself. His
relationship to it was a strained one, resting largely on a belief
that the richness of much of it remained "unaccomplished." He
subscribed, however, to several journals, which ended up accu-
mulating in the Second Office, right beneath old sports pages
stacked on top of political books. *Modest Gifts* would be his last
and, he hoped, best contribution to that world he found to be
lacking. I think he believed he had never been acknowledged as a
serious poet, even though he'd published two books containing
many poems in the past. The world viewed him as a journalist, formidable novelist, and unrivaled essayist, but not a poet.
Now, at the age of eighty, perhaps he would stake a claim in
that often stodgy literary neighborhood and show the neigh-
bors what was what, Mailer style.

Toward the end of the process, John Buffalo, Norman and Norris's youngest son, visited. I'd met Johnny before, when he'd joined them at the Commons restaurant some years ago, but we didn't know each other well at all. He was handsome, twenty-five years old, and a good writer. He'd written two plays and was about to embark on a fresh venture as the associate editor of the revamped *High Times* magazine. That first day he came to Provincetown to visit his parents, John and I chatted in the attic, where I was, of course, glued to the copy machine. We spoke for a while, and as the conversation ended, he said to me, "It's great to have you here, man. The folks could use some youthful energy in the house."

John lingered at the table in the mornings during his visit, reading the paper while Norman and I worked on the book. On one of those mornings, Norris came in and told Norman we should buy a mosquito-killing machine she'd read about. That June was damp and warm, which made it a prime atmosphere for bugs.

Norman hated bugs, mosquitoes in particular. If it were up to him he would eradicate them. A gadget that would aid him in that, at least from his corner of the planet, was therefore a godsend. He bristled at opening the front door to enter or leave the house, because the enormous wisteria vines that framed it and the porch were a haven for mosquitoes. In the spring and early summer anybody going in and out was bombarded by mosquitoes. To Norman's mind, they targeted *him* exclusively and with malice. Truth was, he tended to move slowly, so the bugs had more time to sharpen their attack. He told Norris to get the machine, cost be damned.

John, looking up from the *Times*, turned to me: "The author spends his days plotting the death of bugs while writing his Hitler masterwork!"

Norman looked at me also, deadpan. "I can't believe that my loins produced such a fresh kid."

Days later the bug machine arrived in a large box, and John and I assembled it. It was a bulky device that, according the directions, lured the mosquitoes in with a foul odor and then gassed them to death with propane. A mesh basket collected the bodies. When John and I finally fired it up, Norman was thrilled. He told me to tell anybody who was curious enough to ask that, "These days the author is busying himself with the noble work of killing mosquitoes."

As July rolled around, we were nearly finished with the book. I realized that on the tenth of the month my mother would celebrate her seventieth birthday. Norman suggested we send her one of the original mock-ups of the manuscript as a present. To include with it, he penned a long letter in which he explained that he, at the vastly more advanced age of eighty, hoped that she would enjoy the book in the comfort of her "relative youth." I couldn't help but think that this was a proper gift to send my mother. She had, after all, put up with my meandering around the world and my inability to find any normal path for my life. Now that I was working with an author she'd admired since her adolescence, and in essence had passed on to me in a short conversation many years before, I could thank her for her patience. Norman's idea was a fine one, and my mother was moved by the gift.

Norman's final version of *Modest Gifts* was overnighted to Random House late that month, to return in the form of page proofs some weeks later. As I'd never before prepared a book for publication it seemed to me that the work began all over again. Norman spent another week altering and reediting the 275 pages. Only then did it finally sink in that I had been part of something significant. Norman had opened the door to a world, a literary world, which I had always assumed I would only observe from a distance—if at all. He'd given me a gift, and it was not a modest one.

Modest Gifts would turn out to be a handsome volume, even though its contents were met with varying degrees of criticism, ranging from brilliant to insipid. None of that mattered outwardly to Norman. He had dictated every detail, from how the poems looked on the page to the size of his name on the cover (small and unassuming). Norman spent a great deal of time selecting the precise color of the book's jacket, which was a simple drawing of a woman's face (Norris's) suggested by the silhouette of five birds in flight against a rose-taupe sky. Apparently his effort to find that elegant shade paid off, because months later it showed up in a sumptuous Ralph Lauren advertisement. There was *Modest Gifts*, in clear view, resting on the Park Avenue coffee table of a gorgeous society lady. I hoped, for her sake, no drunkard lurked vomitously in her foyer.

In early fall the first box of bound books arrived. The day was gray, tarnished with a drear that persuades the ocean and the sky to merge perfectly into one destination. Norman had just finished his round of morning calls and seemed to be in a particularly tranquil mood. He sat for more than five minutes in the glassed-in bar off the dining room surveying the shore he never tired of, before urging me to join him to watch two blue herons while away the day on a small red boat, a dory, moored fifty yards out on the tidal flats. The tide was out low and the boat was resting on sand. Given that no one ever moved or fished from the boat, even in gentle seasons, Norman thought it fitting that the dory was finally getting some use. He said the herons must be in mid-migration and decided the boat, which stood out like fire against the dark beige sand, was as fine a place as any to rest. We talked for a few minutes about how long they might stick around and where their journey would take them. He recommended I look into it. We continued to lean quietly together against the bar, observing the birds and their perplexing certainty.

"Do we have a bird book?" I asked.

"I don't know," he said. "But I wouldn't be put out if you took the time to locate one."

The phone soon rang and I reached for it.

"Let it go, pal," he said. "Norris will get it."

I followed his direction and soon the phone fell silent. Some moments later, the doorbell rang. The new books had arrived.

I cut open the box and placed the whole batch in front of Norman. He reached in, grabbed the top one, took a few moments to write something on the title page, and then passed it to me. In his inscription he noted his appreciation of my detailed attention and commented on our "good cheer together." I'd managed to meet his expectations of me, at least enough to inspire this note and, apparently, he'd developed a belief that I could hold my ground in squabbles when necessary. Certainly, I had learned from Norman that a good fight or two was a necessary ingredient to any useful relationship.

As we looked over the book, Norman sporadically burst into verse, reading selections that were as familiar to me now as they had been to him for forty years. He read the poems as if I were a virgin audience, and in a way I was, because he had the uncanny ability to recite text with complete originality each time he encountered it. Norris came down from her study and, as she approached the table, slipped her arms tenderly around her husband's neck while he read, resting her cheek comfortably against his white hair.

"This is the beautiful broad on the cover," he told me with a cocky, prideful grin, as if I hadn't heard him say it a hundred times before.

In years to come he gave the book to friends or acquaintances, almost always with the line "best enjoyed with sipping whiskey," as if to follow his orders would make the read more endurable. Of course the poems read just fine without the aid of libation, because they were smart, honest, and whimsical, but Norman couldn't pass a copy on without the humble stipulation inscribed.

Some months later, when winter settled on the Cape and Christmas was just around the corner, he chose *Modest Gifts* as the present he sent out that season. He wrote notes to old friends he missed and young writers he admired, asking them to indulge him by considering his poems and drawings. To this day I occasionally hear from those people, who say how much they love the book and that they feel privileged that he thought to send them a copy. I mailed off numerous copies of his larger and more staid books throughout the years, but no other book generated the same level of response as the little book of poems with the simple soft cover.

Modest Gifts became Norman's favorite book in some ways, which is baffling, considering his profound body of work. Nevertheless, I cannot count how many times throughout the years I found him poring over a copy at the dining room table with, it seemed to me, as much pleasure as he might derive from watching the clever antics of a favored grandchild whose charms he could not resist.

THREE

The Writer's Table . . . and Other Passions

To look back on my time with Norman now is like peering through a kaleidoscope: vibrant images churn in imprecise order. What emerges as I shadow more than a thousand days with him should be clear, but that is not the case. The memories that do rise to the surface are often as inexplicable as the fog that gathers over the harbor of our town.

My feelings for both Norman and Norris were irrefutable, but sentiment rarely does a good job of defining relationships; that takes effort and time. I seldom knew how a day, or even a conversation, with either of them would turn out. I was abruptly immersed in their world, which revolved around their large, though often absent, family. That family consisted of his nine children and their wives and husbands, and also Norman's sister, Barbara, who came with her husband, Al, and son, Peter. It took me more than a few months to get all of the names straight. Nevertheless, I tried hard, and I got to know them one by one through that first year. Each of Norman's children, at one time or another, told me they were pleased that I was around to help their dad. The consensus was that Norman needed someone around him besides Norris to be an aide, friend, and confidant.

"I've never seen Dad act with an assistant the way he does with you," his daughter Danielle told me the day after I first met her. We were sitting on the front steps of the house, only a few weeks into my tenure. "When I was a kid, he acted downright terrible to his assistants sometimes. It's different with you."

I didn't know how to react to the news that he could be terrible to his assistants, so I simply said, "Well, for one thing, I don't much care that he's famous. I like Norman for who he is, and he knows that. Besides, he makes me laugh."

It was true. He did make me laugh, and sometimes when he didn't, I would only smirk at his stories. He'd feign irritation that I had no sense of humor, but the truth was he appreciated my candor. I came to learn that nearly everybody behaved how they thought they *should* when they were around him, practically genuflecting at every word that passed his lips as if it were gospel. I didn't see the sense in that, said as much, and he liked me all the more for it. I was not impertinent; I was simply being practical. I was there to assist, not stoke the fire.

"Well, he speaks highly of you when you're not here, and you should know that," Danielle said. "He loves your cooking and says you're smart."

"I don't know about the smart business," I said. "I've never felt as stupid as I do around him sometimes."

"Hah! Welcome to the club," Danielle said, and she hugged me.

A sense of ease about being in their home quickly developed. I never knocked on the door to enter the house, and it was clear that Norman didn't like such formality anyway. He'd had his fill of politesse in New York, where his every move was heralded as remarkable and graciousness and propriety surrounded him like a bubble. In Provincetown he preferred casualness and openness. He encouraged me to be candid, because he did not have the time or patience for empty hoopla. He also advocated minimal structure to our time together. We'd work when it was right; I'd come in at no specific time in the morning, just within a half hour in either direction of what was comfortable. Norman didn't revel in routine other than the small personal ones he'd created for himself. Spontaneity was a kind of life-blood for him, not only in his thinking but in how he liked his immediate environment. It was all very relaxed.

Norris showed me how things ran in the house and, in a short time, became comfortable with having me help out however I could. Throughout the first months, a small and confusing twaddle of nerves fluttered in me when I was around her—a sensation, strangely, I never experienced with Norman. Perhaps her beauty, which was engulfed in a vibrant temperament, or the knowledge that she was fighting cancer kept me on guard. I didn't know what to say or do about her health situation, other than be understanding, and that tormented me, because I wanted to help instead of merely utter ineffective words of optimism. Her position as matriarch to a large clan that I didn't yet know well also intimidated me. It was peculiar to be installed in a family and yet devoid of the history of laughs and rows that its genuine members enjoyed. Nonetheless, I managed to conceal my nervousness at being near her in that first year. I put it away for good one afternoon when she shed tears in front of me out of frustration over something delicate and personal. She trusted me enough to allow herself to open up emotionally around me, which informed me that our bond was reciprocal and important and not to be taken lightly. Over the years, I have experienced a greater closeness with Norris than with just about anyone I've ever known, and she has held my hand through fits of trouble more often than I care to mention.

For Norris to relinquish even the smallest control over her kitchen was not easy in the beginning, because she had always done all the cooking in their home prior to my arrival. She had worked tirelessly to fashion an ordinary existence for them in Provincetown, but the gravity of her illness, Norman's age, and her mother's needs forced her to rely on me. I didn't do housework or bills, but I did handle some sticky problems such as doctor's appointments for Norman and management of insurance company red tape. Norman depended on me to deal with this "corporation bullshit," as he called it, but as I did, he developed an irritation at how long the process took. Sometimes he seemed annoyed that I was not two people: one to handle the junk and another to handle him. Judith, in Brooklyn, did a large part of this work, but the difference was that I was *in* the house and, therefore, immediate. When he would look across the table at me with a phone glued to my ear, I could sense him beginning to smolder because it was "cutting into work." While he never came to like the fact that I had absorbed these duties in addition to the research, reading, cooking, shopping, phone answering, schedule arranging, and Xeroxing, he did manage to tolerate it. He was not pleased that his life required that he—or his delegate—devote so much effort to having a prescription filled or scheduling a medical appointment, but he was a logical man. In the end he accepted all of it, and was pleased when I scored one for our side.

Norman was rife with inner contradictions. Surprisingly, one aspect of this revolved around his writing. "Some days I just don't want to go up," he told me. I was new to being around him and I wondered how many people he had admitted this to over the years. Why would he blurt this out to *me*? Later I discovered that when he decided to trust someone, he tended to do so completely, and this startling admission was an example of that confidence. When he first said it, however, I was taken aback at learning that such a great writer as he suffered as others might. His passion for writing was legendary and his elevation of it as equivalent to creation itself was well known. That morning, as he sat staring at his breakfast plate, he said, "The old drive is becoming more and more of a bitch to get hold of." I did not know what to say, and so I said nothing. I just looked at him until he turned his attention back to his crossword puzzle. Over time, I realized his passion for work flourished only while he was in the middle of it. Like every writer, he had to be bloody in combat to find real pleasure in writing. Certainly, also like other authors, he hated the internal fight.

As is often the case with people who are near each other for extended periods, Norman and I developed a rhythm, which enabled me to anticipate what he needed, often before he knew he needed it. He remarked several times that he believed I must be psychic. When he wanted me to handle a phone call, make a schedule change, or simply bring a cup of tea up to the attic, I was usually in the middle of dialing, making the change, or standing next to him holding a steaming cup. Initially we thought it amusing, but then Norman began to take it seriously and said we should never jinx the phenomenon by discussing it. He was superstitious about fortune, and feared that frivolous tempting of it might wither it altogether. For years we regarded our telepathic connection as a good spirit that watched over us.

The line between my private life and my hours with Norman became somewhat blurry. Amplifying that blur was the fact that my partner, Thomas, frequently came to the house to handle various jobs, such as designing storm shutters for the south-facing windows or shoring up the cement wall that protected the edge of the property from the bay.

Norman liked Thomas a great deal, and it seemed to cheer him when he saw us together. I wondered at first, considering the rumors I'd read of his "homophobia," if Norman might be slightly hesitant about accepting a relationship between two men that played out closely before him. This proved to be an unnecessary worry. Norman was anything but bigoted, and as far from homophobic as a man could be. It forever amazes me that such untruths about him prevail. If anything, Norman was the consummate male because he had no apprehension about gay men in any way. He was gentle about my relationship with Thomas, and knew how vital it was to my overall happiness and, therefore, the smooth running of our dealings. He even went so far as to offer counsel to me about Thomas on occasion. Most notably, before a very difficult period in our life came to light, Norman said to me that "Men like you and I can't know the conflict living within Thomas."

I had no idea what he meant. I thought that because Thomas had battled alcohol and depression for years that those difficulties lay at the core of Norman's observation. I would be proven wrong a few years later. It turned out that Norman had exhibited extraordinary, if indistinct, insight into the troubles Thomas suffered more than I ever could or did. I've always had a fair knack for observation—except for what is, sometimes, close. Norman, markedly, had noticed glimmers of Thomas's curiously profound dilemma before any of us—perhaps even before Thomas.

Regardless of the conflicts he observed in Thomas, Norman clearly felt affection for him and was intrigued by his natural skills as a carpenter. When Norman gave Thomas a copy of *Modest Gifts*, he wrote in the book, "This is my idea of construction. Cheers, Norman." Norman had studied engineering at Harvard and had always been fascinated by concepts of design. So it was only natural that when Thomas came to make repairs, Norman offered his opinion about how the job might be accomplished. His theories were delivered in a more vibrant language than Thomas was used to hearing from a client, but he hung on Norman's every word and learned a great deal—as all of us who knew the man did.

"They've been talking for half an hour? Let's be thankful Norman became a writer and not a bridge builder," Judith said when I mentioned to her on the phone one day that Thomas and Norman were outside deep in discussion about reconstructing the seawall. Judith and I both assumed Norman was better with hypotheses than a hammer, but Norman liked to believe he was good with both.

"You know I once did all the plumbing for my apartment in New York many years ago," Norman said to me after praising the job Thomas had done holding back the ocean. "It took me a while, and I found some inventive ways to manage the pipes. In the end, nothing leaked."

"Well, that's the main thing," I said, "keeping the leaks away."

"It is," he said. "And it's never easy."

•   •   •

Norman's breakfast was always in front of him or just finished and pushed to the side of his newspapers when I arrived. Norris usually cooked in the morning, and when I entered the house I'd be greeted by the smell of bacon or the marshmallow aroma of pancakes—which Norman preferred made as thin as crêpes then rolled up like taquitos. According to him, no one, including me, could make a pancake as well as Norris. When she set the plate down, she often let her hand linger on his shoulder for a moment while she asked, "You need anything else, sweetie?"

Their affection for each other was rich, and I sometimes felt like I was glimpsing an intimate act even when they showed each other the smallest gesture of devotion. Granted, they squabbled in that way people do who have been together for thirty years, but their differences played a far second to their deep love for each other. I recall thinking that if the press, who had always been flippant toward Norman and his marriages, could see his real life, they would recant every nasty thing they'd ever printed. Of course he had mellowed with age, but no man merely cultivates noble tendencies out of the blue without having had them in his war chest all along. Sincerity cannot simply be invented.

Once, while Norman and I were working on *Modest Gifts* in the attic office, Norris came into the room and sat on the twin bed Norman occasionally took a nap on when his eyes became weary. It was nestled to the side, under the low, slanted ceiling, handy to the desk. Both Norman and she were in a particularly peaceful mood that morning, and as I sat cross-legged on the floor between them, with the manuscript in my lap, we began to talk. Norman told Norris that he was dedicating the poems in the book to her. He turned to me, his blue eyes flashing with even more spark than usual, and said, "I think we should have your roast chicken tonight." Norman could use anything as a reason for a small party, and although he didn't say it directly, this was cause for one.

"Whatever you want," I said. "Roast chicken sounds good."

"As you know," Norman began, "when I was a cook in the army we used to cook fifty chickens at a time . . ."

Norris rolled her eyes and smiled down at me.

"What?" Norman asked, noticing this.

"If I have to hear about you being a cook in the army one more time I'm going to toss myself out the window," she said.

"Now, Barbara, I'm just telling him that I understand roast chicken." His tone was mock-combative and a sure sign they were off and running.

"You haven't cooked a thing in years."

"That's not true," he said.

"It is true," Norris said, turning to me. "Last time he made his mushroom duxelles, the kitchen looked like a war zone. He managed to use every pot, pan, and dish we have. That was five years ago, and it's taken about that long to clean up the mess."

"Don't listen to this," he said to me.

"Norman, it's true. You cook, yes, but you don't clean up. And the mushrooms were just okay."

"Can you believe I put up with this?" he asked.

Their banter was endearing. As they pretended to squabble in a way that's perfected only over decades, my cynicism about the longevity of love began to fall away. I'd always regarded with suspicion the idea of love being able to cut through troubles, but Norman and Norris cared so much for each other that it was as palpable as late summer humidity. I recall realizing that morning that the ignored moments are often the most vital, the ones that *should* be banked. Most of us fail to pay respect to those tiny threads that are our fabric. I vowed to not make that mistake any longer.

Throughout *Modest Gifts* and our "working lunch" routine, Norman encouraged me to cook more and experiment with foods whenever I wanted. He loved nearly every cuisine, and although he wasn't much of a cook himself, he did come up with a number of ideas he considered helpful and good. In the end he was a very basic man: he loved wine and food and his children and gathering around a table and the company of his smart and gorgeous wife. When all of those fell together in his leisurely evening, he was satisfied.

Food was perhaps the only sector of daily life where our immensely different intellects met on a relatively level playing field. What Norman didn't know about a recipe, I often did, and if I didn't, I would quickly find out. He knew I got as much satisfaction from that kind of research as I did uncovering Nazi exploits for his novel. The search for answers never stopped on the book front or the food front.

"I thought about this last night," he said to me one morning. "What about teriyaki, butter, and raspberry jam? Could we [meaning me] mix them together and then fry a thin breakfast steak in it? How would that taste?" He asked this as if I somehow secretly knew how it would taste and was keeping the answer from him. Raspberry and teriyaki were two flavors he liked a great deal, and he thought there ought to be a way to put them together. The next morning I brought two small steaks with me and prepared his creation. He took a bite and chewed it.

"It's not terrible," he said, "but it's not what I hoped."

Another time, Norman concocted an equally creative lunch dish, which consisted of baby peas, finely chopped broccoli tips, and green beans. The greens were quickly blanched, chilled, and then combined with (yet again!) teriyaki-infused oatmeal. There was a logical foundation for this peculiar creation: He knew he had to eat more vegetables, and the oatmeal would cut his cholesterol. Teriyaki united all of these ingredients to make the whole of it palatable. I made it, and he was right—it *was* good. Not surprisingly, we were the only two who thought it was delicious. Everyone else would look at it with an obvious sneer of distaste forming. It was not a pleasant looking dish, but that mattered little to Norman. For over six months there was always a ready batch of oats and greens in the refrigerator for whenever he broke from work.

When he tired of this combo, tuna sandwiches became Norman's favorite lunch for about a year. He preferred the simplicity of well-drained tuna and Hellmann's mayo—no fancy onion or pickle—on white bread. He also liked his sandwich cut into thirds.

"Why thirds?" I asked him when he set the knife down the day he showed me how he liked it.

"I don't know. Maybe it was how my mother did it," he said. "I suspect it tricks the mind into convincing the stomach that it's getting more than it actually is."

"But *you're* doing the cutting."

"Not after today," he said, and walked back to his chair, satisfied with himself.

Norris sank herself into writing her second book and relished the relief my presence in the house afforded her. Her health problems were constant, if varying from day to day, but her overall strength was gradually improving. Then, of course, out of the blue, she would need to endure the necessity of another grueling surgery, which forced us all to the teetering edge of worry. This vibrant woman, who was Norman's foundation during the last third of his life, was entangled in much greater stresses than anyone outside the old brick home ever knew about, yet she endured it all with humor and grace. She worried about Norman's welfare and she told me that should the worst happen to her, she hoped I would always remain with him. This was not a question. I had no plans of going away under any circumstances. I depended on the two of them as much as they depended on me.

Norman could be a full-time job for anyone around him— Norris had been no exception—but since I was now in the picture, many of his needs fell to me. The dynamics of all of our lives had changed. After some weeks and months of being near him I understood how he was unable, in many ways, to be autonomous. Norris had warned me that this was the case, but I needed to experience his neediness for myself to really understand.

Norman had always had someone—his mother, a wife, a child, or an assistant—to act as a support for the basic elements of his life. This is not to say he was in some measure incapable—certainly not. Having help in life's mundane areas afforded him the opportunity to write, which was immensely important and time-consuming. What most do not realize is that a writer is working even when he or she is seemingly at rest. Norman once noted to me that being a writer was much like being a prisoner serving a life sentence. He was always, always working. He did, however, often show interest in doing some basic things for himself. One thing that Norris and I affectionately conspired to restrict was driving.

"He tore the passenger-side mirror off the car last year turning onto Conway Street," she said, referring to the tiny side street just up the block from the house. "He is always in such a rush. Make sure you drive him when he wants to go out. I won't even get in the car with him anymore if he insists on driving."

"Is it that bad?" I asked.

"Well, yes, sweetie. He's going deaf, and his eyes are not great. He gets in the car and becomes a speed demon. I'm afraid of what might happen. Every time he pulls out of the drive and he sees a car coming, he zooms to get in front of it. It makes me crazy."

"I always like to wait until the coast is clear," I said.

"Well, waiting is not one of Norman's strong points, in case you haven't noticed," Norris said. "Bless his heart." The expression was tinged with exasperation, because any attempt to alter Norman's behavior, even by her, was usually futile.

Undeniably, age had begun to slow him, and I snagged the keys whenever I could. Norman rarely said to me that he preferred to drive himself, even though I knew he sometimes wanted to. He had an urge to control, which he smartly quashed when it came to matters of the wheel. All considered, he also liked being chauffeured, so I encouraged him to appreciate *that* luxury over driving. I never mentioned that it would be safer for the world at large. Norman still retained a certain pride about his prowess behind the wheel, however. "You know, I'm a *much* better driver than Norris," he said one afternoon while we were in my old Volvo. "Don't tell her I said that, though. It would upset her."

We both knew that prickly subjects such as his abilities in the driver's seat were better left out of serious debate, and that was a defining factor in our ease with each other. Norman understood that the bastard edge of age fostered limitations, and he knew *I* knew that—why discuss the obvious? It made for better days for both of us to let some topics fritter away unaddressed.

He was crafty about what he truly required to make it through a day, at least in the realm of directly asking me for help. It took months of small shifts in my role as editorial assistant to all-around aide for me to realize this. Norman would broach things in small doses, so I was usually immersed in a new task before I realized that my work load had expanded. By the end of the first year, to describe my title merely as "editorial assistant" was a half-description at best. I divulged fewer details about my work to friends; a part of me wrongly believed that being "Man Friday" to someone was slightly undignified, even while I greatly enjoyed the company of the man I was assisting. At home, Thomas noticed this was beginning to bother me—and one day, so did Norman.

"I know you wrestle with a notion of intellectual entitlement about yourself as opposed to the truth of your circumstances," Norman said to me. He'd noticed my discomfort (annoyance?) at being asked, yet again, to retrieve a prescription from the pharmacy. "That sense of entitlement will either be the death of you or the force that establishes you."

I didn't really know what he meant by "notion of intellectual entitlement," but I did understand that the essence of his statement was potent: I'd always felt disjointed and unsure about how to find inner success. My duties now, as Norman's assistant, were not entirely what I had envisioned. Devoting half my waking hours to the care and consolation of someone felt both irregular and satisfying.

"I don't know if it's entitlement or cynicism," I said to him. We were sitting at the table; it was just before the New Year, December 2003.

"You need to recognize exactly who you are," Norman said. "No one is going to do it for you. People will point out your flaws and sometimes, if you're lucky, your strengths, but their view will always be varnished with envy or awe. How you manage those distinctions defines you."

Norman was right. We never escape our tendency to harp on what we *can* become as opposed to what we *have* become. The best we can do is find optimism in survival—with some small quantity of dignity attached. I had never been able to embrace advice, either positive or negative, beyond what small lift or ruin it tendered to my self-worth. I questioned everything and had answers for nothing. With Norman, I realized that what counted all along was that I had been *aware* of my confusion— my desire to unearth meaning, but also to be of use. He pointed out that the vast majority tend to exist comfortably without much thought beyond themselves. How one manages the numerous quandaries one encounters is what matters, he said.

Norman never waffled on any issue, and whatever consequence sprang out of his position was handled logically. I could either learn through observation and osmosis or endure stagnancy. I chose to learn a few things and forget the tough small stuff.

In Provincetown the winters can be unforgiving. Hearty comfort foods become important, and Norman, in the winter of 2004, wanted borscht. He had fond memories of the dish from the time he spent in Minsk researching *Oswald's Tale*, his 1995 biography of Lee Harvey Oswald, who'd lived in Russia as a young man. He had been reading the history of Russia, specifically that of Nicholas II, which sparked a Proustian memory in him.

"When borscht is made perfectly, there is nothing that compares," he said. He was eating a tuna sandwich for lunch.

"Beets, beef, broth, cabbage, and onions cooked all together. It's wonderful."

I thought that this was a rather passionate way to describe soup, but I didn't undercut his enthusiasm by saying what I was thinking: "Well, it's probably all they had to eat." Such flippancy would have been met with a sermon about dedication to borscht-making. Instead, I stayed silent.

"Have you ever had borscht?" He asked me. I had eaten it once and wasn't thrilled. Beets were not one of my preferred foods. I told him this, and as soon as I got the sentence out he began shaking his head.

"No, no, no. You must understand the art. In Russia I made it myself several times. Here," he grabbed a yellow pad of paper, "this is how you do it."

He pushed his plate aside and wrote out a recipe splintered with directions as to quality of vegetables, how to chop them properly, and what order to put them in the pot. I noticed his manner was now electric. "First you have to get good beets. Can we get good beets here, do you think? Now, look, you peel them and cut them into chunks, hearty chunks so they don't lose their integrity . . ." He went on like this for ten minutes, and I simply replied, "I'll give it a shot."

Norman meandered from the table after that and headed back upstairs to work with newfound agility. I was left downstairs to ponder the sketch of memory he'd scrawled. "So they don't lose their integrity . . ." Ha! Beets of all things. I set out over the next few weeks to bring his sense-memory of Russia to life.

Making the borscht was not easy, and Norman dubbed my first several attempts merely adequate. I grew fond of the effort involved in navigating his memory in order to satisfy it. When I had a question about method, he would sit back in his chair and reminisce about the mishmash of flavors he'd experienced and the circumstances surrounding each meal. Norman had a quality that made those near him want to please him, and although I noticed its effect on others immediately, I didn't fully realize it in myself until I spent three weeks perfecting borscht. I was going to nail it for him if it was the last thing I did.

After searching everything from the Internet to dusty books and at least one recipe Norris pulled from a travel diary, I finally stumbled on a recipe that Norman declared a success. The secret to capturing the taste he recalled was roasted bones. The oven brought out the illusive essence they contained, and I then stirred them into the broth. The marrow seeped out, and its flavor shaded the mixture perfectly. I added hunks of browned beef and allowed it to simmer for hours. A teaspoon of powerful Russian mustard provided the finishing touch, which set the pot afire.

I went to the attic late in the afternoon after my final attempt and found Norman resting on the twin bed. He was completely silent when he slept—always on his right side, arm sticking out perpendicular to his body—and I was repeatedly taken aback whenever I walked in to find him asleep. He was, after all, fairly on in years, and that detail never really left my mind. I stood a few feet away, watching him for a moment, waiting. Then I noticed his lip twitch, his eyes fluttering open. He slowly sat up.

"Hey, that smells good," he said. The aroma of the soup had permeated the entire house.

"I'm leaving for the night," I said. "Danielle is keeping an eye on the stove." Danielle was visiting again with her daughter, Isabella, for a few days. Norman let out a groan as he straightened himself. His white hair was mussed from the pillow and he struck me as the image of the most comfortable grandfather anyone could ever want. I was glad I'd come up to say goodbye.

"All right then, pal," he said. "I'm eager to try your soup."

"It's ready whenever you are. I'm pretty sure I got it this time. How's the reading going?"

He reached over and used the edge of the desk for support to stand, bending slightly to avoid hitting his head on the slant of the ceiling. The attic was quiet except for the low pound of the surf outside and the light tap, tap, tap of Norris typing in her study at the opposite end.

"Not as good as that dinner smells," he said. "The eyes crap out after a while, you know. See you tomorrow."

"Yes, tomorrow," I said. "Enjoy your borscht."

He did enjoy the soup that night and told me as much the following morning. I'd captured his memory of the broth he loved and resurrected it suitably.

The next day he wrote the first rough draft of a section of *Castle in the Forest* describing the ghastly killing of Russian peasants during the coronation of Nicholas II.

• • •

Whenever Norman encountered foods he didn't like but knew he should eat, he tried to circumvent his aversion by finding an agreeable way to consume them.

We were at the table again one afternoon; I was making a shopping list. Johnny, Michael, and Michael's soon-to-be wife, Sasha, were all visiting. We were planning a dinner for not only the five of them but the Lennons, who were in town also. Mike Lennon was Norman's archivist and close friend. He'd assisted on and edited several of Norman's anthology books as well as an annotated bibliography detailing all of Norman's works through his career. Whenever they returned to their second home in Provincetown from Wilkes-Barre, Pennsylvania, where Mike was a professor, he and his wife, Donna, came for dinner.

"Norman never really wants any vegetable except green beans," Norris said.

Norman didn't like vegetables. He despised asparagus, saying it caused "a disturbing aroma when I piss—which cannot be good." He supposedly loathed zucchini, but he ate them whenever I prepared them because I roasted them with olive oil, garlic powder, and parmesan—cloaking the natural flavor completely. Spinach was out because he said it was "as unpleasant as wet newspaper in your mouth."

Many of Norman's ideas about food had been reinforced through the years by his mother. Fanny Mailer was long gone by the time I came to work for him, but she occasionally still dominated discussions about meals. Consider the roast chicken . . .

Roast chicken was a favorite, but it had to be prepared a certain way. Norman maintained that the bird should be rubbed with butter, salt and pepper, and nothing else, except perhaps a little thyme. "Garlic," he insisted, "obliterates the essence of the chicken."

"Only if you overdo it," I told him. "If it's done right, it *enhances* the flavor; it doesn't kill it." I wanted to strangle him. He had no idea what he was talking about.

No, he insisted, any amount of garlic *ruined chicken completely.* I once asked him, when I had gotten tired of his rant, if he'd ever, in fact, roasted a chicken. He paused and answered truthfully that he had not—at least not in the past thirty years. "But, when I was a cook in the army . . ." He started in again about the fifty chickens for the troops.

Beyond the garlic issue, he also believed the bird should be basted every ten minutes. It occurred to me that he enjoyed saying the word *baste* because it was the only term he was familiar with in the area of chicken roasting. Norris sided with me.

"Norman, no one actually stands by the oven for an hour basting constantly. It doesn't make sense," she said. Nevertheless, "baste" was Norman's mantra about chicken roasting, even though he didn't know what benefit the process actually provided. He was sure that it greatly improved meat moisture, which is, of course, wrong. Basting crisps the skin and nothing else. What's more, opening the oven repeatedly to do it screws up the cooking time. I tried to explain this, but he never accepted it over his established "mother memory." Fanny had basted her chicken, so all should baste.

I finally looked at Norris in shared exasperation. The conversation moved on. Norman assumed I would do it his way, and I let him think this while ignoring him altogether. As for garlic, I used it cautiously, the way one should, and smeared the skin and cavity of the bird with butter and thyme. When I arrived the next morning and asked how he'd liked last night's bird, he said it was perfect. "However you made it last night is how you should do it from now on." That afternoon he uncharacteristically made himself a chicken sandwich for lunch.

When Mike and Donna Lennon were in Ptown it was assumed that they would be over at least every other night for dinner. As Norman and I worked in the morning at the table, prior to going up to the attic, Mike would stop by, often with an armload of books for Norman to sign. They usually weren't additions to his personal collection; they were related to his work. His professorship at Wilkes University in Pennsylvania had segued into a second career involving the literary work of Norman Mailer. This ultimately manifested itself into his main career after retirement as Norman's archivist and, later, official biographer. The books he brought were for foundation donations or private collections he was building for others. Or, I assumed, for Norman's archive itself, which was massive.

Mike had done his doctorial dissertation on Mailer, and through a series of letters and meetings he developed a friendship with Norman. Now, thirty years later, Mike was the sentry to Norman's enormous body of work, not an easy job. He was also the only person outside of family, other than me, who saw Norman regularly. Norman had many other friends

on Cape Cod and off who visited intermittently, but those visits were rarer than one might imagine. Norman liked getting
together with people, but the occasions were always planned
ahead—Mike just showed up and, like me, never knocked. It
seemed to me that many of Norman's friends had a lingering fear of offending him if they were to visit more often.
They had such high regard for the "author" that I think they
sometimes forgot he was just a guy, too. That, of course, was
not a bad thing, considering Norman was essentially a private
man who liked to work a great deal. But he was more open to
spur-of-the-moment visits than people believed, and I think
it led to some degree of loneliness in him that no one ever
talked about.

With Mike he enjoyed an ease that he shared with very few
people. The reason for that: Mike knew Norman inside out.
In all probability, he is the only living person who has read
every word Norman Mailer ever wrote. (Many claim to have
done so, but I have real doubts, due to the sheer volume of
Norman's output.) Because of this, Mike could separate the
"Norman" from the "Mailer" in a way that others could not.
He was the dearest friend to Norman, and there was never a
question about his motive, which was always to care for the
man first and administer to the legacy second. When Mike
arrived, Norman would stop everything and devote his full
attention to him—or, sometimes, gesture to a chair and force
Mike to endure small talk with me while Norman finished
his game of solitaire. That's what true friends do; they wait
for you.

"We've got the conference coming up, Norm," he would remind Norman each year around August. The conference was the meeting of the Norman Mailer Society.

"What? So soon?" Norman asked.

"Well, in November," Mike said. He was a believer in preparing early for things.

The Norman Mailer Society, like other societies founded to preserve the legacy of great authors, was something that Norman told me he initially didn't want but had agreed to only after finding out it was going to happen with or without his consent. He finally approved its existence while he was still alive on the condition that he could have a valid say about it.

"Most authors are dead who have these societies," Norman told me when we were alone. "I feel slightly pushed ahead."

"I think it's kind of a nice idea," I said to him. "The dead ones never get to see how much affect they've had on people."

"Maybe so . . ." and he never finished the sentence.

Norman did come to wholly appreciate the Society and the extensive efforts Mike selflessly put into it. Naturally, Mike was the president; as such, in conjunction with a few other scholars, he organized a thoughtful, meaningful conference each year that celebrated various aspects of Norman's mammoth body of work. Each year the theme varied: The Political Mailer, Mailer the Novelist, The Existential Mailer.

"Do you want a membership?" Mike asked me in the early days.

Norman looked at Mike and pointed toward me: "He's of the drafted variety and probably wants the hell out."

"I don't know. Let me think on it," I said after we both chuckled. When Mike left I said to Norman, "Frankly, the idea is sort of creepy. I mean, you're my friend and we work together. How am I supposed to praise the guy who tells me bad jokes and asks me to buy his toothpaste?"

"You think my jokes are bad?"

"*And* I buy your toothpaste," I said.

"I could tell you didn't want anything to do with it," he said. "I'll tell Mike not to bring it up again."

"No, don't do that. I'll handle it. Who knows, I may want to join someday. I bet I could get a discount on the membership. And just so you know, I don't think your jokes are all *that* bad," I said. "I was making a point."

"Hey, pal, larger audiences than you'll ever know laugh long and loud at my jokes."

Norman's sense of humor sprang to life vividly when he'd tell me about certain incidents in his past. One afternoon, while drinking Pimm's Cup cocktails after I'd fetched him from the airport, we got on the subject of Gore Vidal and their legendary literary spat.

"He was an inspired liar," Norman said. "I never threw a punch. First I threw a drink in his face and then I bounced the glass off his head. A heavy glass. He *thought* he'd been punched. So, what he came up with was 'a tiny little fist coming toward me.' He'll die to have people laugh at his jokes. What he felt," Norman continued, "was a bunch of ice cubes hitting him."

His prime political target was George W. Bush, who, Norman believed, was the worst offender when it came to mangling the language and the country as a whole. Norman summed Bush up by saying that he committed stupidity wantonly throughout the land. It got to the point where Norman wouldn't even acknowledge another Bush absurdity beyond a grunt, as if there were nothing left to say. One day, in August of 2004, however, he did point to something in one of his newspapers and handed it to me. Bush, who had lately taken to calling himself "The Decider," was quoted as saying, "Our enemies are innovative and resourceful, and so are we. They never stop thinking about new ways to harm our country and our people, and neither do we."

"Does he even *have* handlers around him?" I asked.

"It's the most honest thing he's said yet," Norman said.

He saw the humor in the gaffe, but also the brutality embedded in it. It was pure confirmation. Utter contempt for everything, Norman believed, was buried shallowly in the president's head. "The bastard can't help but spew toxin."

As Christmas rolled around in 2005, Norman asked me to retrieve a photograph he'd found the previous June and requested that I hold onto "for sometime later." I had kept it in my desk since then, never giving it a second thought. The photo had appeared in the *Boston Globe*; it was of George and Laura Bush hosting Bill and Hillary Clinton at the White House for the occasion of unveiling the official portraits of the Clintons. It was a rich photograph, even before Norman got his hands on it. The picture clearly shows Bill Clinton lustily locking eyes with Laura Bush while Hillary looks down at the guests with an absurdly oblivious grin pasted on her face. Laura, who appears girlish, if not buttery over the attention, seems ready to leap into the arms of Clinton. The president appears to be mugging his version of a tough-guy toward Clinton. The falseness of all of their expressions (except, perhaps, Bill Clinton's) is blatant.

I dug out the picture and brought it to him.

"Can we make it bigger so I can work with it?" he asked me.

I took the photo to our local copy store and made ten color copies. Norman spent two hours that morning trying out captions in little balloons.

Bill: Little Miss Muffet—it's you and me!
Hillary: How are all your lovely children?
Laura: You're no spider. You are COOL!
George: Cruising for a bruising, Buster!

The final touch was Norman scrawling "Season's Greetings" beneath the photo, which was blown up to eleven by fourteen and printed on heavy paper. I spent thirty dollars on the enlargements and another thirty on stamps and oversize envelopes for Norman's official Christmas card. He was extremely happy with his design and wanted me to spend the entire day stuffing envelopes in order to get his "card" out before the holidays.

"What is that?" Norris asked me when I showed it to her.

"Norman's Christmas card."

"Oh, my," she said.

Norman tried to get Norris to sign the card along with him that season, but she opted instead to send out more traditional ones. She felt as much queasiness about Bush as the rest of us, but believed Christmas was no time for political commentary.

We had been privy to Norman's sense of humor and unexpected swipes of satire before. Around the time he initially found the photo in the paper he felt he needed to comment on how Bush's cohorts embraced and defended the president's every move and statement, and so Norman decided to write a poem to commemorate the ludicrousness. Appropriately, the final draft I have is dated April Fool's Day.

HOMAGE TO GEORGE W. BUSH

A mystery poem (Modern Mystery). 4.1.2005
That ca-ca eating grin you've got
gives away the plot.

Your friends are there to praise
what you say you know up front.

Shrub, you are no small stunt.
Oh, George they say,
your poop is better
than alley-oop.

Your turd has hoots
and toots of steam.
God's truth—your doo-doo
doth smell like ice cream.
But we know what
generates your gleam.

It rises from those Presidential farts
so full of arts, so nobly
steeped in self-esteem
full of the hiss of your self-adoring dream.

Oh, George, your mouth!
Keep licking the cream.

"What do you think?" he asked me. The smirk on his face
equaled the one he conjured in the first line. He'd just read me
a handwritten first draft.

"Well," I said, "I don't really know what to say, Norman.
It's original."

The term *libelous* came to mind, but I didn't say it. It would
have done no good and probably would have provoked him to
lash out at Bush even more potently in his poem. What I did
say was this: "It's kind of *raw*, don't you think?"

"Ah, you're a spoiled darling!" he said, then changed a few

lines. He handed it back with another grin and a healthy hand slap to the table. "There! Now, type it up and let's see what it looks like."

I did, and he went over it two or three more times until declaring it finished.

"What do you want me to do with it now?" I asked. He'd read the poem to Norris, who said she also thought it was in fairly poor taste but no worse than the poor taste Bush exemplified.

"Hold on to it. I'll decide what to do with it later," Norman told me.

What was decided, apparently, was that it would remain on my computer. Norman never asked me to send it out to anyone. A copy did kick around on the dining room table for a couple of weeks, gathering stains, and likely was read aloud occasionally to visitors, but Norman never asked me to forward it to any publications. Simply that the poem had been written was enough for him in the end.

I'd never been around someone who lived the way Norman did, reveling in the smallest things, writing passionately about large issues, and managing to accomplish all with elegance and whimsy. He would suggest I buy the best possible wine for dinner guests and then ask me to make sure we had plenty of Hershey's Bars.

"I can get better chocolate, you know," I said.

"Hershey's *is* good chocolate," he said, "I've never had a taste for the expensive stuff."

That's how Norman was: constantly vacillating between the

fine and the most basic. He never set out to impress his dinner guests, who, in the first year included Pulitzer Prize–winning author and presidential historian Doris Kearns-Goodwin and her husband, Richard; Robert Jay Lifton, the author and psychologist; Christina Pabst, an actress and a daughter of the Pabst brewing family, who became my dear friend; the writers E. L. Doctorow and William Kennedy, whom I barely got to know; and slew of regular people Norman invited to eat and play poker with after dinner. For him, the interaction was important. Posturing by serving haughty food was not. He would ask for meat loaf more often than steak, and care little if that sat well with his guests. It was more that he knew that whatever we served would be less important than the gathering itself.

"I think your meat loaf is just as good as anything else we could feed them," he'd say. "But let's have the pinot noir with that."

So I would make meat loaf, and the guests would eat it as if it were expensive sirloin. To be on the safe side, however, Norman had a luxurious pinot noir as backup.

"Can we get this?" he asked me one morning. He shoved the *New York Times* under my nose as I was making a list for the day's research. It was an article about an Oregon wine that had earned extremely high marks.

"Anything is possible," I said. I'd long ago depleted any interesting choices our local liquor store had to offer. That day I set out to find the wine, and at five o'clock I handed him a sheet of paper with my notes.

"Fifty bucks a bottle, retail," I said.

"The *Times* said thirty," he said, shaking his head.

"That's why it's fifty now. Let me see what I can do." The next day I tracked down the little vineyard in Oregon and called them. I asked for the manager, who got on the phone to apologize. "Yes, it's true," she said, "We just sold the last case."

"Too bad," I said. "I'm calling for Norman Mailer, and he really wants to buy your wine."

"Norman Mailer, the author?"

"Yes," I said. I rarely used the "Mailer Card" when attempting to get something, but Norman really wanted that wine.

"Hold on."

Two minutes later she returned to the phone and said they actually did have *one* case left. By the time I hung up the phone it was slated for shipment, but not to Provincetown. Massachusetts law forbids the private import of wine through the mail. Norman called his daughter, Susan, who was staying at the New York apartment, and told her to expect a delivery. Screw the mail; we'd ship to another state! I called the winery back and told them where to send it. The woman on the phone then told me they wouldn't ship for a couple weeks, because temperature variations during shipment must be considered. She would not endanger her product by shipping when there was a chance the wine could be ruined. Several weeks later, John Buffalo finally brought the case up when he visited Provincetown.

We served the wine when Natalio Grueso, the right-hand man to the Prince of Spain, came to dinner. The tenderloin we served was accompanied by Norman's mushroom duxelles that he had asked me to attempt. I joined them for dinner that night, because Natalio was a fine man whom I liked a good deal and because Norman insisted that timing was everything when it came to his mushroom recipe.

"I can't believe he got you to make that," Norris said that afternoon in the kitchen as I was smashing the water from three pounds of finely chopped mushrooms.

"It's a challenge," I said, pressing the paper towel/fungus sandwich I had made against the granite counter with a rolling pin (it was the only efficient method of pressing the liquid from the mushrooms I could come up with).

"I'm surprised you haven't used every pan, like Norman used to do," she said, pouring a glass of ice water.

That night we debuted the Oregon pinot, and Norman never said a word about it. He did, however, praise the duxelles.

"You did a superb job with the mushrooms," he said over dinner, holding a glass of the well-traveled wine in his hand and tipping it in my direction.

He told me later that he enjoyed the effort to get the wine as much as the wine itself. "I've had better," he said. "Don't misunderstand me; it's very good, but after all we went through to get it, I expected more. Take a bottle or two for yourself."

I did take two bottles and also kept the note the nice woman who owned the winery had sent:

Dear Mr. Mailer,
The vine from which this wine came died the winter after harvest.
This is the last case in existence. I'm happy that it has gone to you.
Sincerely, Patricia Green.

I still have one bottle, stored away for a day when I can sit down to a fine meal and toast Norman's memory without protracted melancholy infecting it. Now is too soon. Like a young wine that hasn't matured, my years with him have yet to find their smoothness. There is too much to flesh out, too much rendering yet to be done.

FOUR

The Remover of Obstacles

My affection for Norman grew wildly in that first year. We arrived at a point where we could say just about anything to each other, and generally did. I was as comfortable being myself around him as I was with anyone, but I never quite got entirely used to being so close to someone whose name popped up regularly in the *New York Times* or on Page Six of the *Post*. Norman would usually just skim an article that mentioned him, generally without comment, sometimes with a grunt, but always with an expression that I could never entirely decode. Occasionally he would appear to be editing it, looking for one inaccuracy or another. He usually found one. After fifty-five years, he was used to seeing his name in print: quotes attributed to him or inane statements about his past marriages, dug up and dusted off yet again.

Norman's fame was unique for a writer. To be fair, he'd elevated it himself with frequent appearances on television talk shows, a run for mayor of New York in 1968, and by directing several movies. Because of this, the scope of his celebrity eclipsed that of his literary contemporaries, which is exactly what he wanted. Norman's competitiveness as a hybrid of writer/journalist/moviemaker/political commentator never subsided. All of those professions tend to be spirited, but wrap them in a single package, and the product was Mailer.

A result of this notoriety was relentless documentation of his personal life, coverage that was often colorful if not downright incorrect. Nearly every article about Norman emphasized his five divorces with as much importance as his literary work—or more. Usually a critique included the tedious retelling of the story that unfolded on a fateful night in 1960. Norman was arrested for an admittedly appalling assault on his second wife, Adele, in the small hours of morning following a big night of drinking. What would have been buried deep within the paper as a domestic brawl, had it been perpetrated by anyone else, hit nearly every front page in America because it had happened to Norman. We talked about that night just once. After taking a long pause, he looked at me and said, "It was a night of ghastly events." Noting his forehead, rutted with affliction, I realized I held him in too high a regard to press further. I had long ago begun to count him as one of the people I trusted most in my life, and this answer was enough. After all, the memory was his demon, not mine; any protracted pains were his to brawl with privately. Norman had virtually no contact or information about his former wife Adele, other than what he heard of her from their daughters, Danielle and Betsy, but he had, without fail, paid her a hefty alimony for more than forty years. It was not my place to judge if that was sufficient penance, and so I never gave it thought. Norman's past didn't sway my reverence one bit.

I liked his fourth wife, Beverly, whom he was married to from 1963 to 1980, a great deal, but I never told Norman that. He had a tendency to get worked up (perhaps with good reason) whenever her name floated through a room. As I was aware of this, I diplomatically avoided mentioning her.

I came to know Beverly Bentley Mailer over the years, out of Norman's range and purely by chance. I first shared a drink with her at a restaurant one summer night in Provincetown, where she still vacationed every summer. I knew who she was when we began to talk, but I decided to omit any mention of my relation to Norman. I didn't want to cause her any distress, so I played the moment as if we were just two people who happened to meet and enjoyed each other's company. I maintained that position for more than a year. When I finally did confess to my relationship with her ex-husband, she was very sweet and said, "I know, dear. I always did. I never wanted to make *you* uncomfortable."

I found Beverly to be an artistic, edgy, captivating woman. She was capricious, slightly crackers, and totally willing to join anyone for a drink to swap stories about Provincetown, a village she loved as much as Norman did. After I confessed to working with Norman, she asked how he was getting along and how Norris was holding up with her illness. She may have been a rabble-rouser, but she was genuine when it came to the essentials.

Her divorce from Norman, which had fallen away to dust everywhere else except in her mind, was a place where time stopped. Whenever Beverly talked to me or anyone else about Norman, she had a habit of speaking in a way that implied their divorce had happened last week. Though they had been separated for more than a quarter of a century by the time I met her, the details were raw for her still, and if unchecked, she could seethe endlessly about her ex-husband. It was a curious phenomenon, and her failure to let their marriage die annoyed Norman. Sitting across a table from him when her name came up, I could see the veins in his forehead engorge with blood. One of his more notable quotes, one inspired by Beverly, was, "You never really get to know a woman until you meet her in court."

Norman was a good father, a detail that remains largely ignored when pundits or scholars consider him. Of all the families I have known in my life, nearly all have at least one child who is damaged in one way or another, rooting their rage in the failure of one or both of their parents. This was not the case with Norman and his kids. Of the nine, none seemed to be remarkably affected, adversely or otherwise, by their father's fame. Possibly, Norman's own growth was interrupted by his rapid shot to celebrity, and he never had the opportunity to manage his own young adulthood before finding himself responsible for children. He was sainted in literary circles at twenty-five and a father at twenty-six. Most men would be wholly derailed by such intense scrutiny at that age, but he wasn't. As he told his son Michael, any questions about his success or failure as a father should be measured in the vein of "quality over quantity." He had been separated from all of his children at one point or another, due to his work, but that in no way affected the level of importance they held in his life. From what I noticed, he offered them unique perspectives from which to find their own pillars.

Although I was not around when they were young, from what I observed as he interacted with them as adults, they had been availed a good life, ripe with freedom, during which Norman masterfully maintained authority. He raised his kids like one might assume a novelist would: every day was an exercise in how never to settle for mere "satisfactory." It was beyond him to claim that he was the best parent in the world, but he did remark once that having a child (or nine) was serious, and not to be mucked around with recklessly. He told an interviewer once, "When one has nine children, it's very hard to get away with a skin game. It's very hard to fool them."

I became close with most of the kids, and they spoke warmly to me about their father. I found myself rather envious of them that first year, jealous that I was coming to know Norman only in this later stage of his life. The more I was around him, the more I wondered what it would have been like to know him in my own formative years. My father, who was a sensible, perceptive man, died when I was seven. I was raised, along with my two older brothers, by a mother who was intelligent and broadminded. Our simple life in Oregon, however idyllic, held me back from investigating much of what pestered my curious head.

We lived on a hill above a tiny town, twenty miles from a larger town that could be regarded as small itself. Lack of exposure to cultural difference and little opportunity to go beyond a basic education were unfortunate consequences. Nonetheless, my two older brothers and I were encouraged to read as much as we were encouraged to know our environment. We lived in the woods, and that in itself taught us to be clear thinking and somewhat studious about nature and our surroundings. I do not remember being unable either to read or to tell the difference between the types of trees that towered over us. When I started school, I found it freakishly easy, and I soon became bored. So, a teacher's aide selected me to help tutor the other children in reading. There I was, teaching other six-year-olds to repeat the name Spot over and over again as they read the insipid *Dick and Jane* books. It was the first time I recall wondering if there was more to education than repetition. That apathy never left me, and it cursed my school life. Consequently, I rarely excelled beyond what was required to appease the bog we called "public education" in the 1970s. Having had quite enough by the age of eighteen, and sick of being force-fed unimportant drivel, I cheated my way out of a math requirement for graduation. I rationalized that I would never need algebra, so I lifted a copy of the three-page test from the a teacher's desk for ten minutes, copied it in the empty faculty lounge, returned the original, memorized what answers I could, and passed with a sham C. I have little regret about the act (other than the obvious shame at my thievery), because I've yet to encounter a need for algebra. Years later, when I told Norman about it, he suggested I might have found a fine life in politics, where a lack of remorse about dubious acts could be put to good use.

The more time I spent with Norman the more I regarded him as a stand-in for a father figure, and wondered what it would have been like to become a man under his tutelage. When I met his children, I got a good idea. I probably would have grown up less afraid, considerably smarter, utterly awed, more irritated about social divisions, significantly more passionate about art and writing, quicker with a quip and a grasp of a glass, physically stronger, and forever thankful my dad was not boring. Norman may not have been a model father in the American sense, but he was never lackluster, never deficient with advice, and always fell into a state of delight when one of his children was near. The only reference I had to having a man Norman's age affect my life were memories of my own detached grandfather.

My grandpa was a quiet man who seldom spoke, except, strangely enough, to recite a poem to my grandmother almost every morning while he rolled his Prince Albert cigarette beside their wood-burning cookstove. I think he must have been quite intelligent deep beneath his outward reserve, but I doubt he gave much credence to it. He was a sawmill worker turned gardener and tended a large and fine garden on our land until he died at eighty-six, after a long day of working it. My grandparents lived near us, just a hundred yards down a half-gravel path. They never wanted more than the simple existence they lived, which made for a decent life. It did not, however, wholly appeal to me. I traveled to New York for a week at age fifteen, and afterward I was never the same. Fifteen is often the age when one begins to place bookmarks in the world for later investigation. I'd tasted a desire to explore beyond the good, quiet existence I'd known up until then. Three years later, when I scrambled east to Vermont for college to crack open my adulthood, I vowed to return rarely to Oregon and instead plowed headlong toward a future full of vagaries. My mother had been hands-off by never insisting I hone my priorities to be more typical, and I admired her for that. Later, I wished she'd been more potent with advice, because I ended up incapable of figuring out much of anything, other than how to merely get by up to an inexcusable age. By the time I landed in Ptown, a third of my life later, I was well beyond where her opinion held serious influence. I was mired in the tedious drear of living paycheck to paycheck, cashing away time and fading hope every Friday while the bank teller did her job. I'd acquired experience, travel, and education in the bouncing-around years, but it was a disorderly muddle, equivalent to an office strewn haphazardly with important unfiled documents. Due to my natural disrespect for organization of any sort, the contents of my den were useless.

When I met Norman, that changed. I adopted a fresh approach to intellectual tidiness, which, in course, set a few of my other off-center priorities on a highway to repair. I found myself motivated by the effect Norman's attitude had on his kids. His children embodied, in part or in whole, everything I aspired to, and they had those qualities directly because of him. The girls—Susan, Danielle, Betsy, Kate, and Maggie—are all smart, appealing, artistic, and pleasant. The boys—Michael, Stephen, Matthew, and John—are vibrant examples of what the best of being male in America is: sturdy, honest, reliable, and perceptive. None of the children is mired in what Norman sometimes referred to as "corporate banality." Of the nine, there are two actors, a filmmaker, three writers, two talented artists, and a psychologist. Not bad for a brood that is the product of a man whose six marriages were splattered across newspapers for fifty years. Norman's children also continually draw strength from one another—something they do even now that their guide is gone. I draw from my time with Norman as well, and count myself as a fortunate semi-adoptive member of that very exclusive clan.

An example of the lengths to which Norman would go to support one of his children was his appearance on the television show *Gilmore Girls*. In 2004 the producers contacted us saying they had written an episode with him in mind. Would he consider being part of it? In the email, they included the synopsis. Norman wrestled with the idea for a day or two, and finally agreed to do it, on the condition that his son Stephen, a fine and accomplished actor, be cast in the part opposite him, as a reporter interviewing "Norman Mailer," and that the TV executives agree to pay Stephen as much as they were paying Norman.

The producers agreed to Norman's requests, and the two flew out to Los Angeles in early August to do the show. For their scenes, Stephen and Norman sat in the fictional restaurant near the Yale campus drinking only ice tea (which Norman disliked in actuality) to the great irritation of the cook. At first the viewer is meant to think she's annoyed that he spends no money and takes up her valuable dining space, but then she blurts out to him, "Norman Mailer I'm pregnant!" which was the title of the episode. Norman gives an appropriately befuddled "Congratulations!" to this news, dead-panning as only he can. They filmed for two days on the Warner Brothers lot, and the entire cast apparently fell in love with Norman, and vice versa, because he returned home with fine things to say about their professionalism—something he hadn't expected to encounter. As far as I know, he never saw the episode in its entirety; that was not his style. Norman had done the job in order to help out his son and that was enough.

Norman knew when to use his fame and when not to, but there was never a question about using it to help one of his kids. He would spread himself thin to attend an art opening or other occasion because he knew his presence would add to the attraction.

Later that August, several Mailers agreed to do a benefit reading performance of Eugene O'Neill's *Long Day's Journey into Night* as a family, to benefit the local theater in Provincetown. Kate, John, and Stephen joined Norman and Norris for the week to rehearse for the reading. I watched throughout the week as the work evolved and noticed the meticulousness with which Norman directed. He was eighty-one years old, but there was no holding him back when it came to perfecting his cast.

"Stephen is going to be in it, too?" Judith asked me from Brooklyn.

"Yes, of course," I said. I was downstairs alone talking to her on the bar phone. "Why?"

"Oh, boy," she said.

"What?"

"Well, sometimes Norman and Stephen don't get on well when it comes to work."

I had no idea about this. As far as I knew, everything had gone well with the TV shoot earlier in the month. Judith then told me about the rumbles she'd witnessed in the past between artist son and artist father.

"What about with John and Kate?" I asked her.

"Who knows?" she said. "But I do know that those two occasionally have issues. He loves that boy to death, but they are too much alike in temperament. Watch out for storms."

Sure enough, halfway through the week, tempers flared. While they were rehearsing out on the deck, I was in the dining room typing a draft of an article that Norman was writing. I couldn't tell what the blowup was about, but it was loud, and there was much banging on the deck's glass table. Norman had a habit of tapping his hand on whatever surface was in front of him. When he read his own work, he tapped softly; when he edited, he whacked more briskly. In making a point during conversation or, in this case, directing, he could pound loudly, and did. His hand was now almost rattling the windows as it repeatedly struck the table outside.

Then the back door from the deck flew open and Stephen zipped across the living room and out the front door on the opposite side of the house, slamming it forcefully behind him. Rehearsal was over. Norman came in and sat across from me at the table. Neither of us spoke. Norris, script still in hand, came to the table.

"You two have to come to terms," she said.

"Barbara, I don't want to talk about it now," Norman said.

"But Norman . . ."

"Barbara, goddamn it. I've got this to direct this fucking thing and I can't do it with you taking sides."

"I'm not taking sides, Norman. I'm just saying you both need to cooperate."

I wanted to fold myself up into my computer and hide until the uproar was over, but I was stuck. Arguments never sit well with me—even when they aren't mine. I gradually got up and slunk toward the kitchen and outside through the side door. From there I could hear the two of them going at it in the house. For Norman it was all about the play, and for Norris it was about the play, too, but more so about family. She forever dedicated her every waking moment to him, to the kids, to her mother, who still lived in the house, and seemingly always put herself second. It was a daunting daily display of selfless efforts. Nevertheless, I couldn't help but think that in two hours they were to be sitting down to the lasagna I'd prepared earlier for dinner. Would it go to waste? In the end it didn't, because the play wasn't entirely the thing; this good family *was*. Fights about art can happen in a family (if indeed your family is ar-

tistic), but the core remains solid. Love, it seems, can be a protector.

Norris left Norman alone at the table and went upstairs. I
wasn't sure where John and Kate were, but I figured the coast
was clear enough for me to return to the table to gather my
computer and leave for the night. Norman didn't say anything
to me when I came in. He was reading the paper. A quiet hour
passed in the course of a minute.

"Well," I finally said, "I guess I'll be headed out."

"So, we've got dinner?" he asked, not looking up at me.

"Yup. Lasagna."

"I don't like lasagna." This aversion was one that had evolved
since noon, when he'd suggested the dish.

"Okay, well, then I guess it's going to be a tough night for
eating," I said. "There's salad too, you know. Mixed greens."

"I only like iceberg lettuce."

I shrugged. There was nothing I could do to magically
change the lettuce into iceberg now. It was late; my day was
done and so were my nerves. There was another dead pause
while I collected my things.

"I'll see you tomorrow," I said. Norman finally looked up at
me. His deep blue eyes appeared weary, but not weary like after
too much reading. I suspected the strain came from the concern
that he'd maybe put director above father out there on the deck,
and now it had to be undone. And he was also, certainly, feeling guilt about having tactlessly battled Norris when she was
clearly in the right, as she usually was.

"Yes, tomorrow," he said. He didn't say anything more about

the food and certainly not about the explosion. For Norman, letting an awkward situation distil without further mention was often the best way to handle it. "Have a good night."

"You, too," I said. I touched his shoulder on the way out as I always did, an unconscious habit that I had developed.

As I passed through the living room, I found Johnny sitting on the couch. He still had his script in his hand, but he wasn't reading it. He was staring at the floor. He was the youngest child, something he and I had in common. I thought perhaps his sensitivity to domestic earthquakes was likely as heightened as mine. I decided to say nothing to him and remove myself right to the Little Bar.

One day, a year or so into my tenure with Norman, while we were taking a break from work in the attic, he asked me how things were going with Thomas. Although he always asked how Thomas was, he rarely inquired directly about the relationship, but this day he put his book down, called me to his desk, and asked me to sit for a talk. Three days before, several days after the blowup over the play rehearsal, I'd taken a day off, one of my first and one of the few. Thomas and I had separated, and I was physically unable to pull myself out of bed. I told Norman that I was feeling ill. Norman was irritated that I needed to skip the day, and this was evident in his tone on the phone. "I've got work to do and now it will have to wait," he had said.

He could be cutting. My personal troubles had been brewing for a few weeks and had culminated in this need to simply check out. Norman sounded distrustful of my excuse that I was not well. I had begun to drink more than ever in the evenings, as a way to alleviate the confusion concerning Thomas that I couldn't face or see clearly. The liquor did its job, but not well enough, and my depression always returned. I wasn't, simply stated, in a very good place.

"You're not paying attention," Norman said without scorn as we sat talking that day. "Something's amok with you."

"We've had trouble, but I'm fine," I lied. I hated lying to him, but I was afraid to admit my weaknesses. Norman was always pragmatic about complexities in relationships—and everything else. He'd faced the government's ire, the rage of several ex-wives, and flying fists in the boxing ring. How do you tell a man like that you are terrified of having further discussions with your lover that you suspect might end badly? By definition Norman was tough, and here I was allowing my limitations to consume me from the outside in.

"I'm sorry. I don't know what's going on these days," I said. I was looking at his desk, and he was looking at me. In the year that I had worked with him we had both come to know when we were holding out on each other, and he didn't accept my reply. He knew exactly what was going on in my head. Any event or rattle of spirit I was experiencing he had endured himself—or at least a variation of it. However, I was so myopic that I could not see beyond myself to know this.

"Well, you have to stop this business and separate it from your work. I need you to be clear. Listen, what you think is tough will be gone the second you decide it should stop. You're smart, and I need you here."

"Okay," I said.

"I need to be able to depend on you."

"I know."

"There's good work to be done here." It was fairly late in the day, and I had to leave soon. From the kitchen below I could smell the pot roast I'd made. "Come back on Monday and we'll get back to the job."

This was Thursday. Was I being sent away for a long weekend?

"You want me to take tomorrow off?"

"The roast will give us leftovers, and I've got plenty of reading to do. You've got some thinking of your own to do. See you Monday."

"I won't be around tomorrow," I said to Judith. It was after nine at night and we were talking on the phone. I was well oiled.

"That sounds like a good idea," she said.

"Norman said he'd just do more reading." I sighed heavily. "I'm tired of all the shit with Thomas. I didn't even want to talk about it with Norman. He's the one who wanted to talk."

"He wants to work and that's all," she said. "He'd never admit that he is concerned for your well-being. Acting indifferent to your troubles is how he makes his point."

"Well, I don't get it," I said.

"Do yourself a favor and get yourself together every day before you go over. Just tell him matter-of-fact and with a straight face that you're better. He'll believe you. Keep your wits about you. You might want to stop being so open with both of them. Draw a line and don't cross it with personal details."

I vowed to heed Judith's advice, and I'm glad I did. The next time I saw Norman, I announced that I was on track and that I'd try not to get lost in my own muck anymore. Soon, our days were back to normal. While I was around him, I played down all that was bugging me. He had been right about the bullshit stopping when I decided it should. It wasn't easy, but it worked. It's daunting to consider how much time it would have taken for me to get a proper grip if Norman hadn't given me the kick that he did. And certainly Judith's clear advice helped—although I could not muster as much restraint concerning the personal as she could, especially with Norris. Judith knew how to deal with Norman better than anyone when it came to work, but she had little knowledge of how to skillfully handle the personal.

Judith McNally became as close to me as anybody in the first two and a half years that I was with Norman, even though we interacted strictly on the phone. She was the only person I could speak to openly about the quirks of our author, the daily grind, and everything else that happened under the roof at 627. Since she'd been working with Norman for more than twenty-five years, she knew significantly more about his varied nature than I did. When it came right down to it, however, Norman knew less about Judith. He knew for certain that she was the product of a strict Catholic upbringing, including her entire education, which made her fluent in religion, but other than the rudimentary details of her personal life, he was in the dark.

"Judith knows more about Catholicism than most bishops," Norman told me.

Judith had shunned her religion long ago. What remained was a deep knowledge that was extremely useful in her work with Norman, who often swerved into that area in his writing. Judith followed Eastern philosophies now, because, she told me, Catholicism had betrayed her. I never asked the details, and it's safe to say she never would have told me anyway; she was selectively secretive. What she did admit to was traveling to Thailand when she had time, but she revealed almost no details about the trips. When she made the pilgrimages, she cut off communication with the Western world completely—us included. Nevertheless, when it came to other parts of her life, she was willing to be a little more open about them with me than she was with Norman.

Judith recognized that I was at a crossroads about many things, which is probably why she let her guard down slightly with me. Most of our talks centered on Norman, but not necessarily the work. Judith cared deeply for him in her aloof, businesslike way, and she depended on me to tell her how he was doing physically.

"How does he look today?"

"He looks tired, but he's okay."

"Well, I'm tired too," she said. "I was up late last night working."

"On what?"

"A piece for Mohammed."

She went on to tell me about the editing work she had been doing for a young journalist who lived in the Gaza Strip. Mohammed Omer had, at the age of twenty, dedicated his young life to reporting on the conflicts there, emailing drafts of his dispatches to her. Judith would edit and publish them to a web page called Rafa Notes. She'd been doing this, and involving herself in other areas of Palestinian rights, for a couple of years. The work was done in the middle of the night from her tiny, one-room apartment on Hicks Street in Brooklyn. When she first told me about it, I was surprised, but not after I gave it a fleck of thought. It was Judith's nature to be hugely private, but she was also an incredibly involved political person. Her politics were left of left, and her sensibilities veered toward the needs of those who she believed were the oppressed. There she was, a former Catholic working for a Jewish author and moonlighting on behalf of the Palestinian movement. She distributed Mohammed's reports because she saw it as the right thing to do. She did all of it under the alias of "Erika."

Judith's efforts on the part of the Palestinians went farther than merely acting as an editor. She told me how she'd recently facilitated the transfer of a young girl named Annya with a leg deformation from Gaza to New York for medical care.

"There can be nothing done for her there, what with the war raging around her," Judith said. "So I rounded up some money and got her over here for an operation. There's a doctor we know who does this for nothing." She told me that since the little girl was turning twelve soon, the ridicule would become merciless. "Children can be horrid to each other, even in war zones."

"Was she hurt in the war?" I asked.

"No. Those kids are taken care of. Kids like Annya are pushed aside. It's wrong."

"So you paid for her to be brought here?"

"Not just me, but, yes," she said. "I thought I told you about her."

"No," I said. "That's amazing."

"No, it's not. Some things just need to be done."

Every so often Judith would tell me more about Annya's recovery, until one day she said the little girl had returned to Palestine.

I never said anything to Norman or Norris about this, because Judith had asked me to "keep it in the vault." Unlike me, she preferred that the Mailers not know some details about her life; I didn't care all that much—especially when it came to talking to Norris. Norman and Norris knew most everything about my life because we were around each other constantly. Another reason we shared so much openness was because none of us was good at keeping secrets. For me, this did not extend to what I knew about Judith's affairs, however. She'd asked me to keep some things we talked about close to my vest, and so I did—much the same way I did for Norman and Norris after I closed the door to leave their home each day.

In 2005, the third annual Norman Mailer Society Conference was to be held in Provincetown. In its first year, the Society had convened in Brooklyn, but it moved to Ptown the second year. That idea had stuck, and the third meeting was again held in Norman's Ptown. Norman had little to do with the event, apart from giving a reading on the final night, at the local theater, and hosting a closing party afterward in his home.

The members, many of whom had devoted a good portion of their academic lives to his writings, descended on the house en masse to see where the Master lived and worked.

I urged Judith to come up to Provincetown for that year's meeting, but she told me she didn't think she could make it.

"My mother lived in Centerville at the end of her life," she told me. "I used to go there to take care of her. I don't have fond memories of Cape Cod." Then she coughed, as only somebody who smoked three packs a day could. The volume of her coughs over the last months had increased, but I never said anything about it. She would have blamed the cough on something other than smoking anyway. As intelligent as Judith was, she lived in total denial of the wolf she courted.

"Provincetown is not like the rest of the Cape," I said. "I really wish you'd come. I know that Norman would like to have you here. Come on, Judith, we'll have fun."

"Let me think about it," she said.

"I think I've got Judith convinced to come up this year," I told Norman the next morning. "She's hesitant about coming to the Cape again, though."

"She's never been here," he said.

"Yes, she has. Centerville, when her mother was sick," I said.

"I mean here to Provincetown," Norman said. "She won't come."

"Why?"

"I don't know."

"You mean that in twenty-five years of working for you she's never come to the house?"

"No," Norris said. She'd joined us at the table. "For some reason she's got it in her mind that she can't leave Brooklyn, even though she goes away to god knows where on vacation very year."

"She's private, Barb," Norman said. "We've got to respect that."

"Private is one thing; stubborn is another," Norris said. Norris cared a great deal about Judith, but always had difficulty with her obstinacy. One of her favorite stories about Judith's inflexibility concerned the destruction of a new computer Judith had bought. She ruined its hard drive attempting to install an incompatible, out-of-date operating system on it because the system was "familiar." Two thousand dollars and several repairs later she finally decided it was more sensible simply to learn the new program.

"Well, I think it's silly," I said. "I'm going to convince her to come up."

"Tell her I'll pay for a hotel if she does," Norman said, probably gambling that she'd decline the offer. Then again, Norman was always offering to pay for someone's hotel, even people who had a hundred times more money than he did.

"Norman will pay for your hotel if you come," I told Judith later.

"Well, if I come, I'm paying my own way," she said and let out another unruly torrent of coughs.

"So you're thinking about it?"

"Can you find me a *cheap* hotel?" Judith asked, "One that allows smoking?"

The day before the meeting of the Society that November, I drove my Volvo to pick Judith up from Provincetown's small airport, which is located out near Race Point Beach. Before she stepped off the ten-foot stretch of curb to walk toward the car, she'd a lit cigarette.

"God, what a long flight," she said. It had been four hours by my calculations since she'd last smoked. Although we had grown close, we had never laid eyes on each other before that day. She was diminutive and spry, a redheaded hundred-pound bundle of knowledge, nerves, and smiles.

"You're taller than I thought," she said, looking up at me as if I sounded short on the phone

Norman had asked me to take Judith for a tour. "Show her the wharf and drive her up Commercial to the end before you bring her here. Introduce her to the town."

He loved to show off Provincetown, even by way of asking me to do it for him. I noticed that he was slightly reticent about Judith visiting for the first time in so many years. When I was leaving to get her at the airport, he was on his way up the attic stairs and had hollered down, "Bring her up when you get back. I want her to see the office."

It dawned on me that he was staging the arrival scene to suit an image he had in his head about how their first meeting in Ptown should play out. He looked slightly anxious as he climbed the stairs. Sometimes Norman could act strange, and this was one of those times.

I drove Judith around for twenty minutes before heading back to the house. The afternoon was gray and turning chilly as we pulled up alongside the boxwoods that delineated the yard from the street.

"It's bigger than I thought," she said as we exited my car. She stood looking up at the old brick house for a moment and then flicked her sixth cigarette into the street. It was not a delicate move.

Norris and Judith embraced in the living room, and Norris immediately began a tour of the house. As they wandered through the downstairs, I dashed up to the third floor. Norman, hearing my feet on the wood stairs, spun around expecting to find both of his assistants together for the first time. Instead, there was only me. A small irritation crept over his face.

"Where's Judith?" He was at his desk, pen in hand. There was no writing on the paper in front of him.

"Norris is showing her the house."

Norman shook his head. "Why? I have to work. She should see the office before I get to work." From the time I'd left to go get Judith, he'd had nearly an hour in which to work, but he hadn't done a thing, other than perhaps read.

"You know how Norris is when people come in the house for the first time. She's showing her around."

"Where'd you take her after you picked her up?" he asked

"Where you asked: past Herring Cove, then out to the pier, and up Commercial to the Provincetown Inn. She said, 'Oh, *this* is the motel he wrote about.'"

Norman had described the Provincetown Inn motel in his novel *Tough Guys Don't Dance*. Oddly, it stands near the true first landing spot of the Pilgrims—which is not Plymouth, as every child in America is erroneously taught. In his book he wrote that while the structure was "no uglier than any other vast motel, it is certainly no prettier, and the only homage to the Pilgrims is that it is called an Inn. Its asphalt parking lot is as large as a football field."

"Well, ask Norris to bring her up. I'll be here working." He positioned himself in a most author-esque way at his desk. I suppressed an urge to chuckle as I went to find the women.

Five minutes later we climbed up to the third floor attic only to have Norris take an immediate detour with Judith into her end, opposite from where Norman sat waiting. He turned around just in time to see them duck out of his sight.

"Barbara, bring Judith in here," he shouted.

"I'm showing her my study!" Norris hollered back, sweet as pie. She didn't realize that Norman was an uncharacteristic twaddle of nerves.

Finally, Judith joined us. Norman, ever the gentleman, stood to greet his secretary with an ample smile. It was then that I realized that they were both the same height. Judith moved close to Norman, who seemed awkward in her presence. Their hug was not fully realized or well executed. Each touched the other in what can only be called an inept embrace, which lasted for no more than a second. Judith stepped back, and Norman sat down in his chair with a thump.

"So here it is," he said, indicating his office with arms spread wide so as to show her the room. Judith turned to survey the book-stoked attic.

"It's just like I thought it would be," she said. I knew she wanted nothing more than to light up. If Norman had still been a smoker (he'd quit forty years before), he would have, too. Watching this encounter play out before me was peculiar. Even after all their shared years, it was becoming clear to me that they knew little about each other. Norman and Judith had basically functioned as a team and had never ventured beyond that point. Judith had worked with him on every book since 1978, but true closeness had never evolved. There in the attic they regarded each other like work associates talking at a company Christmas party before the drinking started. Norman, clearly, was much more comfortable with Judith being a voice on the phone, and she simply looked out of place.

"Oh," she said, turning a bit and walking back toward me and Norris, "The fax machine!" She pointed at the small desk from which I had spent hours feeding thousands of sheets of paper to her via the phone line.

"Yes . . ." Norman said. It was one of the simplest bits of talk I'd ever heard him utter. He was at a loss as to what to say, and so was she. I'd never seen Norman display as much discomfort at the presence of a woman as he did that day, and even now I don't know precisely why. He had more charm in his back pocket than anyone I'd ever known, but still his efforts were lost—or she was merely immune. Finally, Judith asked about the painting that hung in the stairwell, which was of the four boys playing on the beach. Norris had painted it years before, and she began to tell Judith the story. Norman seemed happy about this and turned his attention back to his desk. He never did get any work done that night, and I know this because the next morning no new pages awaited me, and his nearby bed was rumpled. As soon as we'd left the attic, he'd taken a pre-dinner nap. Something had worn him out.

Judith was a vegetarian, and I had prepared a dish especially for her. Norman often bragged about my cooking to her, so I felt obliged to make something worthy of the praise.

"I made roasted polenta with shitake mushrooms for you," I told her as we descended the stairs and wandered toward the kitchen. "I reminded him you don't eat meat."

The main dish that night was a boneless roast that Norman had suggested. "I love it with lots of horseradish sauce. Can you make a good sauce?" he asked, knowing full well I could. If he knew Judith didn't eat meat, he didn't say or didn't care.

"You know she's vegetarian, don't you?" I reminded him.

"Hmm . . . yes. What can you do about that?"

"I'll work it out," I'd said.

Everybody wanted me to stay for dinner, but my patience for family, the Society, and all the other hoopla had reached a peak. Michael and John were visiting, along with Norman's sister Barbara, the Lennons, and Christina: all of whom were to share dinner. I was feeling overwhelmed by all the guests and my obligation to orchestrate the party for the Society members the following evening. Occasionally my weeks were like that: emotionally overwhelming to the point of drowning in frustration. Within the confines of our normal routines I tended to remain even, but with the added obligations, it became difficult. To compound everything, Norman had suddenly developed a need to be informed every six minutes about details he normally would have ignored. It was driving me crazy, so I begged off dinner. I whispered in Judith's ear as she hugged me goodbye for the night that I was "bar bound." "But I'll see you tomorrow," I said. "I just gotta go."

"Believe me, I get it," she said. "Do what you have to do."

The following night was the party, and Judith appeared to have a fine time, which made me happy. The November night was unusually warm, and the members were milling throughout the house and out on the deck. As I sat down with Judith to talk, she looked out at the dark ocean and said, "I see why he's here now." She took a drag from her cigarette, leaned back in her chair, and looked at me. "I see why you're here, too. If I had it to do over again I might consider living in Provincetown."

While we relaxed together, enjoying the evening, I toyed with the idea of persuading her to move up to the Cape. She had recently confessed to battles with her landlords, who wanted to convert her apartment into a condo. Judith was being priced out of her home, but she was putting up a fight. Provincetown was as good a choice as any for a place to go should she lose the fight. Some months later the landlords prevailed, and Judith purchased a house in Kentucky—she bought it over the Internet, sight unseen. For several more weeks she prepared for her move, but before she could finally relocate she ran into even more difficulties, and her plans were abruptly altered.

Before she left Provincetown, Judith gave me a small bronze Hindu Ganesh statue that she'd purchased in one of the shops in town. Ganesh, she told me, is the remover of obstacles.

"It's for your desk, to watch over you while you write" she said as she handed it to me. "It'll help you work, clear your mind. This one is reclining, which holds extra good luck for writers."

The figurine was ugly as sin, but I didn't tell her that. I promised instead to put it right where she suggested: on my desk. I don't know if it has done any good or lived up to its fortune, but it still watches me these years later. What I am sure of is that my opinion of it has changed. I do not think it is ugly anymore; instead I see it as a reminder to keep myself afloat.

Judith gave Norman a version of the Hindu god for his desk also. Later, after we learned that Judith would never return to Provincetown, I noticed that his Ganesh was gone. One afternoon when he was in New York doing press for *Castle*, I searched all around his desk, thinking it must have fallen off the edge, but I couldn't find it. When Norman came back I asked him what had happened to the sculpture. He shook his head and said he couldn't recall.

"I may have put it in a drawer," he said.

In late November of 2007, when there was quiet in the house and a new winter was settling in, I decided to rummage through his desk drawers to locate the statuette to put it back where it belonged. I still could not find it. Ganesh, the remover of obstacles, had seemingly removed himself.

FIVE

Provincetown, Poker, and Friends

Provincetown is not your average small town, and it is not inhabited by run-of-the-mill folks. Because of its isolation at the end of a twisted peninsula, it is a magnet for the offbeat, creative, lost, brilliant, poor, wealthy, and hearty of spirit and soul. From its beginning, outcasts have gravitated to it. In 1620 the Pilgrims arrived and signed the Mayflower Compact, widely regarded as the precursor to our Declaration of Independence, on the ship while it was anchored in Provincetown Harbor for sixty-three days. Only after finding the area inhospitable did the Pilgrims sail on over to Plymouth. Two hundred years later, Ptown was a major whaling center with a thriving economy, and over on Long Point, that final finger of the Cape, was a place called "Helltown," which Norman loved telling stories about. As he told the legend, Helltown was a haven for pirates and whores and the seedy types that followed them. Over time, its houses were floated the mile and a quarter across the water to find new foundations in Provincetown proper. In the 1920s, Ptown morphed again, to become a haven for artists, writers, and those whom society dubbed the "fringe element." People began to migrate here in droves to lead lives free of the constraints heaved at them by a sanctimonious post-Victorian culture. In all of that change, there developed a patent notion of freedom that still inhabits Provincetowners. Now, in summertime, the population can swell to more than fifty thousand, but fewer than four thousand call it home year round, and they are a stalwart bunch. Norman, not surprisingly, enjoyed being merely just one of them.

In the course of his sixty-year attachment to the town, which coincided with his entire career as a writer, he became Provincetown's most renowned citizen. His local fame was due not only to his two Pulitzers (at last count we've had at least four other winners of that award call the town home) or that he'd written more than forty books or even that he lived in the only three-story red brick house in town—which stands out like a sore thumb. Norman was famous around town for being "normal" in spite of those distinctions, and his laissez-faire attitude defined his true local legend. He never sequestered himself or thought himself superior because he was a celebrity. Norman, while not incapable of that kind of thinking, knew better than to indulge in it. Nothing made him happier than to venture out to get a handle on what was happening in town. In his agile days, long before I came to be with him, he was a fixture in restaurants and bars all over town, and his daily runs up Commercial Street were a normal occurrence.

"Oh, I used to see Norman all the time," residents say to me when they find out I worked with him. "He'd always wave or stop to say hello. Such a nice man." One lady told me she had discovered him one morning, many years ago, perched in her gazebo reading his morning paper. "Hi, Norman," she hollered over. He waved back and continued reading, oblivious that he might be trespassing and certain that the lady didn't care one hoot if he was—which she didn't.

To most who live in Ptown, he was just "Norman," even if they didn't really know him, and he was the perfect fit for a town that doesn't flinch at celebrity. Ptown residents were and are proud to claim him as a son of theirs, even though he was originally from Brooklyn. He lent a larger dot to our map and brought a tad more shine to the place, and everyone knew it. Norman and Provincetown intertwined so well because they were alike—with both, you got what you did not anticipate. Townies would boast about having Mailer in their midst, but what they didn't know is that Mailer likewise bragged about living among them. He spoke about Provincetowners as the finest group of people a man could be around, people whose grit he admired.

Norman's loyalty extended beyond what he showed toward people; it reached profoundly into his choice of where he called home. When he first came to Provincetown to work on *The Naked and the Dead* in his early twenties, he was not immune to the town's allure, which infects virtually everyone who sets foot on its shoreline. For Norman that allure never diminished, and indeed grew into a passion. The part of him that commanded he live near the waters of Cape Cod was nurtured by each wave of season. He'd lived near the sea in other states periodically and had certainly traveled the world, but he returned faithfully to Provincetown. Ten years before I met him he had at last made it ground zero for his life. He and Norris moved from Brooklyn to the beach, and he settled in to write his coming works in the shadow of our dominant monument. Provincetown had given him much, and he cared for it as deeply as he cared for anything.

When I would take Norman to an appointment in town—his doctor, dentist, or a visit to the local optometrist—he would often insist that we "drag the town." What that meant was that we'd drive slowly up Commercial Street, usually with the windows down so he could better "see what the town is up to." No matter what the season, Provincetown is picturesque, and this was never wasted on Norman. This ritual of trolling town from one end to the other was one he'd practiced for decades and always found fascination with—one way or another.

"Look at those women . . . " he said to me as we crept along in the bright sun of a summer day. He was eyeing a group of young lesbians who were pretty and tan and clearly thrilled about being in an oasis that readily embraced them. "You think they're gay?"

He wasn't asking me this out of anything other than pure curiosity. Since Provincetown had become celebrated for being a gathering place for gay people decades prior, there was never a shortage of gay visitors. Of course, there was no scarcity of straight tourists, either, so it was not unusual to be interested when one saw an attractive example of either sex.

"Yup," I said.

"They're fine looking." His head careened around as we passed the group. "I don't remember gay women looking like that."

"Things may have changed a little," I said.

We rounded the dog-leg curve near the Coast Guard station and headed into the deep West End. Bikes overtook us on either side, as it was easier for them to keep up speed on the busy, narrow street than it was for my car. As we passed the boat launch parking lot, where I still often went on good nights and bad to mull things over, I told Norman about pausing here for a spell the evening before I came to his house to talk to him three years before.

"It's a good spot to think," he said. "I've always preferred this end of town over ours. It's got more raw meat to it."

"Raw meat?"

"Gristle. Toughness. More root at this end of town, and you can feel it."

We drove on in silence until we neared the Red Inn, an old hotel and restaurant that had been built in 1805 and opened as a guesthouse in 1915. Norman had once wanted to buy it and convert it into a home, but something went awry with the deal and he ended up purchasing the house he had now, at the other end of town. The Red Inn, however, was famous in its own right for having hosted a slew of notable guests, ranging from FDR to Farrah Fawcett. Norman had used the place as a set for the film of his book *Tough Guys* that he'd directed, renaming it the Widow's Walk.

"Maybe I should have bought it when I had the chance," he said as we passed, as he did *every* time we passed it. There was never serious regret when he said this, because he knew he'd landed in one of the finest houses in town, one that he absolutely loved. Nevertheless, the Red Inn also sits just on shore from where the pilgrims first landed, and that, I could argue, made the property even more desirable to an American like Norman. He admired the history it represented. Norman never said this to me, or to anyone else as far as I know, but it was a thought that always entered my mind whenever we drove by it. What some have openly doubted and might reconsider is that Norman was somehow "un-American" because he was critical and questioned certain motives of his government. That notion is pure rubbish. Norman understood what it meant to be an American more than anyone I've ever known, because he put his thoughts to page and his feet to pavement to demonstrate his beliefs. And because it is a fine but flawed country at times, only the latter landed him in jail once—circumstances he chronicled in his book *Armies of the Night*.

In the 2004 election, which pegged John Kerry against the second-term George W. Bush, we drove to town hall together to cast our ballots. Norman, of course, had written about contemporary American issues and, in the process, embedded himself in history itself. He had authored numerous politically centered books and countless op-ed pieces, and as a result his left-conservative views were well known, if not wholly understood by readers. Agree with him or not, his opinions were universally measured as sturdy, prevalent, with a virtually unsurpassed intellectual vitality, and among the finest writings of the twentieth century. Norman was a political giant of American letters, a distinction attached to him as indelibly as his skill as a novelist. He lived to write and to teach through that work, and these passions made him unrivaled in his love of country. To vote with him was a surreal experience, because it is rare to find oneself so close to a man who had prompted abstemious social analysis in several generations of readers. None of that came up for conversation as we made our way into Town Hall to vote. It would have been odd for either of us to mark the moment as being anything more than just two men out voting together.

The ladies who volunteer each election season to mark off names of those who vote in town stood when we entered. It was a purely organic response, and I was certain some of the ladies' politics were not altogether aligned with Norman Mailer's. This did not stop them from demonstrating an act of respect that was totally unexpected by me, and penetrating to witness.

"Hello, Mr. Mailer," one said as he approached the table.

"Oh, ahhh, hi, hi," Norman responded with a jovial, rough voice and smooth smile. He looked around the room at the other people there, who had turned to get a glimpse of him also. He waved his cane slightly to the entire room to say hello, and most made a gesture back. I noticed that every single person in the room was smiling, because their regular voting day had suddenly taken a novel twist. It was safe to say Norman didn't actually *know* a soul in there, other than me, but to watch him as he went through the process of greeting the ladies and nodding to the others, you would have sworn he knew them so well he could recite the names of their grandchildren.

We entered our respective booths directly next to each other with our white folded paper ballots, and I could hear him fumbling around next door. A moment passed as I looked over the sheet in front of me, sure that Norman was doing the same thing. Then I heard him mutter through the plywood separator, "This one's not too sharp."

At first I thought he was referring to George Bush, but then it dawned on me that he was talking about a dull pencil he'd picked up to mark his vote. We're an old town and still cast our vote with an X in a box—no fancy contraptions to pop out "chads."

I never asked Norman how he voted (frankly, I didn't have to), but I'm sure he finally found a sharp pencil with which to check the box next to the less pointy-headed candidate.

Norman loved his town and loved his friends, and I was lucky enough to be a part of his relationships with both.

A few who came to Provincetown to see him and Norris fell into the category of essential. Christina Pabst was one of them. When she entered the house, she entered my life for the long run. Plucky, bright, strong of will, yet tender, she is one of those women who set up camp in your heart immediately. Our first meeting happened when she came to town to act in local theater productions in the summer of 2003, and our introduction was one that could be summed up with: "You don't know this, but you've been waiting for me all your life. Here I am." It was just that simple; she spoke, and I was hooked. Christina and Norman and Norris had a great friendship that had begun twenty years earlier at the Actors Studio, in New York. Theirs was a closeness that was rarely cluttered, and I was lucky to have much of the best of her affection trickle in my direction. When Christina visited, it was, for Norman, as thrilling as if one of his children had come to dote on him.

Christina and I spent not only a good amount of time talking, but hours together in the kitchen. She is a good baker and can make a cookie better than your grandmother. She taught me the basics of making a fine German chocolate cake, which was a feat in itself, because I lack the ability to bake anything well; and I showed her how to make a meat loaf that didn't taste or look like an old football.

"You know, yours is the lobster of all meat loaf," she said to me one day while she stirred batter and I stirred a pot of stew.

"I love this man," she said to Norman, pointing at me. She bent down to give him a kiss while he munched away at his greens and oatmeal.

"Well, don't be fooled," Norman said. "He can be moody and stubborn."

"I'm a quick study," I said.

"And insolent," Norman said, mocking the very candor he encouraged in me.

"I think you've both got it good," Christina said.

Generally mine and Norman's dispositions played off each other in an even way that I'd rarely shared with anyone. I could sense his mood before I even sat down each morning by noting his posture at the table. The curve of his back could signal if he was off, lost somewhere in thoughts from which he sometimes didn't fully emerge during the day, or enraptured by an idea that could float him for hours. If he'd experienced a good night's sleep, it would make for a ripe day; if not, or if he felt his grapple with work on *Castle* was being hindered, it could infect his every fiber. Instinctively, I learned to modify my own nature to suit whatever was called for. To be fair, Norman's temperament was, for the most part, constant. At least once a week, however, I sensed a pall over him, which I would attempt to reach through. I would usually have some measure of success, but sometimes it was futile to try to shift his mood north.

"Rough night?" I would ask.

"Oh, you know, up and down until I finally got to sleep." He would play his cards, allowing me time to unpack my computer before suggesting a task. He would wrestle with the desire to shun writing for the day, happy to do nothing, but his ethic discounted lethargy as a real option. Some days, however, he would throw me a curve ball that could change the direction of our work radically.

"I've decided to put a book together with John," he told me one morning. "Let's get all the recent articles together and see where we are."

I was surprised to hear about this book, but excited that he was doing something fresh. Work on the Hitler book and his political writing had, over the weeks and months, dragged him into a stagnancy that he disliked. The wear and tear while writing a novel is virtually unexplainable, but its evidence is often worn on the writer like ill-fitting garments.

John Buffalo and he had done several father-son interviews that appeared in *Playboy*, *New York Magazine*, and other periodicals. Apparently, in their conversations, the idea of expanding the articles morphed into the prospect of a book. Over the following couple of months of mid-2005, Johnny and Norman conducted interviews with each other, bouncing around questions that were unlimited and uninhibited. It was the ultimate dad-son chatfest, full of gravity, humor, and sensitivity. The interviews were taped, typed by Judith and me, and, finally, edited together with the articles, creating a good book about the state of America as seen from unique generational poles. For me the project was interesting at first, but in the end, frustrating. Norman believed that the book, whose working title was *Hodgepodge*, could be done quickly, without severely cutting into time needed for his novel. He approached it as an uncomplicated project made easy because both Judith and I would do the typing. What remained was merely the job of structuring it.

"I've marked the interview tapes for you two to type up," Norman said, handing me some cassettes. "Send these to Judith, and you do the rest."

It sounded like a good idea. I took the tapes he'd marked and overnighted them to Judith. The problem was that during the interviews, two recorders had run simultaneously (one for backup), and the tapes had been incorrectly marked: backups became confused with master tapes. Since they looked exactly alike, there was no telling them apart. Consequently, Judith and I typed several of the same interviews.

"How could this get fucked up?" Norman asked me when I told him. "You both typed the same tapes?"

"I didn't mark them," I said in defense, "*You* marked the tapes. I typed what you gave me, and she typed what was marked for her."

"Well, we've lost time."

"I told you it would be better if only one of us did the typing."

"No, it's faster if you both do the typing," Norman said. He was irritated.

"Yes, but we didn't know what the other had. You gave us the same material marked differently. But don't worry, we'll sort it out."

Judith and I spent more than an hour on the phone in front of our respective computers one Saturday going over what each of us had for *Hodgepodge* files. Finally, we exchanged transcripts and figured out how to piece them together. I spent that Sunday transcribing the several tapes that had, apparently, not been typed by either of us.

"Here they are," I said on a Monday. I had put all the material into one file and printed it out for Norman.

"Where are Judith's transcripts?"

"They're here. It's all here now. We've put it all on one computer. She emailed me her files and we worked it out."

"But what about the tapes she typed? Where is all that material?"

"It's *here*," I said. "We spent the weekend on the phone getting everything into one place. She *emailed* her files to me, and this is all the material."

Norman's infuriating lack of understanding about how email worked seemed to amplify as time passed.

"I don't know how the two of you messed this up," he said, thumbing through the pages and taking absolutely no responsibility for his actions, which had started the confusion.

"Because we're three hundred fucking miles apart and trusted the goddamn labels, that's how," I said. I'd screwed up stuff in the past out of forgetfulness or stupid mistakes and always owned up to it, but this was not one of those times.

"Well, you two should have communicated better," he said, still removing himself entirely from the equation. "Anyway, it's done now." Norman was the last-word king.

I left the room, angry. I hated the book and I hated being marked with blame; it was as wrong as his mislabeling the tapes.

Much later in the day he called me over to the table. I was in the kitchen preparing Asian salmon for Norris to bake for dinner. His mood, after reading the compiled manuscript, had elevated and he had a grin pasted to his face. "I think we've got a good book here, pal," Norman said.

"I hate the title," I said. I would have none of his convenient charm just yet.

"*Hodgepodge*?"

"It sounds like burnt pudding. No one's going to take it seriously." I was still irritated at being pegged as inept.

"You don't know that," he said. His attempt to sway me back to good humor was hitting a brick wall, and he knew it. His own mood immediately went sour again. I finished the fish and left for the day without saying goodbye. It was a rarity, but I was upset, and he'd have to deal with it. Perhaps I was being stubborn, but I believed that any book with that title would not be taken seriously. The book was much meatier than *Hodgepodge* suggested, and it was my obligation to point this out, whether Norman wanted to hear it or not. He always took my opinion to mind. In this case he assumed I was still seething from our earlier quarrel. I *was* being difficult, but I was also serious about the title.

Our fight blew over, and some days later the name of the book had been changed to *The Big Empty: Dialogues on Politics, Sex, God, Boxing, Morality, Myth, Poker, and Bad Conscience in America*.

"It's kind of a long, don't you think?" I asked him.

"Well, it's not burnt pudding," he said, arching an eyebrow at me. Of course he'd not forgotten my remark. It had never been my intention to scratch at the scab of our earlier squabble by saying the new title was too long, but I had. He was one of the world's most respected men of letters, and I was acting like a moody, flippant assistant who couldn't leave well enough alone.

"No, it's not pudding," I said. "It's a good book and I'm glad I could help with it a little." There was an uncomfortable lag in his response.

"Well, round up all those tapes, will you. They should be put aside for keeping."

I told Judith to send me her copies, but she never did, and I never followed up. *The Big Empty* became an empty matter between Norman and me after that; rarely spoken of and, on my part, a forgettable point. True to form, however, he hit the nail on the head one day when finally we did discuss it a year later.

"You wanted to have more to do with that book, didn't you?" he asked.

"You mean besides typing it? I guess I did, yes."

"Well, what do you think you could have done?"

"You never asked for my input," I said. "I felt totally out of the loop."

"Listen, I did the book for John. It didn't have anything to do with not considering your efforts; you need to understand that. Look at all the other work you've done here. That is no small thing."

And that's what *The Big Empty* was, a labor of love between father and son; it had nothing to do with me or anyone else. As with the best collaborations, there is little room for a third voice, even one that is spoiled by frequently being called upon. My resentment about the book and our fight abated after I finally looked it in the eye and called it for what it was: Norman showing me yet again that there was always more than one direction to take. I might have been closer to him and spent more time working with him than anyone else, but I wasn't his son. What I was was my own man, whom he called on when he needed to. I'd been squabbling with futility. Being caught in the trap of envy was stupid, because I was experiencing Norman in ways that no one else ever would, even John, whom I loved and continue to love like a brother. There is nothing empty about that.

A part of *The Big Empty* dealt with poker and how it relates to individual strengths and weaknesses. That may sound odd to someone who has no appreciation for the game, but Norman considered poker in nearly the same light as he had boxing decades before. He saw it as an exercise in psychology, skill, and guts, but all of that didn't encumber its pleasure as a game. In some ways Texas Hold 'em brought Norman back to the fabric of Provincetown just as it brought him, his family, and friends closer.

There were a few folks in town he liked to have over to the house to play. He found pleasure in hosting games, especially when his sons were around. Matt, John, and Michael all played well, as did his nephew Peter, who had written a book about poker. When they came to Provincetown, and Mike Lennon, too, poker happened! I would toss together a meal, and the players served it to themselves. In the last two years he was in Provincetown, Norman's desire to play Texas Hold 'em became the core of his social life.

"Let's call Pat Doyle," he'd say. Pat Doyle was a woman who lived out near Beach Point, just beyond the main stretch of town. Pat loved the town, like everybody else who landed on its shores, but in her years of living there she'd never met Norman. I'd been introduced to her a decade before, over drinks at a bar, and a long talk about boating and crashed love affairs followed. She had the rare capacity to brighten anyone's spirit, and as with Norman, few were immune to her magic. In 2006, I suggested she and Norman should get to know one another, and when they finally did meet, over a poker game, their fondness for each other was immediate. Norman liked her sturdy character, and she quickly adopted Norman as much more than a poker pal. I think the two of them would have been bound for an affair had she not been a gay woman and he an eighty-three-year-old straight man wildly in love with his wife. They could make each other laugh with a gentle ease that usually develops only after years. When Pat suffered back trouble, Norman gave her one of his fine wooden canes, the only time I've known him to extend such a gift. Pat's back has healed these years later, but I still see her toting that cane around sometimes, doubtless with fine memories of Norman echoing up with every gentle thump of it to the ground.

Norris would play, too, when she was in town. In March of 2007 she had moved a portion of her life to Brooklyn, after weeks of begging Norman to consider the sensible move also. Doctors for both of them were more convenient in New York, and as she put it to me, "I need to be near the children. I can't rattle around in this house anymore. It's just Norman and me, and a part of me is going crazy. It's not good for either of us to be here all the time." This was true; it wasn't good. I'd watched her exhaust herself daily, nurturing Norman while tending to her own enormously serious health issues. Her final decision to go ahead and partially relocate ahead of him was not one made in haste or without sober deliberation and long, drawn-out talks with Norman. He understood that she was somewhat stifled being in Ptown constantly, separated from her children and granddaughter, Matt and Salina's beautiful Mattie James. After the move, each of them traveled to see the other often, and until he could be made to change his mind and join her there permanently, it was a reasonable arrangement.

"People are going to think I'm just the worst," she said to me as we huddled upstairs in her study, going over details of how things would be managed for Norman during her absences. "They'll think I'm abandoning Norman, but I'm not. This whole move is about getting him to come down to be with me, to understand how much more sensible it is for us to be in Brooklyn. I don't know how long either of us has . . ."

"You don't need to apologize to anybody, Barb," I said. "Screw what people think. I'll do what I can around here for Norman whenever you have to be gone. He'll be fine. You do what you need to do."

Norris had survived an insidious form of cancer that no one else had ever endured beyond a few months. She'd earned the right to make changes as she saw fit: to fight to bring her husband with her to Brooklyn where they could both have safer lives. So she went to New York to start the process of their permanent move, and in the process rediscovered a part of her spirit that had been chipped away at by the isolation of Provincetown. In my time at the house, she'd been through at least five surgeries, and the weeks after those operations had been rough on all of us—obviously mostly on her. Once, she had even driven herself home just days after a surgery to be with Norman, because it was the only option. I restated my affirmation of responsibility to both of them while these difficult decisions were being made. Norris should go on ahead, even if Norman was not quite ready to cooperate. Here, in Provincetown, I would do what I could. So, Norris forged ahead unselfishly to lay the groundwork for his eventual move to Brooklyn to be with her.

That was the period when poker sprang from being an occasional event for Norman to being a weekly custom. Occasionally Norman would also venture out to town poker tournaments or Up Cape, to noisy bars where he could barely hear to play. Then one day he decided there could be more to just playing for fun around town.

"What do you know about that television show?" He was asking me about *Celebrity Poker Showdown*, a show on cable that he'd stumbled across one night while flipping channels and now watched often. We were sitting in the bar watching the herons out on the beach, who'd returned for their yearly visit.

"Nothing," I said.

"Why don't you look into it?"

"You want to go on a poker TV show?"

"Let's put it this way: I wouldn't turn them down if they

asked," he said. We watched the birds for a while more and then I left him alone and meandered over to the little office I'd fashioned for myself off the living room.

Over the next day or two I found out what I could about the show and told him about it.

"What do you think? Should I do it?"

"I think the whole experience might sour you on poker," I said. Because I'd worked in television for a few years, for an NBC show and for MTV's *Real World*, I explained what I knew about how productions worked. The poker table would be surrounded by lights that the camera does not see, which would likely wreak havoc on his eyes. The games might be edited, which would almost certainly irritate him when he watched the final show. There would be breaks and time-consuming equipment adjustments that would sap his patience and try his mood. It would not, in all probability, be anything like it appears.

"Maybe you're right. But keep that information handy in case I change my mind," he said. I did keep the names in a file on my desk. Then, not too long after, I read that *Celebrity Poker* was over for good.

"They've cancelled that show you were interested in," I told him the next morning while he ate his omelet.

"Well, it's probably just as well," he said. "It would cut into work too much anyway."

He never brought it up again, but I could sense a slight disappointment that the option to go on TV and play the game he liked so much no longer existed. He was not skilled enough at poker to appear on one of the other professional-player shows, but he was certainly qualified to appear on one that featured celebrities. Truth was, his presence would have lent a new flavor to the show, which seemed top heavy with actors and sports figures. Having a double Pulitzer Prize—winning author like Norman Mailer in the mix would have upped the ante considerably.

When the Norman Mailer Society met each year, Norman geared up for it, but he made the point never to allow it to interfere with his work routine. He liked to host a lunch with the keynote speaker and a few others during the event, and enjoyed being able to feed them. **Norman** loved a good lunch, and hosting people he respected even more. When E. L. Doctorow came for the 2006 gathering, Norman wanted to put out a good spread for him. Doctorow was best known for writing the huge bestseller *Ragtime*, which was made into a successful film by Norman's old friend Milos Forman. Norman, in one of his few legitimate acting roles, played the pivotal character of Stanford White, the architect who is shot in the head in the first scenes of the movie. (Norris plays the woman with him, who screams for a doctor.) Doctorow's history with Norman went back years, to when he was the editor of Norman's novel *An American Dream*, in 1965. They remained friends after, and Norman was pleased that Doctorow was now coming to town. Christina was back also that autumn, and helped me prepare the meal. I was not used to making a lunch for as many as eight, and Norman understood that. Lunch, normally, was a tuna sandwich or a bowl of berries or his oatmeal mixture that no one but the two of us believed was scrumptious.

"Something simple but great," Norman said while we pondered what to have.

"Maybe scallops," I suggested.

"No, they're boring."

"Not if they're baked in a teriyaki cream with roasted shitake mushrooms," I said.

"Never heard of such a thing," he said. "Sounds good. Let's give it a try."

Christina was clued in to my thinking. "You sold him on that by tossing the teriyaki in there, didn't you?" she said when we were alone.

"Of course," I said. "I'm sure as hell not making something elaborate. I'm too damn busy with everything else. This just *sounds* fancy."

The lunch went flawlessly. I cooked, and Christina served the food. Later, Norman declared the scallops the best he'd had in years. Doctorow had seconds. To be fair, the group plowed through four bottles of wine, so my success could have been somewhat skewed by that.

Doris Kearns-Goodwin and her husband, Richard Goodwin, came several times over the years. Doris was enchanting, and she and Norris were close friends. Norman adored Doris, not only because she was a Pulitzer Prize—winning historian but because she is genuinely pleasant. She is as unassuming as anyone you might want to meet, and that was the core of her allure for Norman. They always seemed to be alternately discussing serious issues or laughing over the smallest things. During one meal, Norman asked her about President Johnson holding meetings with his staff while he sat on the toilet. Doris laughed and shook her head.

"What? You won't tell me?" Norman asked.

"Norman, the truth is better suited for after we eat," Doris said.

The night she first visited, Doris spent the better part of half an hour in the kitchen talking with me while I prepared a beef tenderloin and mashed a pot of potatoes. We spoke about the difficulty of getting decent eyeglasses and her selling her Lincoln book, *Team of Rivals*, to Stephen Spielberg for the movies. I told her that her memoir *Wait Till Next Year* had taught me to love baseball. As a kid I'd hated the game. My little league coach, like most, pushed us to win and didn't teach us to appreciate what we were trying to win *at*. Hence, baseball was soured until I read her book. She made me love it again, and I thanked her. That night I learned that she adored mashed potatoes and told me that mine (mashed with tiny flecks of chopped scallion) were as good as she'd ever had. I was glad to be able to repay her in my small way for her good book.

Food was a big part of Norman's friendships, with a fellow author or an old pal, or simply while sitting down to lunch with me. When the kids visited there was always a full refrigerator and fine meals. Norman loved to hold court at his dinner table with his kids, but when one came alone he would insist on taking them out to dinner. It was his way of showing devotion, I think, a way of connecting. When I asked him about it, he said he felt a need to spend time one on one with each of them when he could. He once told me that little surpassed the joy he experienced when sharing a meal with one of his kids.

When Christina was around for yet another visit, she, Norris, Norman, and I dined out together. Norman was in a particularly good mood, and the conversation slipped to writing, of course. He was generous to the point where we, as much lesser writers, were made to feel a kinship with him. He offered a sense of inclusion that we were a part of his elite club. We ate that night at the Martin House, a well-known restaurant in the West End of town, with a fireplace, dusty wine bottles on shelves, and brick-and-stone floors. It had become Norman's favorite haunt because it is one of the oldest buildings in town, harbors an often-encountered ghost, and the food was consistently fine. We sat around his regular table in the tavern basking in the old-world feel of the room. Our discussion shifted from politics to relationships, then to stories about Norman's old friends, who included James Baldwin, Truman Capote, Dorothy Parker, and Lillian Hellman (who still resonated in my head as one of our most important writers). Norman, in his unparalleled career, had known nearly everyone in the literary world. At one point, near the end of dinner and after a couple of glasses of wine, Norman paused and said to all of us, "It's good to eat with three other novelists who obviously understand the world. It's a fine night." Of course his toast was exaggerated, but meaningful. The only one of us who was a published novelist besides him was Norris. Christina and I were merely working our way through early drafts of our first books. Norman had read portions of Christina's, but none of mine.

Nonetheless, he had trust in our abilities to view the world as he believed only novelists can. If Norman was ever a snob about anything, it was writing, so the moment resonated. I finally understood why he was so often praised as being the consummate dinner companion: it was because he truly knew the meaning of inclusion. Even at dinner Norman created masterpieces out of commonplace moments.

The Norman Mailer Society closing parties were fine events attended by people who had read much of his work. After Norman had given his reading, he and Norris would arrive at the house ahead of everybody else, and he'd holler out for me before he even closed the door. For three years' worth of parties, I stayed behind and prepared the house to accommodate nearly a hundred guests. Norman always planted himself in a chair in the large living room, and as the members entered, they beelined right for him so he could sign their books. Norris, ever the good hostess, held her own court on the opposite side of the room in a chair near the fireplace. As I watched her skillfully manage conversations with the myriad guests I wondered if any of them had a clue as to the lengths she went to sustain herself with poise throughout the evening. Norman was elderly, but she was battling greater demons than anybody milling about the room knew about—all the while supporting a man who sometimes didn't publicly pay her enough credit.

It proved to be a terrible idea the first year to encourage the members to bring books with them to the party, because the line lasted through the entire evening and Norman never got the chance to stand or move around, except to excuse himself to hit the bathroom every hour or so. He was virtually trapped. There was no way I could rescue him from the situation, but half of his personality loved being in it anyway, so I never tried. What I did do was kneel down near him every so often to ask if he needed another OJ and red wine—his mixed drink of choice in that period. I also always kept an eye out for any possible oddballs. Luckily, nothing ever happened that forced me to leap across the room to fend off an obsessive admirer, but I still kept watch. Norman had the ability to maintain his humor and his concentration better than any man I've ever met. Watching him entertain, even when he was exhausted, was akin to watching an athlete run his best game. Norman fared well through the three-hour party, but by the time he stood to head upstairs, I could clearly see that fatigue had enveloped him.

The second year, Mike Lennon told the members to drop their books off the day before if they wanted a signature. Norman devoted an hour one afternoon to signing the books as Mike shuffled them one by one in front of him. At that gathering he was spared the work of signing books, but there was nothing to be done about the constant onslaught of adoring enthusiasts.

When he finally managed to say goodbye to his guests near the end of the third year's party, I followed him upstairs after a few minutes to check on him. He'd had bypass surgery the September before, and he'd been slow in regaining his strength. He tired more easily now, and I was more conscientious than ever about making sure he was doing okay. I knocked on the bedroom door, and he told me to come on in.

The room was lit only by his small nightstand lamp, which was fairly dim. He was sitting on the edge of his bed with nothing but a towel over himself, totally out of breath. I didn't say anything for a moment, allowing him time to catch his air. It had not been the climb to the second floor that had sapped his strength; it had been the whole night.

"Are you okay, buddy?" I asked. He lifted his head and said he was fine, just drained.

"It was a good party," he managed to say. I went to his closet and grabbed his robe which was too far away for him to easily retrieve for himself. He looked frail and thin, something that had never been so obvious to me before that night, and not merely because he was undressed.

"Aaah, thank you, thank you," he said in his rough voice when I handed him the robe.

"Of course," I said. I helped him put it on, and I stood nearby. "Are you sure you're okay?"

"Need to get to bed, that's all. Don't worry about me. Thanks for all you did tonight."

"I think it was a success," I said. "Everyone seems pleased."

"I'll see you tomorrow, then?"

"No, tomorrow is Sunday. If you need me to come by, though, I will."

"No, no, not at all. Enjoy your time, pal."

"Good night, Norman."

"See ya Monday."

I closed the door and stood outside, listening. A short time later I went back downstairs to finish out the party. I stayed until well after midnight, to put the furniture back where it all belonged, along with the people I'd hired for the evening. I kept an ear tuned to the upstairs, where I hoped Norman was finally finding rest. That evening, he'd appeared more vulnerable to me than ever before, and I couldn't shake the thought that the party had been too stressful for him. But there was nothing to be done about it, because Norman loved the idea of hosting a party for the members no matter how much stress it involved. There was just no stopping him in that area, and it didn't matter to him that he couldn't enjoy it fully.

More than once he did something or went somewhere when he was not up for it physically, just so he could have the experience. When Ron Howard's production company asked him to consult on the Russell Crowe film *Cinderella Man*, a movie about boxing, Norman jumped at the opportunity, even though it involved heavy travel. Few writers had contributed as much as Norman to the philosophy of boxing, and he was undoubtedly an authority on the sport. Norman had reported on every fight in the 1960s and '70s, including the Foreman-Ali fight in Zaire in 1974, and he appeared in the documentary *When We Were Kings* that was made about that fight. His nonfiction piece on boxing, *The Death of Benny Paret*, is, in my opinion, the most captivating essay on manhood, hope, dignity, rage, love, and carnage that has ever been written. Before Norman made the trip to Toronto to work on the film, he prepared thoroughly, as he did with all projects. I bought every movie Ron Howard had directed, for Norman to watch, and he read pages and pages of material about Jim Braddock, the fighter at the center of the film. We spent three hours watching seventy-year-old silent kinescopes of the fight between Braddock and Max Baer, which happened on June 13, 1935, and which serves as the film's climax. As we watched them, Norman began a running commentary, and I scrambled to keep up in my notes of what he said. I was amazed to hear him dissect not only the fight but what he believed was passing between the two men in their mental battle. Even though the films were nearly as old as Norman, they seemed utterly new as he narrated them to me.

Days later, Norman flew to Toronto, with John Buffalo, to meet with Ron Howard, Russell Crowe, and the other actors to discuss the film. Norman and Crowe became friendly, and when Norman returned he brought with him a black fleece vest the actor had given him. The vest became the mainstay of his second "work uniform," and it was difficult for Norris or anyone else to get it away from him for washing over the following years.

Seven months after the trip, I was contacted by Universal to ask if Norman would like to travel to New York for a private screening of the just-completed movie. Norman, deep into writing *Castle*, declined. Universal, in an unusual move, sent a copy of it to us—not a DVD, but the actual thirty-five-millimeter film. It arrived with a junior executive, who was also the designated security guard for the heavy cans of celluloid. Apparently this was imperative, because virtually no one had seen the movie yet, and Universal Pictures didn't want early leaks about it. Nonetheless, Norman decided he wanted to share the movie with certain townsfolk, and had me invite about fifty people to our tiny local theater for a showing. I contacted the town manager and the man who delivered the morning paper and many in between, inviting them to the movie. The Universal fellow was afraid the press would find out, but I assured him there was no reason for concern. Norman knew his audience and knew his town. Before the movie began, he stood and asked everyone to keep details about the film quiet, and "don't spill the beans." Norman's intention was that his friends enjoy it along with him, and because he commanded an exceptional level of respect in Provincetown, apparently no one ever did say a word. Universal took their movie back to New York that afternoon, and Norman and Norris and I went back to the house.

"Your name wasn't on the credits," I said. "What the hell were they thinking?"

"That doesn't matter," Norman said. "My name was on the check."

He was right; his name was on a fat check, and I knew this because shortly after he came back from Toronto, he'd dug it out of his wallet to hand to me.

"Put this in the bank, will you," he said. I looked down at the check. It was made out to him for one hundred thousand dollars. He endorsed the back.

"I've never held a hundred grand before," I said.

"Well, it's never as heavy as you think it will be," Norman said, and then climbed to the attic to resume work on his final novel.

SIX

Building a Castle in the Forest

Although Norman had been preparing to put his Hitler novel to paper for the entire time I had been working with him, it was not until early 2005 that he resumed writing new text for *Castle in the Forest*. He'd completed the first 140 pages of an early version before I came to work with him, but he remained in research mode throughout my first year with him—he'd done no actual writing of the book. He read voraciously, and I worked with him in the attic copying pages from books that held his notes in their margins. I spent hour after hour on the floor with growing stacks of file folders, into which I sorted those copies, and added to the tall bookcase near me, which already bulged. The files expanded, as did Norman's knowledge about every aspect of Hitler's life he planned to cover and each character he wanted to paint in his tapestry. He would give me endless lists of subjects and names of people to research. The number of books that came in the mail doubled, and I found myself putting together even more bookcases to hold them. This was not easy, because the attic was brimming and we were running out of room.

When Norman started writing again his already amazing concentration amplified. I was awed by his concern for every line and how it sounded to his ear as he wrote on clean, white typing paper. I heard his shallow whisper repeating, repeating, repeating; changing tone, varying strain, stressing and subsequently slaughtering lines only to resuscitate them with droning repetition. All the while his hand thumped at the edge of his desk to music only he could hear. It reminded me of a poet finding the meter of a poem's inner melody. In his escalating deafness there seemed to be an internal symphony booming, which he skillfully translated to paper. He'd always done the "tap, tap" to some degree when he wrote, but as he sank again into this novel, the practice became more pronounced.

A year before I worked with him, we'd bumped into each other on Commercial Street one sunny afternoon. He was taking his daily walk, and I was returning from the post office. We sat for a time on a bench near the library and he asked me, as usual, if my writing was moving forward. He sensed I was lost, which was true, but he didn't spout the usual diatribe that many veteran writers flail at amateurs, which is, "You simply must *do* it," as if those empty words would present a magic bullet. Norman understood that what a novice writer encounters can be cavernous, and not to be toyed with. He'd been there himself and was never afraid to admit it. He instead urged me to take a look at my process and start there.

"You need to speak it. Do you speak it?" he asked me. I didn't know what he meant, and I said as much. "Talk," he said. "Read it to yourself aloud. There's a difference in how words play to the mind from the page and how they sound when spoken. Do you talk when you write?"

I understood what he was asking me, and I did have a tendency to do that, but I had never known why, and believed the act peculiar. I found reading aloud awkward because I have never liked my voice. I recall feeling that day as if he had somehow spied on me. I was too ignorant to realize that he had great insight into what can trouble young writers, and he was coaching me, encouraging me.

"Yes," I admitted. "I do that sometimes. But I think it's strange."

"Well, learn your rhythm. You need to organize the loud and the quiet," he said. "The sounds are the muscle."

Now, years later watching and *listening* to him write, I finally got what he'd been talking about. Norman had been telling me about finding the right words, the right combination of consonant and vowel. Consonants, of course, are hard-clicking, slithering noises pampered by vowels, which tend to slip around them like jelly. Words should flow from the page to the eye with infinite ease, or as harshly as the crack of your skull to a rock.

Before Norman started writing the novel he'd made endless notes on thousands of three-by-five cards. When I read those notes, or the ones scribbled almost illegibly in the margins of his books, I figured out that, in part, he was defining what he *did not* want his book to be. Norman's novel about Hitler would have otherworldly intrigue embedded in it: passion and dirt and fiendish satire. Most writings about Adolf Hitler were barren and intellectual, or soured by the author's own revulsion at the subject. (Who could blame them?) Norman steered his work in a different direction from merely sickness at what had gone on during the war. As I watched him do it, I was exposed to more lessons than I could ever hope to retain.

As his stack of pages grew thicker, the range of what Norman wanted to learn expanded, and its obscurity deepened. In the course of two years, I looked into the particulars of everything from Wagner to measles to Viennese blacksmith shops. I created files devoted to Jung, the brothers Grimm, Karl May, Mark Twain, flour mills, maps of Austria and Germany, silent films, wristwatches, rubber, pellet guns, painting, and early twentieth-century men's homeless shelters. The diversity of subjects was daunting and enthralling.

"I want to know about potatoes," he told me one afternoon over lunch. "I've got Alois into his farm; now he's tending his garden."

Alois was Hitler's father, and Norman was at the point in the novel where the family lived in Upper Austria, near a small town called Hafeld. Herr Hitler was gardening (apparently growing potatoes) and raising bees. Norman thought I should study bees along with him, and of course I did. He literally submerged himself for weeks in countless texts about bees and beekeeping. I would give a list of titles to Judith, and days later, from secondhand bookstores across the country, came volumes about bees and the art of the apiarist. One of the finest and oldest was Maurice Maeterlinck's 1904 book, *The Life of the Bee*, which we both read and which Norman later gave me. To elevate the study to another level, we pored over volumes that pictured the evolution of skeps and went so far as to weigh the virtues of cedar versus pine hive separators—just as his character may have done. Norman made drawings of what Alois would have built for his bees, and produced a twelve-month timeline describing a colony's life, from bustle to dormancy and back. I found sound clips on the Internet that we listened to in the attic together. Norman was captivated by the frenzied dance he heard: the language of the bee. We listened for quite some time, both engrossed in the pulsations. I turned to look at him at one point and his eyes were closed to better absorb the poetry of the hum. An expression of anxious stillness was engraved on his face. Clearly he saw it necessary to take this pause with the larger enterprise of writing his novel in order to better focus on the minutiae. He was writing the story of the most notorious monster the world had ever produced, but so much hinged on the dance and song of the honeybee. Norman said that understanding the largely ignored details makes any idea authentic— grains of sand ensure the mortar of bricks.

Since the novel has been published there have been countless references to Norman equating the rigid structure of bee
society to what Hitler attempted to fashion for his unrealized
utopia. He didn't directly intend this, no matter how obvious
the allusion. He utilized the honeybees in *Castle* in such a way
as to illustrate the bond, or rather lack of one, between Adolf
and his father. I know this because I asked him. I, too, had believed he was making the societal structure equation, but Norman set me straight, saying it was too obvious, too contrived. It
just happens that Hitler's father did own bees, and as the two
worked around them their relationship began its decay—the
true root of what Norman saw as Hitler's drive for impossible
order. Norman's Adolf never appreciated the beauty of the hives
or embraced the work involved, which was a disappointment to
his father. If anything, Hitler would have ended up hating bees
and shunning the beauty they embodied.

As for Alois's gardening and Norman's desire to know more
about potatoes I had a ready answer for him.

"My grandfather grew potatoes."

"So this will be easy for you," Norman said with a hint of
facetiousness. "Why don't you type it up for me so when I get
upstairs I can read all about what you know."

"How thorough do you want it?" I asked.

"From planting to table," he said. "And don't forget variety.
Is there much difference between a potato your grandfather
planted and one from Austria, do you think?"

"I have no idea," I said. And knowing it would irritate him,
I added, "I'll hit the Internet."

Norman mumbled something into his lunch as I left the room. Information, he was fond of saying, is only as worthwhile as the amount of sweat incurred finding it. To his mind, specifics gathered with the instant ease of the Internet could not be trusted. "Stick to your memory and don't trust the computer, pal," he said as I headed to my desk. "If you need to back things up, then get to a book."

"You got it," I hollered back. I was placating him to some extent. I couldn't remember all *that* much about my grandpa's potato patch, but I figured anything I had forgotten would be fairly simple to find on a gardening website.

My respect for Norman's ability to recall just about everything he'd ever learned through his life grew by the day, as did our familiarity with each other's strengths and weaknesses. I found myself amazed at his implacable craving for knowledge, even at eighty-two years old. He'd lived more than twice as long as I had, but he regularly made *me* feel old and slow. Nonetheless, I embraced the methods of my generation and he embraced his.

In our debate about obtaining information, I learned to appease him. Of course, he did the same by pretending not to notice. From that, strangely, came trust. I knew what Norman wanted and I knew how to get it. Norman knew that in the end he'd get answers, even though he wasn't fond of how I found them. I would use books, but sometimes only as support to more immediate information from either my head or the computer. For me the computer was invaluable, but not just because of its convenience. Norman forever attached a rush order to every idea that flew into his head. He hated waiting for anything. While he loathed the computer, necessity dictated that I use one to provide him with what he wanted quickly. There was simply no way around it. I found a happy medium by keeping my online research half-secret or disguising it. I'd note the reference it came from and put that at the top of the page in boldface type, so he'd be sure to see "From the Library of Congress," or something along those lines. It usually worked. I'd leave out any mention of Internet sites, because he would doubt their validity immediately and irrationally. I knew enough to thoroughly corroborate all source materials, and he was just going to have to trust me about that. On the other hand, if I spent an hour poring over a fat book, he would grow fidgety about how long it was taking and constantly interrupt me, thus prolonging the job—which annoyed us both.

The one thing I had on my side was that I could move quickly around the house and he couldn't. I'd dash up the stairs and work at my own pace with my computer in a corner. This strategy kept me safe for about a year. Then Norris bought him a cell phone. Armed with a piece of technology that he had dubbed useless and detrimental to humanity, he discovered one fine use for it: he could call me from anywhere.

"How's it coming?" he would ask from the Second Office or during a pause in his afternoon walk out on the deck. More than once I considered hiding his new phone so I could get the work done without interruption, but I never did.

I typed up what I knew about potatoes and then called Judith. Although most of her work revolved around Norman's transcription, she was an invaluable resource on just about any subject and she didn't need to consult the Internet or a book. Judith just knew stuff. When I mentioned potatoes, she blurted, "Well, you do know potatoes first came to Germany in 1588, don't you?" I did not, nor could I imagine how anyone outside of the International Potato Council *could* know this. But Judith did, and it was, frankly, freakish. Then she told me there were more than four thousand varieties and almost every culture first believed them to be poison and cause for every malady from the common cold to insanity.

"What's he up to with potatoes?" she asked.

"Alois," I said. "Norman has him planting a garden. Norman wants to know all about them."

"You should give him what Nietzsche said, too," Judith said. "God knows he can't get enough Nietzsche."

I had no idea what she was talking about. Two minutes later the quote showed up in an email: ". . . a diet that consists predominantly of potatoes leads to the use of liquor." Suddenly, Nietzsche was funny. I put it at the top of the potato research.

"Where did you find this?" Norman asked. Norman was as educated as any man could be about Nietzsche, but the line took him by surprise.

"Judith," I confessed. "It was in her head."

"Is there anything that woman doesn't know?" he mumbled while slashing a red X through the quote. Unnecessary notes were distracting for him because he was inclined to become fixated easily on just about anything. Consequently, when he crossed something out on a page it vanished completely.

Norman constructed his story around the simple peasant Hitler family. In time he began to trust me enough to tell me where he might ultimately take the story, breaking his rule of never discussing possibilities of where a novel was going. I realized he had no precise route when it came to the outcome of this book. He hated "plot," of course, and was on record as saying so, but there is a measure of direction any story requires, and that seemed at times to be as absent in him as in any lesser writer. Hence, he was open to options—generally his own wildly changeable ones—as to course. He made notes on cards, with snippets of ideas or quotes to thrust the story forward, but he really wasn't positive about anything until it flowed from his pen. From what I could tell when he'd hand me pages to fax Judith for typing, it surprised him as much as it did us what was on them. Sometimes he was categorically excited about the day's work; sometimes he wasn't. He would hand pages to me and say, "Well, let's see how this looks typed."

When he told me he was taking his narrator to Russia for a long chapter to "study," I had the sinking feeling that the Hitler story would swerve wildly off course and perhaps never return to Austria. He'd famously done something similar with *Harlot's Ghost*, an exceedingly long novel that I, admittedly, have yet to finish. He began to pore over material related to the Romanoffs, Rasputin, and Russia, and I wasn't clear what he was up to. Finally, after getting a call from a mildly irritated Judith wherein she asked, "What the hell am I typing every day? Where is Adolf? Why are we rummaging through the Romanoffs?" I decided I would find out. Norman explained to me that even

the devil must endure lessons, and since D.T., his devil narrator, was only a "medium-ranked minion," the Maestro, the
actual Devil, sends him to Russia to learn the art of prolif-
erating pain and suffering. The horror that Norman chose to
illustrate what his narrator learned was the trampling deaths of
thousands during the young czar's coronation. When Norman
explained this to me I began to understand his logic. The idea
was elegant (in a sick sort of way), and I read his new pages
eagerly. Norman had crossed into a shadowy, mesmerizing land
of mysticism and the inexplicable. I mentioned to Norris that
the novel was shaping up as something reviewers were going to
describe as "Norman Mailer meets Anne Rice."

"Oh, God, don't say that to him," she said. "He won't like
it at all. Norman hasn't liked a modern novel in years. Being
compared to Anne Rice will drive him crazy." She was right, of
course—no one knew Norman's literary quirks better than she
did. Norman would have hated the association, but the truth
remained that he'd created a devil who had a sense of humor,
high intelligence, obvious human faults, and a restless conscience. D.T. was a lot like N.M.

Norris was right about Norman not reading mainstream
fiction, no matter what he inferred to the press. Sure, he could
toss names of contemporary writers around with amazing ease,
but in the entire time I was with him the only popular novel
I ever saw him read cover to cover was *The Da Vinci Code*, and
that was only because he wanted to know what all the hoopla
was about. His assessment was that the hoopla was wildly mis-
placed. Norman read every night for pleasure, but the books he

devoured were not mainstream. His favorite pleasure author, for lack of a better term, was Georges Simenon, the Belgian mystery writer whose master character is the French detective Jules Maigret. Norman loved him, saying that writing can be simple and still enjoyable. He asked me to scour the house to find all his Maigret books. Norman was certain that he owned at least seventy of the seventy-five. I searched from basement to attic and found every Georges Simenon book I could. Those I couldn't locate I bought on the dreaded Internet.

Every time a reporter asked Norman what he was reading, he would skirt the question by breaking into his pat appreciation for the greats: Dos Passos, Hemingway, Dostoevsky, Melville, Brontë, and so on. He remarked to several interviewers that Andrew O'Hagan, the Scottish novelist, was probably the finest writer to come along in generations. Norman loved O'Hagan's book *Be Near Me*, and told me that every young American writer ought to read him and take notes. He gave me the book, and I agreed: O'Hagan can fashion a sentence so remarkably well that it mercilessly devours you while simultaneously offering nourishment.

Norris, however, loved modern writers, including Anne Rice. She told me how, years before, Norman had once "cleaned house" in Brooklyn.

"He threw out my novels in order to make space for his own books. He put a stack of boxes on the sidewalk, and of course they were gone in minutes. I mean, who's not going to snap up free books from Norman Mailer's house? Some of my signed Anne Rice books were in there. I could have killed him."

One of Norman's faults, if it could be called that, was that he had a proclivity to be almost too interested in something. If it occurred to him to write countless pages about the Russian royal family smack in the middle of a book about Adolf Hitler, there was no derailing him. After the first "final draft" of *Castle* was sent to Random House, a suggestion came down from his publisher suggesting Norman might want to "consider trimming Russia." Norman said no. For a time there was debate about this, but it was a one-sided debate, because he was deaf to all counsel. Norris read the draft and agreed with the publisher, but Norman didn't budge. Then one day he went upstairs to work while I was in the kitchen. The house phone rang; it was Norman calling, asking me to join him for a moment in the attic. He had something for me to read.

"I've come up with this," he said, handing me several freshly written pages.

I sat down on the twin bed by his desk and read as he watched. This was the only time I recall him watching me carefully as I read his work. His gaze had the same intensity I expected to feel from any *other* writer awaiting feedback, but not from him. Norman had written a caveat for the reader pertaining to the diversion to Russia.

> . . . *If there are readers who will say, "I would rather go on with what is happening in Hafeld," I have a reply. "That is your right." I can tell them. Just turn to page 261. Adolf Hitler's story will pick up again right there.*

I looked up.

"Well?" he asked.

"I've never seen someone break character like this before," I said. "I know it's D.T. talking, but it's also clearly you."

"They want Russia gone, and I want it in. So, I'm submitting this to the reader. Russia stays. Fax those to Judith."

I agreed with what he was doing, but I also thought that the chapter was too long. Readers would become frustrated. "I think you should keep it but trim it."

"I know what you're saying, but it stays as it is."

Norman had, in many ways, a taunting nature. On several occasions he stressed his belief that if others couldn't stick with his choices, trust his methods, "then fuck 'em."

Norris said to me, "He did this with the CIA book and never came back to the story. I tried to tell him . . ."

I agreed with her, because I was one of those who'd become lost reading *Harlot's Ghost*. At the dining room table one morning, shortly after the conversation with Norris, Norman asked me what I thought about that book.

"I never finished it," I said.

"Why?" he asked. He wasn't annoyed, just curious.

"I couldn't keep up with it," I said. "That was a long time ago, but I remember struggling."

"Well, that can happen to a young mind," he said.

"I was thirty."

"Like I said," he responded.

I could have taken that as a left-handed insult, but Norman didn't intend it that way. He knew I was able to stay with complicated prose but was, likely, lacking in the area of concentration—affected by the hideous effects of television. Norman was positive that any mind under its Midas control was irrevocably sapped from the time of infancy of any ability to properly maintain focus. Perhaps he was right, but in my defense my family didn't have a television until I was six, and I told him that. I promised to give *Harlot's Ghost* another try. Then he said to me, "I've always thought the most damning sentence I ever wrote was at the end of that book."

"What was it?" I asked.

" 'To be continued . . .' " he said, and chuckled. "At the time I thought I would, but I never did."

"Why?" I asked.

"The cold war was over. The country didn't care about the CIA. My timing was wrong. Same with *Ancient Evenings*. If I got it out a year earlier, when the Egypt exhibit was still criss-crossing the country and all over the news, it would have done a hell of a lot better. Much is about timing."

In the end, Norman did edit the Russian chapter down by a hundred pages, but only after enough time had passed since the initial debate about it. It was easier for him to change direction if he could resolutely say the idea to do so was his.

By late summer of 2005 the doctors were pressuring Norman to have heart surgery to clear blocked arteries. He wasn't pleased, but he finally agreed. Soon the push was amplified to get *Castle* finished before he went into the hospital. In early September he declared the book done and ready to send to his editor and agent. The title of the manuscript was now *Hitler's Phantom*.

Norman had told me two years before that he would probably change the title, and he did. It went from *The Castle in the Forest* to *Hitler's Mother* to *Adolf's Father* to God knows what else. He finally decided on *Hitler's Phantom* while he and Mike Lennon were driving home one afternoon in Mike's car. As soon as Norman uttered the new title, a rock cracked the car windshield with a loud *thwack*. Mike said it was a sign, and so did Norman, who tended to believe in such things. This settled it; the title waffling was over.

Norman went in for heart surgery in mid-September. A cardiologist at a Cape hospital had flippantly said that the sort of arterial blockage Norman suffered was commonly called "a widow maker." Norris was in the room with him and heard this and was understandably shocked. We were all floored by the callousness of the comment, made in front of his *wife*. But Norman didn't overreact to the diagnosis when I saw him a day or two later. Instead, he said he wanted simply to finish the book.

An appointment was scheduled in Boston with top cardiologists, who had better bedside manner and agreed that the bypass was necessary. Norman became hell-bent on finishing the book before his surgery. Pages flew out of him. He was writing up to fifteen pages a day, and as soon as he finished a chapter I'd fax it to Judith.

"He's banging this out faster than I've ever seen him," Judith said. I was tied to the fax machine and my computer, organizing chapters into a final draft.

Norman's heart surgery loomed ahead and probably tormented him privately, but he seemed most concerned that the novel, as he had originally conceived it, was not going to see its proper end. He'd merely reached a point where it could conclude appropriately. If I knew Norman at all, he was working during the time he was away for the operation and also later, in the rehabilitation facility. He may not have been writing pages, but surely he was mulling further possibilities to include in the novel to bring it to his original, desired end.

After his hospital stay and month-long stint in rehab he returned to Provincetown to Norris's unwavering care. When we'd spoken during his absence he mentioned rough ideas for chapters he wanted to add to better round out the story. I'd scribble notes on my end as we talked, knowing he was doing the same thing. In our first talks after the operation, I noticed a difference in the tone of his voice. Someone familiar with heart conditions said that because his blood was now richer with oxygen, due to unrestricted flow, changes could happen—like this hurried, higher voice. The change initially worried me, but after a few days his tone returned to its old croaky self, and I felt a sense of relief.

After he'd been home for a few weeks he again climbed up to the attic to work. I knew he'd been writing in his head while he was away, because of our talks. Sure enough, notes appeared on margins of the manuscript and he began filling more note cards with prospective new "scenes." In December he said he wanted the novel to be done, finally. What he wanted to write took more than a month. He wrote a hundred new pages, pages that came slower, more deliberately. He took Hitler's story up to where the boy was sixteen. By the new ending, he'd portrayed little Adolf to be, as Norman called him, a "dandy." He was on the track to making his Hitler, at the very least, bisexual.

In due time, the book was finished. The new pages were rough, and Norman again reshaped them. The novel, which had originally been ten chapters in length, was now thirteen. While he wrote the additional chapters he asked me to have another read of the entire manuscript, which I eagerly did. It was one thing to read chapters in spits and spurts, but to read them straight through and tied together was something else entirely. Norman wanted to know if the story rang true to me. Of course that was no problem, because *Castle* was one of the most accessible books Norman had ever written—if such a thing can be said. So many times I have read or heard how people sometimes suffer through Norman's books because of their complexity and because he forces his readers to think for themselves, but *The Castle in the Forest* (he finally reverted back to his original title) is written with humor and a flair of language that he'd never used before. Granted, it was subtle humor, almost quiet, but it was there and it was compelling and infused with elegance. That feature ran all the way up to chapter ten.

When I read the new chapters, the voice of his narrator altered slightly. I mentioned it to Judith, and she said she *kind* of saw it, but it didn't detract from the novel for her. Perhaps the deaths in the story were the reason? I didn't buy it. For me, the voice that had pranced through ten chapters loudly and clearly tinged with sardonic malevolence was now replaced with a formal drone. After I finished reading it twice I told him what I thought.

"Different?" he asked.

"Yes," I said. "I mean, in this latest part it's like there's another devil speaking. It's subtle, but all through the book you have D.T. talking with an amusing superiority. Now he's kind of . . . dry."

"Dry, huh?" He wasn't perturbed; he was curious. He hated people fawning over his work just because *Norman Mailer* had written it, yet that's what everybody did; everybody except Norris and Mike Lennon and me. At that point I knew at least five other people besides us who'd read the book, but none had mentioned this—at least to my knowledge. Norman depended on me to tell him what I thought, without provision, and so I did.

"Well, I'll look at it," he said. "In the meantime, get the pages together and I'll rework the chapter titles."

A week went by and he still hadn't reread the whole thing, but he had broken the book up into new chapters to better accommodate the end material. To crown the ending, he wrote an epilogue that explained his title. The Castle in question was a concentration camp that had been liberated, and this was the name the inmates had given it. I particularly loved the epilogue, but Judith did not and told me as much. I wasn't going to press Norman about what I had mentioned regarding the last pages having a different tone, unless he brought it up again—which he didn't. When he asked me to send it on to his editor again—

with the new pages—I shuddered at what the reaction might be. I was shocked when his editor declared without a hint of reservation, "It's a masterpiece!" I read the whole thing again.

"The last hundred pages just don't sound the same to me, Judith," I said again. She was not feeling well, and much of the typing for the last chapters had fallen to me. Judith was suffering from what she claimed was a bad reaction to tainted Indian food. She inhaled deeply on her cigarette on the other end of the line and told me that if I felt strongly about it I should bring it up to Norman again. "It's your responsibility," she said. Judith had other issues to deal with.

"I'm moving to Kentucky," she told me after a barrage of coughing.

"From Brooklyn to Kentucky? I don't get it," I said.

"Most of what I do is done through the fax machine anyway," she said. "Last I checked, they have phones in Kentucky."

"Is she out of her mind?" I asked Norman later.

"Judith has made a decision. When she does that there's no changing it," he said.

"But Kentucky?" I couldn't wrap my brain around the idea. Judith had been in the same tiny apartment on Hicks Street, three blocks from where Norman lived in Brooklyn, for decades. Her life was citified through and through. To picture her roving around the woods of Kentucky was inconceivable, like an old housecat in the deep Yukon.

"She's taking driving lessons three days a week," Norman said. "That's the most terrifying thing."

She confirmed the lessons to me on the phone. "I didn't

think I would like to drive, but I do," she said. "I never had to learn before now, but my instructor says I'm quite good at it."

"I doubt *that*," Norman said when I told him.

"I bought a house yesterday," she added a few days later—the one she purchased online. It was all getting crazy.

"What is going on with her?" I asked Norris.

"I don't know, sweetie, but she's determined."

"But it's just stupid to buy a house you've never seen and move to a state you've only read about. Is she going nuts?"

"Sweetie, Judith has always been a little bit nuts," Norris said. "We just go along with it."

Sometimes when one party in a group starts to lurch to the left of sane, it's hard to recognize the gravity of the situation. Perhaps because I was the newest member of our little gang I felt there should be some intervention to convince Judith she was making a gargantuan mistake. I prodded Norman to talk some sense into her. "Can't you say anything to her, get her to stop this and wake up?" I asked him.

"Judith is a smart woman. I imagine she knows everything I might say already. It will have no affect if I actually say it."

I had to take his word for it. He had, after all, been dealing with her quirks for a quarter of a century. Nonetheless, I was getting freaked out by Judith's behavior. One night soon after the house-buying conversation, I came home to a ridiculous message from her on my answering machine:

"Did you get the fax today?" she kept asking my machine, as if she were speaking to me and not a recorder. "The fax, we need to make sure that the fax is the right one for the chapter.

I need you to look through your files. Make sure it's how it's supposed to be with *all* the faxes." She wasn't making any sense. The pages were in order, the chapters done. We'd discussed this just hours before, when I'd left Norman's for the day. "We have to make sure everything is in order," she continued, "He's not going to like it if everything is mixed up. I've got to fix it. I've got to fix it . . ." I never called her back. I was too scared of what I might encounter. I could only hope she'd gone to sleep soon after the call.

The next day I told Norris what had happened. I didn't tell Norman, because I believed it might upset him and he'd go plowing through things trying to see what she was talking about with faxes "being all mixed up." God knows I didn't want to go there with *this* book, too. No faxes or chapters were messed up; Judith was.

"She was trying to send a fax here over and over at two in the morning," Norris told me. "I finally had to go upstairs and unplug the machine." Later both Norris and I spoke to Judith separately. She was back on track and claimed to have been tossed through the ringer by new antibiotics her doctor had prescribed. She said they'd made her loopy.

"I've never heard such bull," I said. "Antibiotics don't mess with your head like that. Something else is going on." By now Norman was aware of the bizarre behavior and told us not to pressure Judith too much about it.

"She's explained the problem and we should accept what she says and leave it at that," he told me.

Norris and I could both see that he had doubts about what

really was going on with Judith, but we didn't stress the point. Judith had been with him and stood by him for years. Norman would handle this situation the way he handled most everything he couldn't easily fix: by waiting it out. A few weeks passed with no replay of Judith's peculiar behavior. Maybe the medications had been at fault after all?

I was still irritated by what I saw as a problem with the last portion of *Castle*. Norman was still working at getting his strength back, so I didn't bug him about it. However, now that Judith seemed clear again, I brought the situation up with her.

"Well, do what you have to do." She clearly was not into debating if Norman's book was headed for magnificence or disaster. She was not physically well again, and with her driving lessons and impending move to Kentucky she didn't seem to care greatly about work. This was not normal, because Judith, of all people, took Norman's work so seriously that she lived and breathed it.

Finally, I decided to bring the issue up with Norman again.

"I still think it sounds like there's a different narrator at the end, Norman," I said.

"You feel strongly about this," he said.

"Yes, I do. Maybe I'm just too close to the whole thing."

"I'll tell you what. I'll reread the last half."

"Fine."

When I showed up the next morning he sat me down and told me that I had been absolutely right. The last chapters were different in tone from the bulk of what preceded them; levity was completely absent. That afternoon he set out to make it right. It took him three days of edit sessions to recapture the voice that had faded after his heart surgery and to repeal the dourness that permeated the later chapters. I keyed in his new edits on my computer to make a brand new draft to send to his editor. Judith was, for the most part, out of the picture now, low with illness. She was occupied with doctor's visits and was, as she told me, crushingly tired. Norman said it was best to give her a break, time to mend; she'd more than earned it. He thought that perhaps her troubles were related to simple overwork.

Norman didn't merely tackle the end of the book; he also made another edit pass on the early chapters. I ended up with a huge amount of work, and for days all I did was fashion his manuscript *again*. My respect for the work Judith had done for twenty-five years was elevated to an even higher level. I was now accountable for this last huge drive in assisting Norman in completing his seven-hundred-page novel. It was not uncomplicated, but it showed me that writing is never static but forever alive and evolving.

On May 2, Judith called to tell me she was not going to be available for a couple of days: she was checking herself into the hospital for tests. Her normally burly voice was deficient to the point of being a shadow of itself. She finally admitted that her health probably had nothing to do with bad food but was "likely hepatitis-related." She was positive the doctors would be able to take care of it after the tests. Judith had a way of putting logic aside where her health was concerned, or into the area she labeled off-limits to us. It was infuriating.

Norris urged Judith to be checked for more serious issues, and Judith, more or less, laid down *her* law: that Norris was not to make further suggestions. Norris, justifiably, was hurt, because if anyone knew the difficulty of facing a ruthless illness it was she. She was angry about Judith's attitude, and told me as much. I couldn't say anything to Judith beyond the basic, which was: "Let me know if I can do anything." She tossed my concern aside also as senseless worry.

"I'll call you in a couple days," she said.

I woke early two days later. I'd had a bad night's sleep, full of fitful thoughts racing in my head—dreams that made no sense at all. I got up at five, made a pot of strong coffee, dawdled around for an hour, and then finally turned on my computer to check my email. Peter Levenda, Judith's oldest friend, and a writer we all knew as the rock of her life, had written me a short note.

Dear Dwayne,

Judith passed away early this morning. I don't have any firm details right now but I will be in touch with you later when I know more. I am hesitant to call the Mailers this early so I have opted to send this to you to tell you of the sad news. I'll be in touch later.

Peter

I got myself together after a brief period of shocked sadness and headed to the house. When I arrived, Norris met me in the entryway. She'd received a call from Peter minutes before yet didn't have any more details than I did. She said she had just told

Norman that Judith was dead. He was upstairs in his bedroom getting dressed. I was still stunned by the news, but it was more or less an upset that I had prepared for, unconsciously, since Norris had told me about her clash with Judith the week before. I simply hadn't wanted to believe that Judith was so ill.

I went outside to the deck and sat in the sun with a cup of coffee. Norris came out for a minute and we talked. There was little to say, however, and she left me alone to think about things.

Understandably that morning, Norman had a melancholy hovering over him, but he remained strong. He'd known all along also, I believe, that Judith was seriously ill and that she'd never make it to her house in Kentucky. That's why he'd never questioned the absurdity of her decision. He knew it would have been ineffectual and, in the end, of no importance. That was the thing about Norman; he simply knew things. I don't know how, but he did.

Little work was to be done that day. I spent the morning and afternoon trying to get details from Peter, who was in transit from Florida to New York, where he intended to handle Judith's affairs. I didn't hear from him until I received a lengthy letter the next day.

Fri, 5 May 2006 2:52 pm
Rather than tie up the phones calling everyone, I thought I would send you this email to brief you on what I know (and mostly don't know) at this time and you can forward the information on to Norman and Norris as you see fit.

You probably already know as much as I do by now, but it is important that the Mailers understand what is happening to Judith's property. The City of New York has sealed her apartment, since she has left no obvious will anywhere. Neither I nor anyone else can get into the apartment at this time. I have emails from Judith saying that I am the executor of her estate, but in the absence of a written will it seems an email will not hold water.

On Tuesday the City will return to her apartment and conduct an inventory of her assets. We can be present during this inventory, but there is nothing we can remove. What they will be looking for is any evidence of a will; but barring that they will inventory everything and await the State's pleasure.

I have been desperately trying to find out if Judith has any living relatives anywhere who could be considered beneficiaries of her estate. She had cousins here and there, some in Massachusetts where her parents lived before they died, but I don't know who they are or what their names might be. If you have any clues, please let me know ASAP.

I will try to talk to the hospital, but it is possible they won't talk to me since I have no legal status. While Judith wanted to be cremated, the law does not permit that in absence of written instructions (do you believe that?) so she will be buried regardless of her wishes. I would like to arrange a funeral service of some sort for her, but in absence of a will it is entirely possible that this will have to be a memorial service rather than an actual funeral. Again, I just don't know.

I am afraid that the costs of this might be prohibitive as well. Had I control of her assets, then I could pay for the service out of her account; however, it seems that this may not be possible, in which case I will be looking for alternative ways to cover this. I am hoping that the Mailers would be able to cover these expenses, but I have no idea of their current financial status, etc, etc, of course, or even how to approach them on this, so . . . you would know more about this than me. I await your advice.

I feel that the service, whatever it might be, should probably be held in New York, but I am open to suggestions. Although Judith named me as executor in her emails, if I have no legal standing on this then I am really not in charge anymore, except morally I guess. Judith was my oldest and dearest friend, someone I've known since 1972 in thick and thin—but the legal obstacles are surprising and intimidating and have thrown me for a loop. I haven't had time to mourn yet.

Peter

I showed the email to Norman and Norris as we sat at the table that afternoon. Then, as we discussed the fact that none of us knew anything about any relatives Judith may have had, I told them about her work with Mohammed and the Palestinian child's medical care. Neither Norris nor Norman had any idea about this, and at first I felt I'd broken a promise by telling them. Afterward, however, I knew I'd done the right thing. Norman and Norris were both surprised, although Norman not as much as I thought he might be. "I could see her doing that," he said.

The talk then moved to arrangements for her memorial service. Norman and Norris agreed that their Brooklyn apartment would be the best place to have it, as soon as we knew what was happening with Judith and where she would be buried. As it turned out, it would be nearly a month before we knew anything about what the state would allow, because they had control over her body, her apartment, and everything in it— the unpleasant result of Judith dying without a will and without heirs. There was some back-and-forth between Norman's lawyer and the state about what rightfully belonged to whom. Some of Judith's property was directly linked to her work with Norman, which made for a convoluted situation. In the end, both Peter Levenda and Mike Lennon were allowed to enter her apartment to retrieve what was relevant to her work. The state took everything else, and Judith remained in state custody for nearly a month while they did their work.

Norman's method of dealing with the death of Judith was to dive into his final two weeks of work on the manuscript. He did it stoically and spoke about her little. I knew he was in a private, intricate place. No one is immune to the loss of someone who has been so close, so relevant, and so integral for that many years, and Norman was no exception. He did ask me a week after her death, knowing that I was still somewhat at a loss for what to think or do, if I would consider taking on her workload. I told him I would never be Judith, and he understood what I meant by that. I would do what I could, but frankly she was irreplaceable. I was still struggling with my feelings about losing Thomas as well, and so the thought of compounding my days with trying to be a stand-in for Judith didn't set well with me. So, I did the thing I was quite good at, which was to submerge my confusion about Judith dying by drinking even more when my day with Norman was done. I went to the Little Bar every night after I left his house, to obliterate my ache about her and what had transpired with Thomas, whom I deeply missed being able to talk to—especially about Judith. The bar was less expensive than seeing a shrink. Or so I believed.

At the end of May a memorial for Judith was finally held in Brooklyn at Norman's apartment on the same day she was buried somewhere in New Jersey. I didn't go. Norman and Norris went down to Brooklyn for two weeks, and the service was held near the beginning of that stay. I chose not to attend because I needed to clear my mind and put Judith to rest in my own way. How I did that, how I finally managed to begin addressing everything properly, including my confusion about Thomas, was to stay in their house, sleep as much as I could, and stop drinking. I knew alcohol was becoming a crutch for me, an excuse to remain dormant. I did not want to find myself twenty years down the road in a situation similar to Judith's. I wanted to produce and maintain a better mind for work; I wanted to be a better man, one deserving of the tutelage I was receiving from Norman.

I tossed my last glass of vodka off their deck into the bay and went to bed early on the warm night of June 1. I'd had quite enough.

Norman's book was done, and Judith was gone, and at last I understood that I was the driver of my life and not a passenger. I had responsibilities to myself and to Norman, who was regaining his strength by the day. Nevertheless, I noticed that more and more he was dogged by heaviness in his breathing. The situation had grown worse since the surgery—the surgery that was supposed to remedy his ills and allow him to live strong for many more years. It was obvious that some troubles had not been addressed—his arduous struggle for air, for one. I knew I would have to be more attentive where he was concerned, give more consideration to him than I already did.

SEVEN

Mail, Media, and Matters of Men

In the days after Judith's death we were in a holding pattern. Judith didn't have much beyond a meager savings, and the contents of her minuscule apartment, which she would have wanted sold and the money donated to good causes. I believe it was a tragic end for a woman who had contributed quietly, yet extraordinarily, to the literary world. She was an unsung hero, and we all knew that. Norman and Norris did what was in their power to ensure that her few possessions were dispersed respectfully.

As for Norman, after he returned from Brooklyn he dove back into his routine, as I expected he would. Some mornings, however, I would come in to find him sitting near the phone in the bar, looking out to the beach. I wondered if he had intended to dial Judith's number, as he'd done every day, before remembering she was gone. Even the strongest and most pragmatic of us experience road bumps in change. But Norman adapted to the absence of Judith over time and life settled into a new normal.

Sometime this week we should do the mail," Norman said. He uttered this once every two months or so during my tenure with him. "Arrange the letters so they're ready."

Generally the letters had already been sorted by me into stacks, and placed on the window ledge in the dining room, clipped together. In the middle of the table there were invariably a few he'd opened and tossed aside, which sometimes became lost under newspapers and magazines. "I'm sure there are more letters than this," he'd say, digging out a few from beneath the *Times*, old torn-out crosswords, and back issues of *Scientific American* magazine.

"There are. They're over on the ledge. Shall I get them now?"

"Oh, yes," he'd say, and then go back to his game of solitaire. I'd get the letters, go through the bunch, insert the newly found ones from the table into the correct stacks, and present the lot of them to him.

Even some of his children told me that they did not know

that Norman tried to answer *every* letter that came to him. Half of Norman liked getting mail and the other half detested it. Mostly he hated the time it took to write answers, but once he'd sunk himself into the job, he did it with enthusiasm. At least six times a year he would spend an hour after a lunch, usually while devouring a Dove Bar ("there is *no* better dessert"), going through his mail. A few people wrote to him all the time, and at least one man, who now lived in Israel, wrote a letter to Norman every day for a year. "What's this all about?" I asked Norman, holding up one of the Israeli's letters. "Oh, he just needs to do this," Norman said with no further explanation. Norman read only one per week from the fellow, and asked me to put the rest aside to "file." That didn't mean in the trash; it meant in an actual folder we kept. Norman never liked to throw anything away, and the man's letters are now probably in the Norman Mailer archive in Texas. In 2005, Norman sold everything that had accumulated over the course of his career to the University of Texas in Austin for $2.5 million. That sale ensured that his letters and written works would thrive in perpetuity. Mike Lennon oversaw the transfer of over a thousand boxes containing nearly forty thousand letters to and from people ranging from Mohammed Ali to Alan Ginsberg to John Lennon.

Prisoners wrote to him, too, hoping that the Great Norman Mailer would write an *Executioner's Song* on their behalf or, more often, help them publish their tales as he'd done with another prisoner more than twenty years before.

Norman was notorious for having spearheaded the release of a prisoner named Jack Henry Abbot in 1981, with whom he'd corresponded. Because of that, Norman was dubbed a hero, in prison circles. The reason Norman took on Abbot's case initially was because the prisoner struck him as a fine writer. This attribute would normally be far down on most people's list of reasons to help someone, but not Norman.

"He was an excellent writer, no doubt about it," Norman told me. "The situation was not good in the end, however." Doubtless, this was one of Norman's larger understatements: Abbot ended up murdering a waiter/playwright in Manhattan shortly after his release.

Prison mail still trickled in these twenty-five years later.

In early 2007, an email arrived asking me to provide a regular mail address for Norman Mailer. The notorious murderer Scott Peterson, recently imprisoned for life, wanted to send Norman a letter. The email was from a third party who claimed to be speaking on Peterson's behalf. We kicked the request around for a day or two, and finally Norman said okay, forward the house address. When Norris found out she was understandably annoyed at Norman's irresponsible approach to the request, and told me I shouldn't do it. I told Norman what Norris said, but he waved his hand and overruled her: "He probably won't write anyway."

The issue was forgotten for months. Then, a week after Norman left Provincetown for his final journey to Brooklyn that following September, a letter arrived from San Quentin addressed to him. As Norman had always insisted that I open all of his mail to decide what was worthwhile and what was junk, I opened the letter. It was from Peterson. In it he professed respect for Norman's writing and wrote that he had read once, and agreed with, an observation by a journalist who said of Mailer that "there may never be a figure so powerful." I immediately thought this guy was sly. And creepy. His letter had all the earmarks of one penned by a sociopath. To top it off, his penmanship resembled that of a suburban high-school girl's.

Norman was having a rough time of it in Brooklyn in September and October of 2007, and he had more immediate issues than answering some letter written by an imprisoned psychopath. I slipped the two-page letter into my pocket, deciding to show it to Norman when I next saw him, thinking it would be good for lively conversation. That visit would come some weeks farther down the road, so I figured that for the time being I'd mention the letter in a phone call.

"Peterson finally wrote back," I told Norman that evening.

"Who?"

"Scott Peterson, the guy who dumped his pregnant wife in the ocean in California two years ago. Remember? It was a huge case. He wrote us earlier asking for the address."

"Oh, yes, yes," Norman said. "What does he want?"

"Well, it's basically a fan letter. He says he read in the paper that you were ill, but he doesn't trust anything the media says. He gushes, but he's sly. The guy is a textbook sociopath. It's amazing."

"Do me a favor and bring it with you when you come," Norman said. "We'll take a look at it."

I took the letter home and put it in a black leather box I keep on my desk for important items and forgot about it until the morning I made the trek to New York to see Norman that last time. Just before I left my apartment I stuffed it into my travel case. But when I arrived in New York, at the hospital, I knew Peterson's letter would be the last thing Norman and I would talk about. However, Norman had asked me to bring it along, so the letter made the three-hundred-mile drive to New York with me. It also made the return trip; unopened and unread by Norman. There was no time, no need to bring it up—more pressing issues filled that two-day stay.

Most letter writers were not as obsessive as the Israeli writer or the prisoners, but some were. When I first absorbed the task of handling mail (Judith had always done it before I came to work with Norman), he told me that there were some he called "the usual suspects."

"Let's put those someplace safe, just in case," Norman said. In case of *what*, he never told me. I collected the letters and stacked them in the attic for "whenever." At some point they disappeared, likely by Mike's hand and into the archive. I only know that one day they were gone.

The normal correspondence was enough for Norman. He felt obliged to write notes back to people even though it consumed much of a day. Again, Norman was so riddled with duality about what he *should* do and what he *wanted* to do that he would wrestle with this conundrum until the mail pile became so towering that he had to dismantle it. To answer the mail, he typically opted to dictate into a tape recorder, which I would then transcribe while he was upstairs working. This should have been a straightforward approach, but Norman could make the seemingly simple complicated.

"I'll name this letter A-one," He'd say into the tape after thirty seconds of "testing, testing . . . one, one, one, two (COUGH, COUGH), two (COUGH), three . . . (AAA-HEEHMMMM). . . . Excuse me. Let's see. . . . Oh, yes, letter A-one."

Click! The machine would go off. A moment later it would click on again, followed by a long silence. "Ah, yes, okay . . . Dwayne, this is letter A-one. Dear Frank *A-r-d-u-n-b-e-r-g* . . ." And so it went through twenty or more letters.

"Norman," I said, after listening to him spell names for an hour, "you do realize that I have the originals in front of me when I'm typing, right? You don't need to spell names aloud."

"Yes, I know that, but what if they get lost and we need to get the names correct?"

"Well, good point," I said, "but if all the letters get lost, which I highly doubt, then we won't have the address to send the responses to *anyway*."

"Then maybe we should start making copies and keep them separate so the worst never happens. Then, we'll have backups," he said. Norman always liked to have backups for everything— at least in theory. In reality, he was horrid with organization (hence my presence, but, frankly, I wasn't great with it all the time, either). He was eternally cursed with the thought that things might "go missing." This was justified because occasionally one or two letters *would* go missing, usually shuffled into his morning newspaper. Several times I dug through the recycling bin for a letter he was positive he'd read a few days before.

"I put it right there," he'd insist, pointing to a spot near the mound of newspapers that grew like unruly yard weeds in my absence.

"I'll check the trash bin."

"How could it end up there?" he'd ask, oblivious. I got to the point where I would just look at him with a blank stare. His mess on the table was explanation enough.

"You need to make sure that pile doesn't get too big," Norris said to me. "He likes to stack."

"I try to handle it when he's working or in the second office, because he always wants to oversee the process."

"Well," she said, shaking her head, "however you manage to do it, you should do it more often."

Norris was right; it did need to be done more often. So, sometimes I would go ahead and attack the pile while he was present. Norman would immediately perk up and say, "Now make sure we don't lose anything." I'd say, "Okay, sure," and continue, but Norman had the kind of mind that could be easily engaged by what was happening *right then*. He'd point at an advertisement: "Let me see that." Sometimes the ad had the word "SAVE" written on it for some unclear reason.

"What the hell did I want this for?" he'd ask. Then, shaking his head: "Oh yes. Now I remember. Can we find out more about this?" Inevitably the ad was for an exercise contraption or remarkable new vitamin supplement.

"Sure," I'd say and set the paper aside for later. This would play out over and over until the "toss" pile shrank and the "save" pile grew.

"Please don't let him order any more books on vitamins or exercise equipment," Norris said. "We've got a basement full of machines and a million books about pills he's never cracked. We've got to keep an eye on the mail. Throw out anything that says 'Miracle Cure.' He's going to drive us to the poorhouse." To her great credit, considering all else she had to manage, she kept a keen eye on Norman's occasional frivolities.

"I'll do what I can," I said conspiratorially. For years I edited the mail, as did Norris, if she got there before it was plunked down in front of Norman. His astonishing intelligence did not always prohibit him from being a sucker for con ads and rubbish.

Once, during work on *The Castle in the Forest,* he decided a form letter would be best for answering a fat batch of mail. "It'll save hours," he said.

He wrote a pleasant, concise note explaining his reason for not writing more: because he was working on a novel. He suggested I put it with each letter and then he would write a short note at the bottom, sign the form letter, and we'd be done with the batch. Perfect idea! However, when he gave me the form letters, many were scrawled with long notes. He'd been unable to resist expanding his response beyond a simple gesture. His handwriting was nearly impossible to read sometimes, and I knew I was in trouble. I stupidly said, "Well, I hope they can make this out." He took a letter from my hand and reread what he'd scribbled.

"Hmm . . . you're right. Maybe you should type up each note and attach *that* to each form letter," he said.

"But doesn't that defeat the whole idea?" I asked, kicking myself. I'd created a new mountain of work.

"It won't take you too much time," he said.

Norman had more faith in my ability to read his writing than I did. I was going to have to be fast on my feet to get out of this one. I knew this presumably menial task would take, at the very least, most of a day. To compound the problem, some of the letters were already close to three months old, and another day's delay was troublesome to me. It kicked up an irrational guilt on my part.

"When they see that I take a while to write back, they will, in turn, take their own time to write again," he said, attempting to quell my anxiety.

Wrong. Within ten days of a "Mail Day," we'd be bombarded with responses to Norman's responses. It was a wicked mail loop, and I felt as if I were at the center of it.

"I think we should just send them as they are. Your handwritten note will mean more," I said. I was trying to get out of all the deciphering and typing. Saying this would inspire the belief that, yes, a handwritten note from Norman Mailer was unique and important. Norman did not commonly think that a letter from him was history-worthy, but facts were facts.

"Perhaps you're right," he said.

Fortunately he didn't latch on to the real reason for my suggestion, which was that I simply didn't want to wade through forty pages of his handwriting. It was my least favorite task, because I had to train my eyes for an hour to be able to slip into a kind of netherworld of interpretation.

"Let's send them out, but let's also *Xerox* the originals, so we have my responses," he said. "They'll be good for the archive."

Photocopying the letters was, obviously, much less work than retyping them, but it still involved more time than we'd originally planned.

This was just one of several methods employed through the years to deal with the river of mail that never ran dry. Other systems involved Norman simply writing on the bottom of the originals and having me return them—all history was mailed away that time! Occasionally he would simply dictate a line or two as I sat at the table typing into my computer. That method, inevitably, was time-consuming also because he could slide into a story—one having nothing to do with the letter—and before long two hours were gone to good conversation.

The books that arrived from fans to be signed were endless. At least three would come each week requesting an inscription, which he always provided. They were usually accompanied by a self-addressed stamped return envelope, but sometimes not; some had cash stuffed between pages to cover mailing costs. Inevitably one or two would come with no monies of any kind, and Norman would grumble, "I guess I'll pay for this one." Moreover, when an obviously elderly fan *would* send cash Norman usually stuck the bills right back into the book.

"They need this more," he'd say. "Leave the five in."

I was used to having reporters in and out of the house for interviews ever since I started working with Norman. There were endless requests for interviews, most of them coming to us through Judith, who had been his ultimate press filter. She was exceptional at weeding out worthwhile inquiries from unnecessary ones. Norman loved his privacy, but knew he had to continually nurture his name and reputation, and that meant talking to reporters. He had a vigorous sense of humor about the whole process. Once, after hanging up the phone, he sat across from me shaking his head. I asked him what the conversation had been about.

"Oh, someone wants a fluff interview," he said. "Not interested."

"Why?" I asked.

"It gets odious," he said. "They all want to know the same thing: 'What's it like to be Norman Mailer?'" He then demonstrated the ego involved in answering such silliness by jabbing his fingers under his armpit, bringing them to his nose, sniffing deeply, and saying, "What's it like? Aaahhhh. It's better than roses!" and letting out a loud laugh.

After Judith died, the task of maintaining Norman's schedule fell fully to me. I didn't mind, because I'd already had a large part in its maintenance anyway. My days were now beginning to fill with queries about the Hitler novel. The number of interview requests was growing by the week. As Norman and I went over possibilities, he suggested "Media Day."

"Schedule them all into one afternoon," he said. "That way I won't lose too many hours of work."

"Work" at that point consisted mostly of reading more German books for volume two of *Castle*, research on the blunder of Iraq, and the occasional blog to the Huffington Post. Arianna Huffington was a friend of Norman's, so when she invited him to join the "blogosphere," Norman accepted due to his respect for her. Blogging was relatively new and, to Norman, it smacked of being a frivolous way to publish. After all, the writing lived strictly on the Internet and was therefore "tinged." He finally relented and gave it a try when John was visiting. The short essay would be a statement about Iraq, Bush, and the entire war mess.

"You should give it a shot, pop," Johnny said. Norman turned to me and asked what I thought.

"The life expectancy of any article is forty-eight hours, at best," I said. I tended to agreed with his notion that venturing into blogdom might have little effect in the long run, if any.

"Why?" Norman asked, fielding our opinions.

"Because I think it is disposable journalism that generally gets buried under rants and pointless comments."

"No," John said. "Not always. Sometimes it changes things. Sometimes it sticks around for a while."

"Yes, you're right," I said. "But only if your name is Norman Mailer. For the most part I think it's just fence talk with global eavesdroppers."

"Well, not to point out the obvious, but *I am* Norman Mailer," Norman said to me. Johnny smiled.

"Good point," I said, trumped.

For two hours and six or seven drafts, Norman Mailer, the

creator of the "New Journalism," ventured into the "Newest Journalism," on May 17, 2005.

"I want to do one more pass," he said when I handed him the third revision of his fifth or sixth draft.

"You know, one of the foundations of blogging is supposedly spontaneity. From what I can tell, not a whole hell of a lot of rewriting goes into it."

"That may be true," Norman said, "but venue has little to do with good writing. The better this is, the better those who follow me might be." Norman eternally educated through example.

Fifteen minutes later I brought my laptop around to show him his first published blog on the Huffington Post.

"That is fast," he said. He then reached for his stack of cards and began to toss a few hands of solitaire. The new experience had had no effect on him in the least. To Norman it was all just *writing*.

The media days began to fall into place—usually Tuesdays or Fridays.

"Why then?" I asked when he said that he preferred those days.

"Less interruption, Norman said. This made very little sense, because as long as I'd been with him, no day was any different from others, except football was on TV on Sundays and he liked to devote an hour or two to that. Norman was a creature of unpredictable routines and surprising repetition, if a label must be attached. He was predictable, but only to a point—his brain was the wild card. When a new idea came to him he could change direction quickly, and I would be taken along for the ride. I might arrive one day believing I would spend my hours typing, and end up researching silent turn-of-the-century Yiddish movies or, on one occasion, two hours narrowing down the brand of roast beef hash his mother served him for breakfast in Brooklyn in the 1930s. That indeed happened, and it was challenging and enjoyable.

I got on the phone with the young woman in the publicity department at Random House, Jynne Martin, and informed her of our desire to fit most of the interviews into our selected two days. "Do you think this will be a problem?"

"No. They'll come when I tell them," she said. "After all, he's Norman." She was right; no one ever did question the days.

As weeks passed and the schedule took shape, the countries represented by the press grew from the expected North American ones to include most of Europe and half of Asia. Phone interviews accumulated also, but took on a life of their own. "Phoners," as we called them, were scheduled the same way as other interviews, but calls from foreign reporters demanded a protocol. Each reporter calling from whatever country had to be screened by me before Norman would talk to them. Norman urged me to assess the interviewer's ability to speak English before he took the phone. As noted, Norman was hard of hearing, and broken English on top of that tried his patience. I had a perfect score when it came to foreign callers, until I walked in from an errand once to find Norman several minutes into a Q-and-A from Greece. Norman was raging at the poor woman five thousand miles away: "*I cannot* understand what you are saying. I was told you spoke English. Clearly, you do not!" He slammed the handset down as I rounded the corner.

"I couldn't understand a goddamn word!" he said.

"Well, who the hell was it?" I asked.

"The Greek! I thought you screened her."

"Well, no. She's not supposed to call for another hour. It's only two thirty."

The routine was that reporters would call and I would answer and chat for a few moments. If they passed muster, I'd hand the phone to Norman. If not, I'd veto the interview with an important-sounding excuse.

"Well, call back and suggest they get someone else. God knows what would end up in print in Athens if I'd have kept talking!"

I located the number and called Greece back. After much jumbled apologizing by the rattled reporter for aggravating Mailer, her editor got on the line and I passed the phone to Norman.

"This one's as clear as a bell," I said with my hand over the mouthpiece. Norman took the phone as if nothing had happened. As fast as he could become annoyed, he could also switch to being pleasant as pie. It was not often that he morphed into his famed old terror self, but it did happen—usually only when he was faced with stupidity. For him, journalists trying to interview him in fractured English fell into that category.

The reporters who came to the house tended to arrive with controlled terror in their hearts, especially when Judith was alive. She prepared them with rigorous rules as to conduct.

She always cc'd me with her correspondences, so I would know whom, and how many, to expect at the front door. Late in the summer of 2003, I got a note from her saying that a journalist named Karin Davison was to visit the next week.

Davison, an accomplished reporter for a German television network, was constructing a two-hour retrospective on Norman, slated to air months down the road. I'd never heard of her and ignorantly assumed she was just another member of the press. She would come, get her story, and leave. Nope.

Karin was incomparable. Her interview was smart to the point of academic and her sensitive charisma unearthed the regions of Norman that I knew generally lay dormant when he spoke with the press. Her examination of him proved more thorough and truthful than any I'd seen yet.

We all took a liking to Karin, and Norman invited her and her crew to join us for a drink. We gathered around the bar off the dining room and she told us stories about famous people she'd encountered over the years—from every major world leader to Elvis Presley. She'd met everybody twice, and no one had truly rattled her but Elvis. Apparently he had such an effect on her that when it was time to begin the interview, she couldn't talk—she managed only grunting sounds that, she said, were so disjointed that the King of Rock and Roll recoiled. She also confessed to having served as the composer Leonard Bernstein's part-time assistant and confidante in the last years of his life, and the loss of him had affected her deeply. I am sure that revelation underscored the beginning of our friendship—one that has endured for years now. She was one of the few who understood the personal intricacies of my position with Norman and respected its complexity.

Karin is one of a small number of journalists Norman had serious affection for. She visited the house several times over the next couple of years to speak with Norman for a variety of reasons, and ultimately he chose her to give his first significant interview about *The Castle in the Forest*. She also brought John Hemingway to the house for a shared interview. John was the grandson of Ernest Hemingway, and Norman was happy to meet him. He'd known John's father, Gregory, quite well in the past, but said he never knew about the man's inner struggles.

Gregory Hemingway, from all accounts, was profoundly troubled, mired in conflicts revolving around transsexualism. Perhaps due to the social mores of the time and the domineering legend of his father, Ernest, Gregory never found equilibrium for his life. He died seemingly broken as "Gloria" Hemingway, at a Florida detention center for women after being arrested for public drunkenness in 2001. At the time we met him, John Hemingway was researching his father, probing for answers to riddles that plagued his childhood, which he wrote about later in his book *Strange Tribe*.

As John was preparing his memoir, Karin was producing a documentary about the Hemingway family. Norman never met Ernest Hemingway face-to-face, as is often assumed. He told me that the one time he did have the opportunity to meet Hemingway, he backed out. Norman decided to not step off the elevator on Hemingway's floor at the hotel they were both visiting, and returned instead to his own room on another floor. He told me he'd feared the worst—that they would have nothing to talk about. Also, he detested the thought of navigating his way through the throng of sycophants who Norman assumed likely swarmed around the author at any given moment. Norman was young then and Hemingway was exceptionally famous, emperor of the literary world. No meeting between the two ever happened, but Norman did write about him, and penned one remarkable piece titled "A Wandering in Prose: For Hemingway, November 1960." He had included it in *Modest Gifts*, and read it aloud to me over lunch once with a reverence in his voice I'd rarely heard. When Karin brought John Hemingway to Provincetown, Norman was excited to host them both and grant the interviews. He was eager to tell John what he knew about Gregory and contribute, as best he could, to the young man's understanding of his father. The night, as one might imagine, ended in a drinkfest. Mailer and a Hemingway twice removed hit it off while hitting the bottle with abandon. The next day, John Hemingway had to be physically assisted into a taxi so he could catch his flight to Key West. Norman, when I saw him that same morning at the breakfast table, sported a peculiar shade of green himself.

"It was the grappa," he moaned to me over his uneaten eggs. Grappa or proximity to Papa, I wondered?

"It was *everything*," Norris told me. "I haven't seen him drink so much in years."

On average, during the publication blitz, we would host a slew of reporters at the house three times a month.

Everyone from major American papers, weekly news magazines, the BBC, Danish News, and the Japanese, Italian, Spanish, and Belgian press came. The living room at 627 became our own United Nations of communications. When a renowned French celebrity academic arrived with his crew to tape a show on "Mailer's Intellectualism," I found the man to be generally appealing but excessively self-involved. He was pure TV personality, right down to his designer pants, half-open shirt, and perfect hair. His interview with Norman more closely resembled a monologue *about* Mailer, in front of Mailer. Norman seemed to comprehend only every third word, due to the man's accent, and occasionally looked bewildered. His knowledge of Norman's work seemed to me to be somewhat askew. My opinion was validated later on when I ran across an interview he gave about *doing* the interview with Norman, wherein he stated that the main character in Norman's *Tough Guys Don't Dance* was gay! (Frankly, all anyone has to do to find out the truth about that misstatement is read the second paragraph of the book in question.)

Finally, the interview was over. As on every media day, I had placed a plate of cookies on the coffee table. The Frenchman grabbed a Nestlé Tollhouse Chocolate Chip Cookie, took a bite, and informed Norris it was the best cookie he'd ever eaten—in America *or* France. Norris looked at me, I at her, and we both suppressed an urge to laugh. The cookies were less than an hour out of a plastic package.

A British reporter, anxious about meeting Norman, mistakenly put salt instead of sugar in his coffee as he waited with me in the kitchen. To be fair, it wasn't really his fault, because the salt and sugar were next to each other in small bowls. (We never used a salt shaker in the house.) When he choked on his first sip, I was embarrassed and apologetic; I should have never had the two near each other. I thought he was going to have a coronary, but I managed to calm both of us in time for the sitdown. I felt terrible about the episode, but the nice gentleman ended up with one of the best interviews Norman gave that week.

Nearly every journalist was slightly on edge when he or she came to the house. The glut of them came after Judith had passed on, so I couldn't blame their nervousness on having dealt with her—although when she was around, that used to up their anxiety level considerably. To interview Norman, to come in contact with him, was, for reporters, like meeting one of the inventors of the profession they'd devoted their lives to. Norman, along with Capote, was considered the father of "New Journalism." He took an otherwise often dry business and turned it on its ear by inserting opinion and "self" into it. Truman and Norman gave permission to an entire generation of writers to buck normalcy and flail opinion and "story" around abundantly in their reporting, bringing style and sometimes bravado to stoic newsprint. I once asked a journalist from a large paper who had, I knew, spoken to every major writer, celebrity, and political figure alive what the huge excitement was about interviewing Norman. He raised his eyebrows, inhaled deeply, and said, "Well, he's Mailer, for Christ sake. It doesn't get any better than this."

All of them tried to get something out of Norman that no one else had. Their questions were always smart, and each interviewer left with the feeling that they'd gotten a unique take on the Master. Truth was, Norman had been doing this for more than fifty-five years and knew exactly how to tweak any statement to make it sound fresh and spontaneous.

Norman and I had a ritual on press days. He would read the paper at the table, play solitaire, and do crosswords until the media members arrived, while I arranged the living room to more easily accommodate cameras and other assorted equipment. When the doorbell rang, Norman scuttled into the TV room to collect himself and wait for me to get him. In the meantime, I confirmed the names of the reporters and their crew and scribbled notations on a Post-it note, which I would then slip to Norman. I'd add details such as "red hair," "paisley tie," or "very tall." By the time Norman wandered into the living room he knew exactly who everyone was and, generally, the correct pronunciation of their names. The Post-it notes became invaluable.

Reporters were regularly amazed at how easy going the "Literary Lion" was when they met him. Norman's first words were usually "Oh, please call me Norman." Over the course of my years with him, countless reporters told me Norman was unlike what they had expected. He was mild-mannered, gracious, and outright welcoming. Unfortunately, prior to this round of media, little of that side of him appeared in stories, because to be pleasant is not sexy—it doesn't sell papers as well as legend and controversy. With this latest media blitz, most articles were suddenly bloated with praise about Norman's cordiality. I figured it was about time.

Random House scheduled a tour for Norman to publicize the book around the time of its release in January of 2007. The tour would begin and end in New York, and in the middle he would make his way through San Francisco, Los Angeles, Sacramento, and Chicago. Because the stress of travel was a lot for him to endure at the age of eighty-four, John Buffalo went along to ensure that everything went smoothly and to see to it that his dad was fine.

Preparing Norman for travel was a feat unto itself, and not because he was elderly, but because he was downright nervous. He would never admit this (even to me), but his anxiety surfaced the closer we got to departure day. In 2005, I'd purchased several small notebooks that he kept in his shirt pocket to scribble notes in on everything from character studies for the novel to dinner and what kind of wine we should have with it. When trips came up, the notebooks would appear frequently and he'd furiously write reminders in them, to himself and to me: "Dwayne, don't forget the following: The Latin book, the three Iraq pages, my pills, razor, playing cards, schedule, typing paper, pens . . . 2 ties only this trip. . . . Do I have clean shirts? Check with Norris. . . . Will I need shoes? . . . Is the speech enlarged for reading? . . ." And on and on they would go. Of course I had already considered most of these items, because what he needed rarely varied for each trip, but when I checked the notebooks I always found a laundry list of worries.

"You're all set for your trip, Norman," I told him. "You don't need to stress about these things."

"I want to make sure," he said. "Keep the list handy."

"Of course."

The closer it came to the time he would depart, the more protective of him I found myself becoming. This man who had been so open and helpful to me as teacher and friend had become lodged in a branch of me that I'd only imagined a grandfather could inhabit.

His overall health was becoming worrisome and the clatter of age more apparent. It pained me to witness, but I was determined that I would never, under any circumstances, broach the subject of his health with him in any overly concerned tone. When he prepared to go away, both of us sensed the coming disruption, and I became more attentive to him. I think both of us couldn't wait until his return, so life could settle down again. I know this feeling was not one-sided, because while he was away I would get a call from him several times a day. He didn't necessarily need anything specific, but talking to me was, apparently, a tangible link to home.

Norman made only one live television appearance to promote *The Castle in the Forest*, besides the Charlie Rose program on PBS (which he appeared on eleven times over the years), and that happened in March of 2007. His publisher wanted to know if Norman would consider appearing on *The Martha Stewart Show*.

"What does she do on that show? Doesn't she cook?" he asked. I told him yes, she did cooking segments, but she also interviewed actors, singers, politicians, baseball players, writers, and, on at least one episode, a bird trainer. Martha wasn't Oprah, but her show was respected.

"She's got a huge audience," I told him. "It couldn't hurt, and it airs at a convenient time."

Norman, always willing to try something new, agreed to the proposal. He was certainly no stranger to television; he just hadn't done it *live* in a few years. By the time he left Provincetown he was mildly excited about the prospect. He headed to New York the next week, several days prior to the show, to be with Norris and prepare. Jynne had also scheduled a series of press conferences with reporters at the publishing house the day before Norman appeared on *The Martha Stewart Show*.

To review the broadcast now is to see the generally female audience appearing to fawn over a pop music star, not an eighty-four-year-old writer. Norman said later that when he looked out at them, many dressed in pink or red (for reasons he could not figure), he experienced a pleasurable reaction.

"I thought I'd be facing a bunch of women expecting me to make a pie," he told me on the phone. "I was surprised. They were genuinely interested."

"Of course they were. How was Martha?" I asked.

"Who?" Norman was not fazed by his fame or anybody else's.

"The *host*." His hearing was really getting bad.

"Oh . . . oh fine, fine. Very pleasant. I think I've met her before. I'll have to check with Norris." Norris was much more than just Norman's constant caregiver; she was often his memory for details of their long and unparalleled social history.

The audience likely hadn't read much of his work, but what they *did* know about Norman Mailer was his name, and he easily seduced the lot of them with his charm and his ever-twinkling blue eyes. For the broadcast, he wore his now-famous Russell Crowe vest, dark blue sweatpants, and Uggs, and appeared every bit the amiable, grand author he was. Moments into chatting with Martha, the audience appeared to be as engrossed as any scholarly crowd to have the chance to hear a writer and intellectual they probably knew only as an American icon. They all received a copy of his book, and I would bet most of them went home and immediately read it—Norman had that effect. As Judith stated once, "Norman is his own best PR firm."

I received a phone call one afternoon that was completely different from any other request for an interview: the actor Tim Robbins explained to me that he was making a documentary about changes in war through the twentieth century and its effects on the men who fought. Unlike the Iraq war that Bush had forced troops into so irresponsibly, World War II, Norman's war, clearly had meaning and purpose. It was a good idea for a documentary, because little attention is generally paid to the feelings of men who are obliged to fight wars. I told Norman about the request, and he first wanted to read everything I could find about Robbins. After he went over the material, he agreed to the project.

Tim Robbins had interviewed both Gore Vidal and Kurt Vonnegut prior to visiting Provincetown to talk to Norman, and so he'd done his homework about war as it pertained to Norman's generation. As Tim said to me when we went to buy coffee for ourselves and his young crew, "Guys Norman's age knew what a cause was, and they were willing to go all the way. Now, there is no cause. Only blind patriotism." I agreed with his sentiment and knew Norman did also, but Norman's take was complex, and he laid it out in detail during the two-hour filmed dialogue.

I lurked in the background as I usually did while they taped, and then went outside for a few minutes to call Thomas. Tim Robbins was Thomas's favorite actor and I wanted to be able to give Thomas the chance to meet him. Our relationship had improved, finding its way closer to stable. There was still a haunting, unnamed void, where our life together was concerned that I couldn't find a label for. I assumed, and hoped, our situation would mend itself over time. With my clean head, I had less of a desire to force issues and instead embraced newfound patience. While Thomas and I were far from perfect in our relationship, we were on the track to getting better.

When I made the call I discovered that Thomas was having one of his bad days again. He had locked himself away from the world and didn't want to go out. This was not abnormal for him at the time; I knew there were demons that ran deep in him. But since he could not find a way to tell me about those demons, I remained a concerned observer, gentle with him and careful not to exacerbate their stupefying gnaws at his soul. The practice of leaving him to work through his depression alone had become rote for me, and I generally pushed his befuddling behavior aside. But on this day I pressed him to rouse himself and enjoy the experience of meeting someone he admired. No. Thomas wasn't going to come over to meet Tim Robbins.

"I just don't get it," I said. "You're going to hate yourself for hiding today."

"I know," Thomas said. "I just can't go out today."

I was irritated, but figured he was the one who would have to always kick himself for not mustering the power to get out of bed. How often does someone get the chance to talk to their favorite movie star in a relaxed one-on-one environment? I had even told Tim about Thomas. Tim said, "Oh, I'd like to meet him." I don't know if he was being truthful or just pleasant, but I passed the message on.

"He says he'd like to meet you," I told Thomas. "He's a really nice guy. We spent forty-five minutes driving around town talking. I wish you'd change your mind."

"Why would he want to meet me?" Thomas asked.

"Well, ask yourself this: Why *wouldn't* he want to meet you?" I hung up the phone. None of it made any sense to me, and it pained me that I couldn't devote enough of my energies to be of help to him. But Thomas had to find his own way even as I was finding mine.

Thomas never met Tim Robbins. Over the following days he emerged from his depression and returned to work. Life improved. We were on our way back to the ease we'd mislaid the year before, but there was still one more obstacle to overcome, one that Norman had commented on long before: ". . . we can't know the conflicts living within him."

"It's good to see Thomas is around again," Norman said to me one morning when we were out on the deck enjoying some sun. Thomas was upstairs repairing a leak in the bathroom.

"I'm glad he's around here more, too" I said.

"Last year . . . you never had anyone else in your life, did you?"

"No," I said. "That wasn't possible. I was unable." It was the truth. I had been utterly stalled.

Norman and I didn't normally discuss matters that were so directly intimate, but this day was an exception, and I felt he was concerned for my overall well-being. He, of course, knew and appreciated that I'd taken steps to improve my life in the time I'd been with him, but he was also concerned about how his assistant would fare in the end.

"He's good," Norman said. "But you'll always have difficulty."

"I know," I said. "Scares the hell out of me."

"It should," Norman said, "but it shouldn't stop you, either."

I put the talk aside, thinking that I would always have it to refer to when I found myself mired in indecision. I appreciated Norman's opinions on personal matters when he offered them, so they tended to stick with me. He was correct about the difficulty I would endure with Thomas, but not entirely.

I would now, more than anything, love to tell him how in the end Thomas became better and more alive than either of us could have imagined. But maybe Norman did see how it would play out all along. I don't know. It would have been just like Norman to keep what he knew secret and then later tell me, "Well, I thought you should find out for yourself what was right there in front of you."

EIGHT

Shifts

There was no denying it: Norman was aging in front of me. He had faced a million obstacles, both personal and political, and had balked at none of them, but clearly age was a new ballgame. To do battle with it, Norman utilized his sharpest weapon, which was his intellect. In his life, if he didn't win a fight, he at least made a loud racket that let everyone know he was serious about the match.

He surrounded himself with youthful people, those with electric minds. That didn't mean he held court exclusively with the young—far from it. His idea of youth had nothing to do with age; it had to do with state of mind. Norman disliked stagnancy in all forms. Consequently he plodded onward through all the impediments old age presents. Perhaps that's why at the age of eighty-four he decided to direct another movie. Even though he had trouble breathing and suffered derelict knees, he still believed he could helm a film of his 1967 play *The Deer Park*, and do it better than anyone.

Even when Norman did show strains, no one around him adopted a patronizing tone or attitude. First off, they wouldn't have lived to walk out the door if they'd tried, and second, on his worst day Norman still emitted an authority that floated around him like vapor. He never merited fuss, but we who were close to him did become more protective—as is human nature. Norris was adamant that Norman be well cared for at all times, thus in 2007, I began spending even more time with him. With her schedule, my being around more often became important. Honestly, there was little additional that I could do, but sometimes just the presence of someone you trust can make all the difference. Norman's health could take quick turns, and I never knew what I'd face each morning when I arrived.

Perhaps the first time I truly became aware that Norman was growing old happened in 2004. I'd worked with him for only thirteen months then and rarely, if ever up to that point, been overly concerned about his age. That changed one day when I fetched him from the Provincetown airport after he'd gone to Mexico for his son's wedding. Norris had to miss Michael's wedding because she was in the hospital for yet another round of surgery. Nothing in that week had been easy, but both of them missing the wedding was completely out of the question, so Norman traveled alone.

As I stood waiting for him to climb down the steps from the small airplane that serves Ptown, I was surprised to see a bandage on his temple. He was moving slower than usual, placing more responsibility on his two canes than when I'd seen him off. He'd been gone for a week and although we'd spoken nearly every day, I missed him. The last thing he'd said to me the day before on the phone was, "It will be good to see you, pal. Can't wait to get home." Now here he was: wide smile, eyes tired but sparkling, and a cut on his head. As he moved toward me, I remember thinking that he looked old. His bend and measured swagger was pronounced, and the rather soiled patch on his forehead sealed the image. Norman looked like he'd been in a bar brawl.

"How does the other guy look?" I asked as I shook his hand. I took his small carry-on bag and put it into the back of the Volvo. We both climbed into the car.

"Ha! Like a fucking marble sink," he said, arranging his canes next to his seat. "I took a fall in the bathroom last night at the hotel." I could tell he was slightly hung over, too, which didn't help matters.

"How's the pain?"

"Not bad but not that good," he said and let out a "whew" as he settled into the car. He was beat, but his mood was okay.

He was still a tough guy, but he was an eighty-two-year-old tough guy. At that age, Tough Guys Don't Bounce. He also seemed to be irritated with himself for having fallen, more than at the actual injury. His self-assurance was, I sensed, slightly dented.

"Mr. Mailer?"

I had just started the car and about to drive away when a woman approached the passenger-side window. She was in her sixties, pleasant, and obviously delighted about spotting Norman Mailer in the parking lot of the airport. Norman rolled the window down, and his entire demeanor changed from slight personal irritation to subdued thrill at being recognized. Right in front of me he slipped into his parallel famous self.

"Hello, hello," he said to the woman, whose hand had slipped inside the car to greet the author.

"I am so happy to see you, sir," she said. She wasn't an over-zealous fan, but she was a fan. A man in his late thirties, who I assumed was her son, stood behind her holding her travel bag.

"Why, thank you," Norman said, "Thank you. Nice to see you, too."

"I just love your books, Mr. Mailer, and I hope I'm not bothering you, but I saw you and I wanted to tell you that."

"Oh, no bother at all."

Since laying eyes on him a few minutes before, the only thing I could think was that I had to get him home as soon as possible. The dried blood was obvious on the bandage, which needed to be changed. This was a bad time for a fan to show up.

"I reread your book a few weeks ago and I just loved it," she said.

"Which book?" Norman asked.

"*The Executioner's Song,*" she said. "It was so real and so truthful. You really brought me into the story."

My heart rate escalated. Something inside that usually stayed dormant, a need to protect, sprang up. My body language was clear as I tapped on the steering wheel. My foot revved the gas. Couldn't she see the bandage on his head? The woman continued to talk for a minute. Then, coming out of her monologue, she switched topics.

"What happened to your head?" she asked.

"Oh, I had a little run-in with some furniture," Norman said, ever the pro at downplaying the urgent. "It's nothing."

"Gracious!" she said.

"Well, thank you!" I popped off a little too intensely in her direction.

"Oh yes, of course, you have to go. Well, thank you, Mr. Mailer."

"Yes, yes," Norman said. "What's your name?"

The woman said it and then introduced her son. More handshakes.

The transmission lurched slightly. The two nice people said their goodbyes and made their way toward the entrance to the terminal, finally leaving us alone.

"Don't do that," Norman said, shifting into an aggravated state. He was irritated at me for rushing him away. "That woman needed to say hello." His voice was tired.

"I know, I know," I said. "I'm just worried about your head."

"Well, let me worry about my head," he said.

"Sorry."

Our happy reunion was now dampened with annoyance on both sides. I turned onto Route 6, aiming for home. Neither of us spoke until we were near the house.

"Norman, I didn't mean to interfere," I said. "I was just worried. I still am."

"Listen, it's not the first time I've hit my damn head," he said. "But thank you for your concern."

"I know it's not, but it's the first time since I've been around. It looks like a hell of a bump."

"Well, there was quite a lot of blood," he said. He sort of lightened up a bit when he said that, as if the amount of blood spilled validated his stamina. The Tough Guy was back and even smiling a little as I swerved the car into its usual spot in front of the house.

At the dining room table a few minutes after I'd put his bag away and found the first aid kit, I sat down next to him. Norman pulled the dirty bandage from his head and put it on the table.

The extent of my care for him, which ran deep, did not extend to dabbing his wound. It was up to him to tend his injury and up to me merely to be near—no matter how much he fumbled. I sat still and watched him as he helped himself.

"Have you told Norris about this?" I asked.

"Yes. I didn't go into much detail. Don't *you* go explaining too much either, pal," he said, dabbing a towel over the cut that topped a purple bump on his head. "I'm depending on you for that."

"I know," I said. I never told Norris about how bad the cut looked that day. As he rebandaged himself, I thought about another time, a few weeks before, when I'd cut my hand in the kitchen. Norman wanted to help *me* out by playing kitchen battlefield medic.

"Let me see that," he'd said, taking a gander at my cut. It was clear it would be difficult for me to put a Band-Aid on it one-handed.

"I could butterfly-bandage that for you." He was making reference to a dressing that sounded too large for such a small slice.

"No," I said. "It's not deep. I'll manage."

"Listen, I used to do this in the army," he said. He wanted to help me, but I couldn't allow him. I was embarrassed by my mishandling of the knife, which clouded my thinking, and I returned to the kitchen.

"Suit yourself," he'd said.

Now our roles were reversed, and I watched him take care of his head.

"Facial cuts bleed more than anywhere else on the body," I said when he'd finished.

"I was a boxer," he said. "I know that."

"I'm glad you're back, Norman."

"Me too, me too," he said, and nodded his head a little. "Do you mind putting that stuff in the trash?" He was pointing to the old bandage.

I was relieved he was home, but I found that he was, some-how, slightly different. Physically he appeared the same as always, but a weariness had drifted over him that I suspected was settling in for the long haul.

By 2005, Norris had moved her mother into an assisted-living complex in Orleans, which is a larger town thirty miles from Provincetown. Norris's own unsteady health, combined with her mother's age and Norman's irritation at having Gaynell in the house, had dictated this sensible move. The mixture of the two of them—vastly different octogenarians under the same roof—was an incredibly stressful situation for Norris. I knew from the start that Norman wasn't terribly fond of Norris's mother. He thought it was fine that she was around during the hard periods Norris had endured, but small conflicts inevitably arose between them.

Gaynell was a year or two older than Norman, but no two people were such opposites. Nothing, aside from their mutual love of Norris, ever surfaced that indicated they had anything in common. Norman disliked playing nice with Gaynell, but he did it because he was a gentleman and loved his wife completely. As for Gaynell, she didn't seem to think much of Norman either, but she was far beyond saying anything about it directly, because she was a good Christian lady. His rank as one of the world's most revered writers was lost on her. Or, if she cared, she didn't show it outwardly. She did have a way of making comments about him to me that spelled out her opinion more or less succinctly.

"I don't know how you can help him on all those big books he likes to write," she once said to me, shaking her head slightly and gazing upward toward heaven. Ouch! It was an innocent enough remark until I thought about it. "All those big books he likes to write." Did she think his work was a hobby? I could tell she was calling him, in her way, a blowhard. She didn't seem to appreciate that Norman had written more than forty books and that they'd paid for the very chair she sat in while daintily skewering him

Norman was equally passive-aggressive.

"Ah, hello, dear," he'd say in a voice so syrupy that you'd swear he was part maple. "What are you going to *do* today?" He knew she never did anything except read Christian novels and nap, but he always asked this as she passed him in the morning pushing her red walker.

In Gaynell's opinion, I think, Norris had married the devil—plain and simple. But as her good Southern Baptist way dictated, she always held her tongue. Norman, more or less, didn't give a darn what Gaynell thought or believed. For more than a year, life simmered in this way between them, until Norris moved her mother out and rediscovered a portion of her own battered sanity.

The irony was that both Norman and his mother-in-law were similarly afflicted. He had trouble walking, and so did she. He was deaf as a wall without his hearing aids, and she was headed in that direction herself. Her heart was pretty strong, and Norman's was recently refurbished. Both of them were still mentally vital—although Norman was ahead of her in that game. I happened to like Gaynell a great deal and did what I could to entertain her or help Norris with her when I could. I also enjoyed her devious streak—even the part of it she aimed at Norman. She loved my cooking, and since dinner was a big part (the largest?) of her day, she was always curious as to what I was making. When she came into the kitchen to investigate my bubbling pots, she would sneak Snickers candy bars from the freezer, where we kept them—not good for a diabetic. I usually pretended to ignore the crinkle of the tiny packages that she herself couldn't hear and the bulge of her sweater pocket when she left the room. I figured it was not really my place to monitor the sugar habits of an eighty-five-year-old lady.

One evening I brought sushi home and offered her a taste. She wasn't big on new foods; mushrooms had been a milestone.

"I don't know," she said in her hesitant Southern drawl.

"If you don't like it we'll just throw the rest of it away," I said. She bit into the rice and shrimp delicacy and chewed. A grin spread over her face.

"It's good," she said, and stuck the other half into her mouth. She declined a second piece, but I'd made her day happier by coaxing her into trying something new.

Gaynell was infatuated with Thomas. He was often working around the house, and she would watch him through the window, straining to lift a board or sweating over a project in the sun. Thomas was not hard on the eyes, no matter what the eyes' age. His skin was olive-bronze, his hair longish and thick, and his eyes as soft as a girl's. He was good about spending time talking with Gaynell, something that spoke well to his overall gentleness. He had sensitivity toward her because he'd lived in the South himself, when he was younger, and knew that some of its customs were different from ours in the North. She said to me, "You know, if I had a son, I'd want him to be just like Thomas." I wasn't sure if she knew that Thomas and I were more than just "best friends." It made me happy to know that this straitlaced Baptist woman, who was painfully sheltered in some ways, would have liked a son just like the man I loved. Later, after she moved out, I found out that she knew our whole story, because Norris told me she was sad at hearing the news that Thomas and I were "having problems."

Once *The Castle in the Forest* was in bookstores, Norman's self-imposed work load diminished. He still read every day, still did groundwork for the second book about Hitler, but his rush to complete or invest himself in projects took a backseat to a period of relative repose. My time with him became more focused on his day-to-day needs. I had long ago cast aside my feeling that to be an all-encompassing "personal" assistant was somehow undignified. I realized that Norman's respect for me had lent foundation to my *self*-respect. More than I'd ever thought possible, he'd ushered me through vital essentials of understanding myself and the events that lurked in my past.

A day after I returned from seeing my mother in Oregon, Norman and I were together in the attic as usual and he asked how my trip had gone. I told him it had been fine, but I'd come back to Provincetown with new information about my dad's death, which had happened when I was only seven. I told Norman about the long illness my father had endured, the endless trips to the Mayo Clinic, and the several operations to remove a snaking cluster of benign tumors strangling his spinal cord, growths that had developed after a fall from one of his greenhouse roofs when I was two. Nothing had worked to cure him. After a consultation at Palo Alto Medical Center, where they'd given him bad odds for surviving another operation, he opted not to return for one. He came home for the last time not long before Christmas. He wanted to spend that winter with us, his sons, and not risk losing that time in hospitals having procedures that might not work for him in the end anyway.

My dad spent that Christmas with us, and I remember it was a long winter, snowier than usual, and therefore grand for boys. Through that December, my parents entertained more visitors than they customarily did; Grandma and Grandpa came over often, and extended family and friends were invited for dinners. It was a good Christmas.

After the New Year, my father made a difficult choice and died at home on a January night that, yet again, brought a heavy snow. That next morning, a good neighbor, a rancher, plowed our long driveway so my father could be taken away by a large black car with no windows. My two older brothers and I watched from the living room window of my grandparent's house as the hearse left our hill.

I told this to Norman. During my visit, my mother and I had finally, these thirty years later, discussed that night and the morning that followed.

"So, he took his own way out," Norman said

"Yes, he did," I said. Neither of us used the word *suicide*, but that is what we were discussing, because I had learned that my father had taken sleeping pills.

"Most men never face their life directly like that," Norman told me. He went on to say that in most religions, and much of society, a choice like my father's is viewed as shameful, when it should not be. Ultimates are hard, and that one is the hardest. Some decisions we, as the ones left behind, cannot fathom. Some things a man can't change. He once wrote a response to a quote by Emily Dickinson that "We cannot ponder life for long without searching for the possibilities within death. This may be the only obsession which is worth its weight upon our heart."

"I think his decision was brave," I said. "I admire what he did, if you want to know the truth. I always suspected, but I was never sure. I don't know how my brothers feel. I think they know, but we've never spoken about it . . . "

"Men in your position are often angry."

"I was raised well. I don't have anything to be angry about."

"It doesn't always raise itself in clear ways," Norman said. "From what I can see, you spent a good portion of your life in search of a base."

"Not so much anymore," I said.

"Keep in mind that large decisions are not always clear, even when men like your dad make them. Maybe his larger idea, even if he didn't know it, was for you to learn to manage obstacles better than he did. That is not a bad lesson in the end."

I don't know if loss can be graded. Certainly the loss of a

child must be the worst, followed by the death of a spouse in a marriage that is still young and vital. Then, I would argue, comes the fissure carved into the mind of a boy who has lost his father before finding a sense of himself. It is a hollowness that goes unnoticed from day to day but shows itself to be rabid over years of looking for balance.

I felt suddenly exposed, a rare situation for me when talking to Norman. I wanted to say aloud to him how much I valued his words, but I didn't, because there was no need. He patted my shoulder for a moment while I sat near him at the desk. That was enough. The gesture was one that he never knew held more weight than any compassionate touch I'd received in decades.

Norman had been assured that the opposite would happen, but from the day he returned home from his heart surgery there was no marked improvement in his breathing. The doctors said he was suffering from asthma and prescribed a regimen of pills and inhalers that seemed to do nothing except further clutter up the dining room table. From what I observed, the medicines made Norman's breathing worse. That his physicians were seemingly unable to nail down a proper course of treatment for him drove me crazy. It drove Norris crazy, too, I know, and I once flirted with the idea of throwing all the drugs into the trash bin—I was curious what a medication-free week might bring—but I never did it. Instead, Norman and I set out to do research. He figured that if he boned up on facts about what was ailing him, from his breathing to his eyesight, he might have a better chance of beating the odds. We started with foods. I looked into the health benefits of tomatoes, proteins, grains, fruits, and anything else that came into his mind. If their benefits could be found in pill form, he'd opt for that—he was used to popping a lot of pills each morning; how could a few more hurt?

Because of his failing eyes, Norman developed a near obsession with lutein. His eye doctors had diagnosed him with macular degeneration, which we knew meant inevitable blindness. Lutein, found in tomatoes, carrots, squash, leafy vegetables, and spinach was the best weapon against rapid advancement of the disease. Needless to say, Norman was not going to suddenly eat piles of squash and spinach, which he hated, so I bought him lutein capsules. I got the best ones I could find, and for months he took them each morning with his OJ. The prospect of blindness bothered him tremendously. We visited his eye doctor often, and once on the drive back Norman said, "He says I could be blind in fifteen months." He paused and looked at the scenery and then blurted out: "Another fucking expert!"

We sat in silence for a half a mile or more. I didn't know what to say. I knew he didn't embrace "experts," and he certainly didn't like to dwell on their inaccurate conclusions. One of his favorite observations about experts was that at best they were right only 50 percent of the time. With those odds, anyone could be an "expert" on *anything*. Finally, after a moment, he turned to me, now more upbeat. The brief doom had passed.

"Hey, let's have salmon tonight."

"Shouldn't we call Norris in New York?" I asked.

"No, I don't want to worry her just yet; there's plenty of time for talking later. Let's set up a poker game and we'll feed the bastards your good fish." He chuckled a bit, and for the rest of the trip home he talked about surviving a harrowing helicopter ride with the mother of his third wife, Lady Jeanne Campbell. His rather eccentric third mother-in-law was not, Norman said, an "expert" pilot.

Norman did tell Norris later what the eye doctor had said. There is little to be done, however, for macular degeneration. His particular diagnosis was the less virulent, "dry" form, but any form of the disease leads to no good end. To make work easier, he decided to stick to larger texts. He was reading for the second book, and the typeface in them was not always large enough for Norman to read comfortably. So, I spent a lot of days in front of a copy machine at a store downtown, tearing pages out and feeding them into it by the hunk. I hated destroying books. One or two I refused to ruin.

"This kills me," I told him. "I love books too much to do this."

"I love books, too," he said, "but it has to be done."

Norman didn't love books. He loved what books *contained*. He had no love for the volumes themselves. He still wrote all over them, mangled pages to mark his spot, and tended to stack them in piles around him on his desk as if they were masonry bricks.

"Well, I'm not ripping this one apart," I said, holding an ancient copy of a Göring biography. "I'll copy it page by page."

"That will take a long time."

"Well, then it will take a long time, but I'm not going to trash this book."

"You're an obstinate son of a bitch," he said.

I copied the book on my own time and didn't destroy it as I had so many others. In the end, I saved that particular volume from destruction, but my effort didn't matter, because Norman never read the enlarged copy I'd made. Just never got to it.

It was not only his breathing and deteriorating vision and worsening arthritis that slowed Norman down. Before he had his bypass in 2006, the doctors insisted that he have his teeth taken care of, which meant removing bridgework to ensure there was no infection. That whole process went on for several months. Dentures in, dentures out. They never seemed to fit comfortably, and this bugged him to no end. After several rounds of ill-fitting teeth, he commissioned his dentist to get them right no matter what. He visited her nearly every week for fittings while they were being made. She then enlisted the assistance of a "dental arts specialist," a man who fine-tuned dentures. Because Norman was not a man who liked to wait for services like overnight mail, he asked that I deliver his teeth to the artist personally. So, with my friend Astrid, I ended up making the forty-five-mile trip several times. We'd leave early in the morning with Norman's teeth safely resting in a small box on Astrid's lap. I was to deposit them into a suburban mailbox that was actually a gaudy, recycled Harley Davidson gas tank. We'd make the drop and then while away three or four hours at the mall, waiting for a phone call saying it was time to pick up the teeth. We managed four or five rounds of this drop-and-grab routine and never encountered the toothman face-to-face. Because of his request that I use the "deposit box" instead of giving the teeth to him personally, I can only assume he was a kind of recluse. I often wonder if he ever knew whose pearly whites he was tweaking.

On one of my first trips to the mysterious denture guy, Norman handed me a stack of magazine inserts, those irritating, stiff postcards inserted between pages. They infuriated him.

"Throw these in the mail somewhere along the way," he said. I looked down at the cards. Each was scrawled in Norman's unmistakable hand with only one word: *KILROY*. Norman had been collecting them for weeks.

"I hate these goddamn things and this is a good way to protest," he said. He was serious, but he also had a sly gleam in his eye. He'd get back at the bastards for screwing up his magazine reading, by God.

I put them into my jacket pocket and said I'd handle it.

"Make sure you mail 'em out of town," he said. "If it's ever traced back to me I don't want to have to say *you* were involved."

I never knew if he was serious about the "traced back to me" line, but he was certainly serious about lashing back at the magazines, making them pay the postage. To be honest, I never mailed the cards, because I admired the people I knew at our post office too much. I figured it was enough simply to get the cards out of Norman's sight. I let him believe they were sent back to the offending corporations instead of to the trash, where they actually went. The one time he asked me how the mailing had gone, I told him the cards were where they belonged. It was the truth.

Norman's interest in life never waned; he never seemed wedged in a rut. There was always something that struck him as interesting. The mail never stopped, plans for the next Norman Mailer Society meeting were always ongoing, and requests for him to speak or travel to events continually flowed in. I fielded all the inquiries, putting the details in front of him so he could make a decision. He never wanted to give the impression that he was beginning to slow down, and so would have me send a note requesting that he be put on the roster tentatively—we'd be in touch later with a firm confirmation. Some events, such as the New Yorker Festival and one at the New York Public Library featuring him and Günter Grass, Norman quickly agreed to and did attend. He wasn't ready to fade, and the drive to ensure that his stature and name were still clearly in the mind of the literary world and the press was as strong as ever.

While events were penciled into the schedule and plans for speeches and interviews were executed, I couldn't help but wonder if he was taking on too much. He assured me he was able, just moving a tad slower now. I slated the events, said yes to interviews, marked travel dates on the calendar, and hoped for the best. I didn't want the excitement about travel and appearances to fade into something that Norman "used to do when he was stronger." He wouldn't have any of that kind of thinking, and so neither would I. I'd sit across from him in the afternoon when he'd finished his lunch and watch him read a magazine, the old eyes as fascinated as ever in everything that found its way in front of him.

"See what you can find out about this poetry event on the Internet, pal," he said, sliding an article in a literary journal in front of me.

"It's happening next year," I said. "There may not be too much up on the web about it yet."

"Well, look into it anyway. We should keep on top of it."

NINE

Days Out . . .
and the Secret Book

Norris and I discussed at length what would happen during her necessary absences. We decided that most everything should remain the same while she was away—no visiting nurses or professional therapists—except I would extend my days with Norman when it was merited. So, I began to arrive earlier to make breakfast and stayed a little longer into the evening. It turned out to be good for both Norman and me. I enjoyed spending time in the kitchen or just sitting with him at the table while he read or plowed through the stack of mail that arrived each day around three.

Some nights he would join Mike Lennon at Michael Shay's, the restaurant a block or two from the house, within walking distance even for him. The car was still out front, but Norman rarely drove it himself anymore. He knew his reflexes were not as sharp as they had once been, although he never said it. Mike usually picked him up if they went to dinner, but some nights Norman would wander out alone for a bite when Norris had to be away. He liked to chat and charm the waitresses while devouring a plate or two of oysters with a glass of wine. Oysters became his favorite food. I don't think it had to do only with the trickiness of his dentures; I think he genuinely loved them because they perfectly embodied his seaside surroundings. The silky, raw Wellfleet delicacies nourished him in abstract ways.

Norman's tastes had altered over the four years I'd been with him. His former devotion to investigating new recipe ideas began to lessen, so I put more effort into the few dishes he truly preferred. Salmon, meatloaf, pot roast, chicken, and my thick, smooth-as-silk mushroom soup were favorites—as well as his morning omelet with cheddar or cream cheese. He was eating less and less, and his weight began to drop. I felt responsible for helping him stop losing pounds, but I didn't know how. If he wasn't going to eat much, there was little I could do other than increase calories, which I did with butter and cream when appropriate. I told him I was going back to our old favorite method of preparing his meals, and he slapped the table and happily declared, "Good, goddamn it!" I'd like to say the maneuver to infuse more calories worked, but it didn't. Norman continued to lose weight as the early months of 2007 passed.

Days Out . . . and the Secret Book

What was not getting thin was his desire to stay active with work. Since 2004, Mike Lennon and he had conducted interviews that focused on Norman's thoughts about God. I'd transcribed the interviews throughout the years, and they remained mostly dormant on my computer, waiting to see light. Now, with *The Castle in the Forest* done, Norman's interest in the project was beginning to be revitalized. He and Mike again hunkered in the attic to record Norman's take on all things theological. Norman, not a theologian by any stretch, nonetheless had absorbing ideas about the nature of divinity and man's place in the universe. The theories discussed in the manuscript were literally Norman's inner source material behind everything he'd ever written. His writings, which range from Marilyn Monroe to Hitler, tend to incite questions about fate, and force the reader's own introspection. To begin the whole process, Norman had me print out the chapters of *The God Book* for him to reedit.

More than once when the subject of *The God Book*, as we called it, came up, he told me it would likely be published after his death; hence his previous leisurely pace in getting it done. I think he knew Mike would finish the book if fate dictated, a job he was exceptionally suited for. If anyone had complete, coherent understanding of Norman's processes, it was Mike. In fact, since the death in December of Robert Lucid, a professor and trusted friend Norman had appointed as his official biographer, Mike was the point man in all matters Mailer and now Norman's sanctioned biographer.

The God Book began to shape into a viable manuscript. Still,

247

Norman had doubts his publisher would have much interest, because it was not a "big" book. It was not a novel or an in-depth political tome; the subject was ethereal and obscure. Norman had written about World War II, political affairs, sex, drugs, Vietnam, movie stars, and the spooky art of writing, among other matters. He said that this volume probably wouldn't be easily accepted into his inventory of serious, noteworthy accomplishments. Granted, he'd interpreted the story of Christ in his 1997 novel, *The Gospel According to the Son*, but I did agree that this book might be viewed as a vague vanity project. I figured it would, if published, be embraced only by pure Mailer fans and a few curious readers searching wildly for meaning. Random House would likely not be clamoring for it. We were both wrong.

One day in the late spring of 2007, while having our regular morning chat, Norman suddenly said, "I think we should send the book to David today." David was his editor. I said okay, and forwarded it via email at eleven that morning. At three we received a call saying they wanted to publish the book immediately, for an October publication. For the next two weeks Norman labored through edit session after edit session and title after title. For a project that had been pushed comfortably aside and somewhat neglected, it now had new life.

The final series of edits did not come as easily for Norman as they had on other works. Still, in January of 2007, he showed no signs of forgetfulness or tentativeness. His ability to retain ideas remained strapping when he worked, even slightly sharper at times. He took his time with the work now; certain words were considered more intently, sentences and paragraphs were structured and restructured to achieve their ultimate potency. As he toiled away he rarely even suffered from aphasia, that momentary void one can experience while searching for a term or specific word, as most people as young as forty occasionally do—including me. Norman could grab a word from his armory without effort, and his acuity remained astounding.

Nonetheless, in April and May I began to notice a mild slowing in this regard. He'd grapple with finding the ideal word as he dictated a letter, and seemed to take longer to recall the name of someone he'd read about in the paper the day before. I said nothing and did nothing, because there was nothing to be done except remain present. He commented on his own new lack of swiftness several times—usually in a half-frustrated, half joking way. "Damn it! I just talked to him! What's the dentist's receptionist's name again?" His brother-in-law, who'd died more than a year before and was a riotously intelligent documentarian, had, in his last year, grown forgetful, which drove Norman crazy. But Norman had been very fond of Al Wasserman and missed having him around each summer. When Norman found that he, too, was now often befuddled about where he'd left his glasses or a book or his wallet, he would say to me, "For Christ sake, don't let me go Wasserman on you!" Norman had a way of popping off something funny, sentimentality be damned.

When *The God Book* manuscript was in final reworked shape to be sent to Random House, Norman was still digging around for an appropriate title. Nietzsche, Norman's old favorite, once commented that "all priests are liars," and Norman had quoted the remark in the book. The line embodied much of what he believed about the intangibility of faith. Priests, fundamentalist preachers, reverends, vicars, rabbis, prophets, and any number of clergy threw around the concept of faith as if it were something one could discover as easily as finding eggs at the grocery. According to Norman, faith was not tangible, not bone solid, and certainly not purchasable. Also, it cannot be truth per se. So the Nietzsche line became the title for a day or two: *All Priests Are Liars*. The idea tickled Norman. I liked the title, too, appreciating that it would probably provoke every fanatic in the country. Norris didn't much like the idea, though, so Norman dutifully scrapped it. He went back to work and finally he settled on a title that more clearly defined the book: *On God: An Uncommon Conversation*. It ruffled no feathers, and it also, sadly, didn't rustle up sales in the end. He should have stuck to Nietzsche.

Although he was actively reading and thinking about the second volume in his Hitler series, I realized one day that he was probably not going to get too far into it if indeed he ever started to write it. Norman took years to rev himself up to face the nuts and bolts of actually writing a book. Even *On God*, which had been mostly dictated, had taken nearly four years. Most writers need to let time pass while ideas fall in and out of line, marinate to achieve balance. A writer's "work" is frequently pondering the value of certain notions and how they'll affect the overall tone. When a writer is awake, he or she is often actively working, even if simply staring out a window. There were also times when I noticed Norman in conversation with someone and, for a second or two, he would radically depart from the situation in his mind. I knew he'd abruptly and inexplicably gone to work—if only for a moment. With a nearly unnoticeable flicker, he would spring back, and the person he'd been talking to wouldn't even realize what had just happened. He did this with me all the time, except I always knew, because he'd simply stop whatever it was we were talking about, whip out his notebook, and write like a crazy man for thirty seconds. Then he'd apologize for the interruption. He knew I understood his process, that he couldn't risk not putting a thought to paper the second it came to him. He did it blatantly with me because he knew I wouldn't be put off by the surprise severance of our talk. Besides, in the end, the little book he wrote in was always handed to me later to type up. The interruptive burst was just a preview.

The afterword Norman wrote for the completed *On God* was among the last of his essays, and I noticed in him an extraordinary determination to get it right. He worked for several days on it, tweaking draft after draft. He wanted it to be an airtight closure for a book that would probably be reviewed with scathing doubt as to his authority to speak about God. The piece was intended to fully explain any notions of divinity that he touched upon in the main of the book. He finished the last draft of the essay on a Friday, and I printed it for him so he could inspect it over the weekend and make some small final edits.

"You can type it up again on Monday," he said before I left. I knew he was going to have dinner with friends for the next two nights and that people would be around on both days, so I made no plans to stop by.

On Monday morning he was not up yet when I arrived at ten o'clock, so I made coffee and poured his orange juice so it would be waiting for him on the table, but he didn't come down until well after eleven. In the interim, I looked for the essay to see what kind of changes I would have to make, but I couldn't find it anywhere. I decided to wait to ask Norman where it was. He ambled slowly into the kitchen, his cane plunking on the tile floor. He looked tired. I assumed he'd not slept well, or that the weekend with friends had been more stressful than usual.

"No good sleep last night?" I asked. He shook his head no and bid me a rather bland good morning, which was uncharacteristic.

"I'll make an omelet for you?" I asked.

"Yes, yes, but not for a bit. Let me get some orange juice first." That was an odd thing for him to say, because he knew I knew his morning ritual as well as *he* did: OJ, paper, pills and vitamins, a short break, and then food with coffee. We'd done it hundreds of times. I was just asking what he wanted for later on.

"Sure . . ." I said.

I followed him into the dining room where he sat hard into his chair and proceeded to fight for breath. Then, he swigged down his pills with the juice. He was not talkative in the least this morning, which was also rare. He never failed to ask how my day or weekend had gone, and sometimes he pointed out news on the front page of the *Times*. Today, as I went back in the kitchen to cook, all I could hear was a struggle for air and the *swoosh* of one of his inhalers.

I went back into the dining room with my own cup of coffee and sat down. A moment passed with neither of us talking. He just looked somewhat blankly at me and shrugged, indicating that his breathing was abnormally difficult this morning.

"Did you do the edits?" I finally asked.

Norman unfolded the newspaper, looked at it, and then put it aside.

"What?"

"The edits. You were going to do your final pass on the afterword. Did you get to it?"

There was a withering to him, a paleness. Moreover, he'd not shaved, which was peculiar, because he usually did. Norman was always well groomed, even when the effort was not an easy one.

"I looked around and I can't find the pages. Where'd you put them?" I asked. He looked at me with his tired, deep blue eyes and shook his head.

"Must be here on the table," he said. He continued to sip what was left of his orange juice.

I stood and went to the side of the table, looking again through the stacks of weekend papers, old mail, and magazines. The pages were not there.

"I can't find them," I said. "Where did you do the work? Did you do the edits down here or upstairs?" I returned to my seat. He looked at me again and his center seemed off, as if he were searching for a thought that had dashed away or was too complex to fully wrangle.

"I don't know . . ." he said. "Shit."

Then it hit me. He *didn't* know. He didn't recall when or if he'd done the work. He couldn't nail down the order of scattered moments. Norman had never done this before, not with work. Yes, he'd forgotten his hearing aids, his favorite pen, his notebooks, and even his teeth in the glass upstairs, but he'd never forgotten anything about work. We sat in silence for a minute more. It seemed like an eternity, because I didn't know what to do. I simply watched him finish his juice and, finally, reach for the newspaper—which also seemed to hold no interest for him. I didn't press him, didn't even move. Rain was streaking down the large bay window at the end of the table and the wind was battering the house lightly. Norman just looked at the paper and said nothing. He'd almost fully caught his breath, but he remained dimly disconnected.

"I'll be back in a few minutes," I said, standing. Norman didn't respond. He simply continued to read the headlines.

I grabbed his empty juice glass and put it on the island in the kitchen as I headed for the stairs to go to the attic. I needed to be away from him for a while, needed to quiet the fears that were suddenly noisy in my head. I climbed the creaky stairs to the office and sat at his desk. The heating unit was clunking and clacking and there was warmth in the room, but also a chill. The windows had always been screwy up there, allowing for drafts and even sneaky gusts. I looked down at his disheveled desk. Norman had forgotten if he had or had not edited the final essay for the book. I was unable to do anything but ponder how I was going to handle this. His muddle was so atypical that it stung me. Should I call Norris, who happened to be away attending to her mother? Should I wait it out and pretend nothing had happened? Was it me who was crazy? Perhaps we'd never even *had* the discussion Friday. . . . No, that was wrong. We *had* talked about it; it was Norman's idea that I leave him the pages.

After about five minutes I shook off my confusion. I knew the best thing I could do was to cage my panic and act normal. I feared I would fail him that morning by not being strong, by letting my stress about the situation overwhelm me. I put that thought aside after a moment because I knew I must get myself together—help where I was needed. I owed it to him. I owed it to myself.

I returned to the dining room and sat down. He'd put the newspaper down and was looking at the wall, thinking.

"Hungry now?" I asked.

Norman looked at me and said he was; maybe an omelet would be nice today.

"Then an omelet it is," I said. I noticed he was not wearing his hearing aids yet, so he likely didn't hear the anxiety in my voice. "How do you want it? You want it with raspberry jam and cream cheese like last week? Do you want to try that again or do you want cheddar?" He sometimes liked a "sweet omelet" as an alternative, like a sugary egg crêpe.

"Cheddar?" he asked. I could see clarity returning, a sliver of interest about breakfast. "How about we do only cream cheese this time? Not too little, not too much."

I wasn't going to let this go. I wanted to keep the tides moving until his thoughts were smooth again, centered on breakfast.

"I could make cheddar *and* cream cheese," I said. I knew this would drive him to say that uncomplicated things should not be messed with. One had either cream cheese or cheddar.

"No, just cream cheese. One ruins the other."

"Yes," I said.

I breathed a sigh of relief as I went into the kitchen and left him to his paper, which he'd picked up again.

Food was a flimsy subject to use to get him to focus, but it had worked. He was now drinking his coffee, and a normalcy was creeping back. Nonetheless, I was still at a loss for answers about the edits that he'd either completed or not over the weekend.

I put his eggs in front of him with one piece of white toast cut in half diagonally, which resembled wings sprouting from each side of the folded omelet. I'd always served it this way, made it look as inviting as possible. Norman enjoyed that aspect about my food; he liked the flair. He smiled and said, "Ahh, ahh, yes. That looks great. Thank you, thank you."

He ate his breakfast, and I went to my small office off the living room to figure out where the pages might be.

"Oh, Dwayne?!" he bellowed, and I immediately got up and went to him. Not only were his thoughts back but so was his booming voice.

"Yes?"

"Check on my desk in my bedroom for the pages," he said. "I seem to recall I put them there."

"Sure, pal," I said and went up to his room.

The five pages of text for the end of the book were indeed there. I turned on the lamp and looked them over, curious if he'd made many changes. There were new marks on them and my question was answered. He'd done the edits.

I brought the papers down with me, and he pushed his half-eaten food aside to concentrate on the work for a moment.

"Yes. Oh yes, yes," he said, his voice full of recollection. "I did want to go over this one last time. Yes . . ."

"When did you work on this?" I asked, hoping to get him to find the answer that might further erase the uncertainty that had nipped at him.

"I guess yesterday," he said. "Yes, yesterday afternoon I worked on this. Now, let me just see . . ."

He dug his Pilot pen from his shirt pocket and began to work.

The incident was not followed by any similar ones for quite a while. What had occurred was the first of very few instances of forgetfulness, but it raised a flag for me that I should pay close attention. What had reared its head was common and natural, but painful for me to observe. I told Norris about it and that it had happened only that once. I said that maybe it had been related more to a lack of good sleep than anything else. Now, these years later, I still prefer to believe the natural vacuities of old age didn't visit Norman that morning, but they did, albeit briefly. He wasn't like other men, which is why I was so stubborn about accepting the truth. For Norman to experience fog in his thinking about work was, honestly, beyond my scope of comprehension. Nonetheless, from that morning on I became watchful for any further hints of age's unforgiving torment.

Norman moved on from that morning at the table and so did I. The incident slipped away into shadows, far from the forefront. There was work to be done and it was pointless to hamper daily dealings with worries of what *might* happen, what *could* change.

Norris was healthier, more alive than she'd been since I'd met her, as she carved out a portion of her life in Brooklyn again. Some people felt they were in a position to offer their opinions about Norman living partially alone for short periods. They made the egregious mistake of saying to Norris that they thought Norman should have full-time care. They saw his labored effort to walk, his windedness, his weight loss. Norris and I recoiled at this uninvited advice. Neither of us was stupid; neither of us was neglectful or ignorant about his state of health. The children came when they could and were, obviously, aware of everything also. As a further testament to the respect they held for their father, they all agreed that he should call the shots; he should manage his life the way he wished.

Norman did not want any professionals visiting the house. He insisted he didn't need them, and his decision to stay after Norris had begged him to move to Brooklyn was one that he stood by. To his thinking, which was logical, if something should go wrong or if he should, as he put it, "kill myself falling over the goddamn stair rail," then so be it. What outsiders overlooked entirely was that while Norman was growing physically fragile, he was still a man fully able to make personal decisions. That alone merited utmost respect. Norris and I spoke about the interferences, and while these few outsiders believed they had Norman's best interests at heart, it was clear to me that they were more concerned about the legend than the man. They missed the entire point of Norman's life, his message. Freedom, autonomy, independence—they are the pinnacle of what any man can hope to attain. For us to hinder that in any way would have been, for Norman, equivalent to psychological homicide. Norris was irritated, as was I, that anyone outside of family would dare to question their decisions about their occasional unusual living situation. Norman loved Norris more than anyone he'd ever known, whether she was in the house or spending time in Brooklyn. I know this because he told me often, and on top of it, I continually saw the proof.

The kids visited as much as they could throughout 2007, but they had their own lives now, their own families. They knew I was around to help their dad with his work when Norris happened to be away. Aside from Norris and the children, writing was the most essential aspect of Norman's existence, and the drive to do it never subsided as he aged. The children knew this, having watched him toil intensely their entire lives. It didn't matter what was happening with family or anything else, Norman always had a project, constantly worked on *something*.

For much of the time I spent with Norman he had been compiling yet another book that was unknown to almost everyone—and still is. The book was not one that readers might normally associate with literature produced by "Norman Mailer." It was a book comprised of arbitrary aphorisms and quotes, tidbits of knowledge and, sometimes, whimsy—both his and other writers'. It was a pet project, rather like *Modest Gifts* had been at first.

In early 2004, I'd found fifteen pages under the Ping-Pong table in his office that were clipped together. The papers had been there so long that they'd accumulated a layer of dust and had started to curl in the dry heat of the room. I read them, curious as to what they were. Norman had always discussed projects, both old and new, with me, so finding what was clearly a work in progress was a surprise. On the first page was a quote from Abraham Lincoln, written in the language of the time:

The true role, in determining to embrace or reject anything . . . is not whether it have any evil in it, but whether it have more of evil than of good . . . There are few things wholly evil or wholly good.

Under it was Norman's unmistakable handwriting:

This is the perfect antidote to political correctness

What was conspicuously missing was any explanation for the pages. They seemed random, one having no relation to the next. I set the folder aside, went back to work on my Hitler files, and waited for him to come up. When he did, I picked up the folder.

"What are these?" I asked. I put the stack of quotes on the desk to show him.

"Squibs," he said brightly, as if I had any clue what that meant. "I thought I should respond to some of the quotes I stumble across here and there."

He thumbed through the parched papers, reading the comments and his own responses to them. Of course he edited several before handing them back to me.

"When did you start doing this?" I asked. I thought the idea of someone firing back at all those lofty quotes we often see was an innovative one.

"Oh, I don't know. Maybe two years ago."

He told me Judith had typed them up, but the Hitler research had forced him to put the idea aside. "Do me a favor and keep this nearby," he said, pointing at the pages. "I may want to revisit them."

I put them on the bookshelf by the fax machine and forgot about them. Some weeks later, during our morning meeting at the table, he fished a wadded mess of clippings out of his shirt pocket. They were quotes of the day, torn from the *Boston Globe* comics page; he'd been collecting them since the day I'd run across the dusty pages. On each one he'd scribbled a line or two.

"Type these up, will you?" He plopped them down next to my notebook. "Oh, hold on." He reached into his back pocket, grabbed his wallet, and produced five or six more he'd stuffed between bills. "These too."

It was not easy to decode his responses to the quotes because he squeezed a lot of words into the small space around each one. Norman forever denied that any piece of paper had two sides, preferring instead to write all over a page using asterisks and arrows and other marks to cryptically denote where his transcriber should go next. He apologized, because it was clear his handwriting on the mangled pieces of paper was worse than normal. He began to read each of them aloud and, in the process, reedit and rewrite them, which made them more muddled to my eyes. Unfortunately, even though he'd read them out loud, it was still a major task to translate them into clean pages.

"This is going to take some time, you know," I said.

"There's no rush. Let's keep a running file of them and see where we are in a few weeks."

I didn't know then that his handing me crumpled papers would become a weekly ritual that would last nearly two years. In time, the pages grew into a manuscript. The book, because indeed it is one, is a volume that to this day, no one, less Mike Lennon, John Buffalo, Norris, Danielle, I, and perhaps one or two others has ever read.

The Quote Book (as we initially referred to it) is a book of aphorisms, axioms, maxims, and idioms. It was the project Norman turned to for several years as a kind of distraction from his normal writings. It became his private amusing passion, something he enjoyed as much as searching for palatable poetry or diddling with football statistics.

"Here," he'd say with a happy tone, "I've got more for you." He would place a handful of wrinkly snippets in front of me and ask me what I thought of each one. He both hated and loved the fact that I was frank with him when I said his sense of humor tanked or when a response he'd written was vague. What else was I supposed to do? I couldn't lie or laugh emptily. Usually, if it was merited, I did laugh.

"Judith rarely laughed at what I say," he said. "I have to say it's much easier to drag one out of you."

"I'm only about half as smart as Judith was. Obviously you don't let that impede your attempts."

"Get those typed," he'd say, pointing at his latest pile of newspaper pontifications and feigning irritation at my insolence.

I never told him I could always see his reaction when I left him alone at the dining table after our banter. Directly across from his chair was a large mirror that dominated the room and hung just low enough and to the left to frame his reflection. Whenever I walked away from one of our talks there, I would turn to see his amused expression in response to our exchanges as he picked up his cards for yet another game of solitaire.

The Quote Book blossomed. When it was already fat, he handed me a book of maxims by the French author François de La Rochefoucauld. For Norman, La Rochefoucauld was the king of all aphorists, and so the book was rich. Norman had put a check mark next to more than a hundred quotes in the book and countered each of them with a keen response. Rochefoucauld's maxims ended up comprising an entire chapter of *The Quote Book.*

"I think this could be called a chapbook for writers," Norman said.

"How so?"

"Well, the quotes make the reader think. There's nothing like a short hair of an idea to feed the process when you need to work."

He believed the book would prove useful, especially to young writers. In the introduction of the book he wrote this:

> . . . we enjoy a race of thought when encountering a good epigram, or an aphorism. Their function is to fortify our powers of criticism. It is left to poetry to evoke our sense of how far away we are from the center of existence.
>
> The epigram and the aphorism offer, therefore, more direct virtues. The epigram is forceful, declarative, and upsetting to many cherished conventions. It delights in savaging our preconceptions. In contrast, the aphorism often finds a door in the wall of an old problem. Nonetheless, it, too, is opposed to ambiguity. Both do their best to clarify large or small matters that too many have taken for granted too long.

I had never given much weight to the belief that two minds, clearly of different caliber, could rock along in comfortable tandem. The odd communication that we shared, which Norman likened to telepathy, seemed more delicate now, more important, yet we still avoided discussion of the phenomenon as little as possible. He continued to believe that we might squash it with any talk about it. So we'd simply utter a quiet "Oh, yes" when we faced it. "I swear you've got a sixth sense," he said to me hundreds of times.

For a period in July and August of 2007 my cell phone would ring each morning as I approached the same spot on the road to his house, near a small convenience store called The Patrician. It didn't matter what time I'd actually left my apartment.

"Ah, good morning," Norman would say. "Could you pick me up a *Post* on your way?" He liked the *New York Post* because they had the best sports page. (I also saw him reading "Page Six" faithfully.) I would stop, get the paper, and be at his house three minutes later.

"That was fast."

"Well, as usual, I was right next to The Patrician when you called."

But that unvoiced tie ran deeper. When things became complicated with his health, he didn't need to tell me how he was feeling, and I never needed to ask. All he had to do was look at me and I would hear volumes. His personal frustration was evident, and I would simply nod, yes, and continue with what I was doing, because that was how he wanted it. Silence was the best strategy; repeating hollow words amounted to futility. Norman hated the unproductive question as to how he was *feeling*. After a phone call with a friend he would sometimes slam the phone down, turn to me, and say, "I'm eighty four. That should be enough!" He hated to talk details about what ailed him. More than once I heard him rake someone over the coals for calling to "check up on him."

"Listen, it doesn't do any fucking good to ask how I'm doing," he would say to the person. "This is a waste of your time and, more important, it's a waste of *mine*." His voice was still as strong as always when he was cranked up. Doubtless, those on the receiving end immediately shriveled—as they should have. Norman's health was no concern of theirs beyond whether or not he was breathing. What they could not see was his expression after he lashed out, a mixture of rage and satisfaction that he'd laid down his law. Norman would then pass me the phone to put back in its cradle, as if to let go of the device would lessen his seethe.

In the entire last year of our time together I never asked him how he felt. I'd ask him how a doctor's visit went, if he preferred one kind of vitamin over another, what he wanted to read, to see, to hear, to talk about, or what he desired to eat—but never how he felt. He occasionally spoke to me about his ills, but it was never maudlin talk, never remarks full of woe or despair. What interested me, what interested *him*, was what there was to *do* each day, what more there was to learn.

I was unhappy that Norman's taste buds had begun to diminish, but he'd discovered his slippery oysters, and they satisfied him. He simply couldn't get enough of the local bivalves. Since he was Norman, and his thought process was inimitable, he had the notion that they were more than food—they were untapped art. Norman said oyster shells had portraits concealed on them, craggy faces etched by sea and sand. The images he saw fascinated him, and he became intent on drawing out their jagged beauty. What he saw was not far removed from his own sketches, the faces that occupied the pages of *Modest Gifts*. Each time he ordered a dozen oysters in a restaurant he asked the waiter to box the shells, and those of his guest, if he had one. He'd then carry them home and put them on the kitchen counter. The problem was that by the time I got there the next morning, the shells, with their remaining bits of flesh, had begun to smell.

"I brought more shells home," he said each morning after a night out for dinner.

"Yes, I know." The stench had met my nose moments after I walked in.

"Would you mind putting those outside with the others?"

"Not at all!" I hustled the stinky things outside.

On the edge of the deck near the wall of the house was a volcano of old shells being cured by the weather. The pile grew and grew, awaiting the artist.

I hated the shells. I hated washing them off in the sink and carting them to the smelly pile on the deck. However, the idea of what could be done with them made Norman happy, and so I held my tongue, and my nose, and helped.

Finally a warm day arrived wherein he shuffled himself out to the deck to enjoy the sun and watch the beach and water. I was sitting on the steps just near him when he hit the glass patio table with the flat of his hand and declared we should start separating good shells from bad. I gathered a bunch and we sat together scrutinizing each one, gauging its potential.

"Ah, here, look at this face," he said, holding one up. It was squiggly and rough. From the messy lines, bumps, and crags a ripe face was clearly struggling to emerge. Another sported sad eyes and a droopy nose; the next was mottled and dented deeply above a mouth curled sideways. He set the good shells to one side, the merely adequate to the other. This went on for half an hour, until we'd inspected each shell and he had selected fifteen or twenty good ones to work with. I put the rejected shells into a new pile that Norman dubbed "the possibility batch."

"Make sure the gardener doesn't toss those away," he said.

Later I went out to buy an array of pens for him to draw on the shells with. (That past Christmas, Norris had bought him an entire paint set for when he decided to sink himself into the project seriously.) I found six or seven fine pens, each with varying thickness. He doodled away for a bit, showing me how each face sprang up and out to life with only slight coaxing and shading. He ruined several of them because his artistic intentions weren't yet well defined and the inks didn't always flow easily on the course casing. Shell was more porous than he'd assumed, and Norman's colors bled. Noticing this, we pondered a sealant. I suggested hair spray, which he agreed just might work. We tried it on one oyster shell and it did indeed act as a protectant, but not well enough.

"It's unnatural," he said. His sense of smell, which was more heightened than most men's, was offended by the plastic scent of hair spray. He was, however, wholly at ease with the aroma of decaying oyster flesh.

Throughout the oyster art experiment he'd been talking seriously with his son Michael about directing the film of his play *The Deer Park*, which he'd originally penned as a book in 1955 and adapted for the stage in 1967. There was no digital copy of the script in existence that we knew of, and so I set out to key the entire play into my computer so he could make the changes he needed. When I finished, Norman converted it into a script that could be used for film. The process went relatively quickly—about two weeks—and in the end we had a script that Michael could produce and Norman could direct. He intended it to be an avant-garde work, set in a theater where the actors, in an unknowing hell, were doomed to repeat the play for eternity. As Norman described his vision of it to me, I immediately thought of Sartre's *No Exit*, a play I had read in college, admired greatly, and performed in twice as the Valet, a minion and nephew of the head valet, the Devil. Shooting of the movie would begin later in the year, November.

Bringing *The Deer Park* alive reenergized Norman. It dealt with, on the surface, Hollywood, where cravings for sex and love dodge each other within a swirl of dubious characters who gnaw at one another like cannibalistic roaches. Much of the story unfolds in opulent bungalows, which exacerbates the sensibilities of the often morally devoid protagonists. Norman's film would be the definitive version of his play.

Most of the work on the script was done in the dining room, for two reasons: one was that it was now difficult for him to climb the stairs each day to the attic, and the other was that Norris was with her mother in Brooklyn, so we could keep the table as chaotic as we wanted without being admonished. When guests came for dinner, I'd simply shove everything to the far end. Those who came were probably fascinated at seeing his work in progress anyway. Norman's paper piles could be interesting—even to me after all this time. Of course when

Norris came back, I moved most of our stacks to the bay window ledge. She disliked clutter, but after thirty years of loving a perpetrator of it, Norman, she'd grown used to it.

One day that April, when Norris again happened to be down in Brooklyn, Norman decided to take the day off from his scriptwriting. I was planted at my end of the table, typing away, when he appeared late in the morning looking unusually sprightly.

"I'm going out for lunch today," he announced. He quickly played several rounds of his complicated solitaire until the clock neared noon and then plunked the deck of cards on the table with a thump.

"Well," I said. "I'm at a good place to stop. Where do you want to go?"

"I think I'll drive myself."

I ceased typing completely. One of my fears was just this: Norman going for a drive alone. Norris hadn't taken the car on this trip, and it was sitting in front of the house, driven only occasionally by me.

"I don't want to have to bother Dwayne if I need something this week," Norman had told Norris. "Leave the car."

Norris and I were in a sort of cahoots during her brief absences. If His Highness needed to go someplace, I would drive, period. Norman surely knew Norris and I had the pact, but he never mentioned it. Now, even if he did know she and I had discussed the matter, he didn't care. He wanted to go out to lunch. Alone.

"Norman, it's no bother for me to drive. Where do you want to go?" I pressed.

"I'd rather you spend the day finishing up the script," he said. "I'm going to Wellfleet. Lunch out sounds good to me." He didn't want company and he wanted to drive himself the fifteen miles to Wellfleet.

I had no choice but to swallow my urge to struggle it out with him. While he got his canes and located his wallet, I suppressed a small panic. I trusted Norman in nearly everything, of course. His advice was invaluable, his teaching had penetrated deeper than any I'd been exposed to in any classroom, and his warmth toward me resonated. None of this, however, made the moment easier. The stories Norris told me about him acting like a mad racer pulling out ahead of approaching cars and once ripping off the side mirror as he misjudged a turn abruptly came to mind. It was not high season yet and our streets were still relatively empty, so the chance of his plowing into a throng of tourists was small. That aside, it was still not safe for him to be touring the Cape in a car he wasn't terribly familiar with. I feared for oncoming vehicles and unsuspecting small animals.

Norman stood and headed for the door. I pressed the "Save" key on my computer and closed the top. The script could wait.

"Do you have your cell phone?" I asked, following him to the front door. He patted his pocket and said yes.

"Where are you having lunch?" I asked.

"I think the Wicked Oyster," he said. He opened the front door. I moved closer.

"Are you sure you don't want company today?" I asked again, cheerfully.

"No. I think there's plenty for you to do here," he said. He sauntered out and down the steps, gripping the porch rail. I stayed close behind.

"Going to be mosquito season soon," he remarked, moving toward the car and looking up. "Maybe you should check the basement today to make sure the bug killer is in working order."

"I think we've got time before the mosquitoes come back, Norman," I said. He was at the car, climbing in.

"I'll call later," he said and shut the car door with a wave. I stood on the brick path watching him fumble with his key before starting the Toyota and revving the engine. Norman never wore a seat belt, and today was no exception. I only mentioned once that it might be a good idea for him to put one on while we rode together, and he said, "Why?" he asked. "Are you planning on diverting from the road at some point?"

Norman pulled away and turned up Allerton Street. He was driving out of town, out for a nice lunch alone, and there was nothing I could do.

The first thing I did was call Norris in Brooklyn.

"He's gone to lunch in Wellfleet."

"Well, sweetie," she said, "I guess there's nothing you can do about it. We just have to wait."

I was surprised she was so calm, but Norris had the capacity to know what she could and couldn't manage, something I was still in the process of learning. Debating an issue with Norman was more or less fruitless.

"Let's just hope for the best," she said. "And keep an ear out for the phone if he calls."

I spent the afternoon finishing the script. At four I noticed that it had become cloudy, along with a light rain. I hadn't heard from Norman since he drove off hours before. He must be having a very long lunch. A half hour later I decided to call it a day. I packed up, got in my Volvo, and began to search town. I thought maybe he'd driven back from Wellfleet by then and was now enjoying an afternoon drink somewhere. I had no luck searching the usual haunts and finally dialed Thomas.

"Norman's out driving by himself," I said. "He left over five hours ago."

"Oh boy," Thomas said. "What are you going to do?"

"What *can* I do? He's out and I have no idea where. Keep your eyes open for him." Thomas said he would.

I then called my friend Tony. He knew Norman and exactly what the silver Toyota looked like. Tony called a few other friends and within a matter of minutes there were five sets of eyes patrolling Ptown for Norman Mailer.

By six thirty it was dark, and I had yet to hear from him. He'd said he would call when he got home, and it was not like him to go back on his word, even regarding something as simple as this. Thomas took me out to dinner an hour later, and on the way we drove past Norman's. The car was still not there.

"He's probably drinking someplace," Thomas said. "You should cut him some slack."

When I got home several hours later I found an email from Norris:

If you haven't heard from him, Norman is at home. He went to
the Lobster Pot, and something went wrong with the car and he
couldn't get it out of Park. It is in the lot. He took a cab home.
I guess you'll have to deal with it tomorrow. He had kind of a
hairy start to the trip, but was glad he went. He needed to get
out of the house and see that he could do it. I do worry about
him, but know, too, that he can't give up his manhood altogether.
I'm glad he's coming here on Friday. I think he is, too. He
misses me, and I miss the old coot, too. So don't worry. He's
home in bed. Talk tomorrow.
Love, N.

I was relieved. I sent a note back:

I just got home. I went to *Montano*'s with Thomas for dinner.
On the way we took a look up toward your house and the car
still wasn't there. That was at about 7:45. Thomas pegged it.
He said, "he's probably in a bar someplace." I said I doubted it.
I was wrong. Good to know he's out having fun. What the hell
good is it to live in Ptown if you don't have fun once in a while?
Love, D.

Norman was home. A part of me, too, was indeed glad he'd
ventured out. The man worked hard and never took time for
himself, other than to play solitaire or attack his crosswords.
He, more than anyone I knew, deserved to take a day off. The
next morning I wrote as much to Norris:

I'm actually glad he got out and staked his claim, once again, on the roads and towns of the Cape he loves so much. I'm thrilled, in hindsight, that he decided to take a day off and do something new. Sure, I was worried for obvious reasons, but overall it was kind of exciting. Here's to men who have lunch and hoist a few at the Old Colony! Not to worry about the car. I'll round up Thomas and we'll figure out the problem and bring it back. I've no idea why it wouldn't get out of park . . .

Norris answered my note a few moments later:

Yes, I'm sort of proud of him in a perverse way, and you can tell him that for me. He won't believe it coming from me.
More later, XX N

When I went to see Norman later, I asked about his night. He'd driven to Wellfleet for lunch after touring the side roads of Truro to see what surprises they held.

"It occurs to me that in sixty years I've never given much thought to what happens in Truro," he said about the town that borders Provincetown. After a long lunch and two glasses of wine he drove back to Ptown. He dragged the town, checked out a few back roads, and become hungry again. He parked at the main town lot and had an early dinner at the Lobster Pot restaurant. After, he wandered next door to the Old Colony Tap for drinks. Norman had filmed scenes for *Tough Guys* in there and once told me it was "the most honest barroom in town."

"You need to retrieve the car," he said. "The damn thing wouldn't start. I had to take a cab home."

I didn't say I knew all about the car from Norris and instead just told him I'd get Thomas and we would bring it home. I was relieved that he hadn't been able to start the Toyota, because by the time he'd tried he must have been well into a fine buzz. I deduced, since the car started immediately for me when I finally found it, that he'd not realized the engine wouldn't turn over unless the driver has placed a foot on the brake pedal. Mystery solved—and Provincetown's streets had remained safe for one more night

"By the way," Norman said, "I shared a cab last night with your old roommate." I couldn't figure out who he was talking about.

"Scott," Norman said. "He was in drag. He said he was hosting a game show or some such thing."

Scott was not my "old roommate"; he was my ex-partner. We had moved to Ptown together eight years before and separated five years after, when Thomas came into my life. However, in the first weeks after Scott and I moved to Provincetown, Scott became famous for impersonating Cher, of all people. Clubs in town paid him well, and he had fun doing it. In off months he hosted a bingo game in drag on Wednesday nights at the Little Bar. Apparently, he'd been on his way there when his cab was diverted to pick up Norman. In Provincetown, that's how it is if you happen to be in a cab: the driver picks up other fares along the way and you're often willy-nilly supplied with travel companions you might not normally encounter. I was weirdly mortified about the convergence of Norman and Scott in a taxicab, because I'd never gone into much detail about my personal past with Norman. It just never came up—until now. Again, I was too silly to realize that Norman understood the oddities involved in living in an unconventional town like ours better than I ever could. He'd been here for sixty years, and nothing, including donning a dress and singing for money, surprised him in the least.

"He makes a good showgirl" was all Norman said. "Is there anything else you haven't told me?" Then he let out a genial chuckle.

A few days later, after I'd put Norman on the plane to New York to be with Norris for a week and sit for a press interview, I bumped into Scott. He told me about sharing the cab ride with Norman.

"He was a little drunk but seemed to be having a good time," Scott said. "I see why you like him so much. He isn't anything like I thought; he's a nice guy. He said he'd sign a book when I asked him." I knew Scott barely owned any books—he was not a big reader—much less one by Norman Mailer.

"Well, he *is* that way," I said.

"I invited him to bingo next week. You think he'll come?"

"With Norman," I said, "you never know."

Norman did not, in the end, attend drag bingo. He wouldn't have been able to hear the numbers called over the noisy music and general craziness of the bar. Nonetheless, I would never presume to think Norman would have discounted the idea altogether.

● ● ●

Work on the script for *The Deer Park* was done by the late spring. We had a working draft that I planned to forward to Michael in New York.

"Get Michael on the phone and let him know it's coming," Norman said.

"I'll send him an email right now."

"I think you should call," Norman said. "I don't trust emails."

His distrust of email was heightening for no reason lately—and driving me crazy. If I spent time on the phone trying to leave voice messages with every person he wanted to touch base with, I would have had to spend three quarters of my time with a phone stuck to my ear. It didn't make any sense. I was growing tired of our disagreement about communication methods. We were clearly of different minds about this.

"I'll do both," I said.

Generational differences rarely divided us beyond petty irritations. Norman was not a man who believed a person couldn't adapt—except when it came to technology. He maintained that it was fundamentally evil. Overall, he lived in the time the calendar said, and his six decades of work reflect that. He knew more about the politics of any given era than just about anyone, and had written about it more than most. Norman was an eminent voice who remained relevant in both the twentieth and twenty-first centuries. In April 2007, *The Paris Review*, in one of the few times in its history, conducted an interview with him, forty-five years after having done their first. Of all the writers they could have chosen, his wisdom about the work and life of a writer was unequaled.

Norman's body was visibly affected by the razor wire of old age by that time, but his mind certainly was not. He spent two days talking to the writer Andrew O'Hagan, the young author he admired over most others. Norman's brilliance flashed again for a new generation of readers during that interview and didn't lose a beat or fail to have impact. The article was followed by an appearance he made in June at the New York Public Library, where he and the brilliant German author Günter Grass spoke about writing, the life of the writer, and what their duty is to truth. The event was praised as extraordinary by everyone who saw it. Norman was enthralling when he spoke: clear and dead on. It was his last major public appearance and one of his most potent. Norris told me Norman hadn't lost a flicker of himself, and wooed the audience with as much style as he ever had.

In August, Norman broke a technological barrier—ironic considering his unconcealed abhorrence of technology. Earlier in the year the Edinburgh International Book Festival organizers had invited him to fly over to speak and host a book signing. Norman's health dictated—after much sober thought—that he decline. Traveling long hours on an airplane was too hard for him at that point, and as he put it, "voyaging is hell." The good Edinburgh people proposed an alternative.

Norman could still appear as their keynote speaker and, amazingly, also sign books. They proposed a broadband Internet-video connection through which Norman could speak directly, live, to the audience and sign books. The signature system, called *Long Pen*, had been invented by the writer Margaret Atwood. It consisted of a pad, rather like the screen of a laptop computer, and an attached stylus. When the time came, Norman wrote his signature, and three thousand miles away an exact facsimile of what he'd scrawled appeared in the page of a book, flaws and all. It was a remarkable invention, and we were informed that Norman Mailer, the man who adamantly stated that technology offered "little good to the world," was the first author to use it to sign books transatlantically.

Andrew O'Hagan, being Scottish, was again tapped to do the intercontinental interview with Norman, which happened before noon on a Sunday for us in Provincetown. Norman was to speak to an audience of more than eight hundred.

I arrived an hour before to help the technician set up our "studio" in the small room off the kitchen that Norman mostly used to nap or watch football in. We connected to the UK, and Andrew appeared on the video screen.

"Hello, Dwayne," he said. Andrew and I had become acquainted over the course of the year, and so we chatted casually for a moment. Then it occurred to me that the entire audience was more or less privy to our discussion. Our voices were booming throughout the theater in Scotland as eager book enthusiasts settled into their seats to watch and hear Norman Mailer. I ducked away as quickly as I could and rounded up Norman.

He sat in front of the video screen for the discussion with Andrew, and as soon as he did his internal fame switch flicked on. Norman morphed in a matter of seconds into his vibrant, public self and fired through the interview without a hint of difficulty. The interview was followed by a Q&A with the audience that went well but had a rough moment or two. Norman, hard of hearing, needed me (who was crouched down next to him on the floor, out of sight) to repeat a few things. Scottish brogue, while beautiful, can be difficult to decipher even for young ears. Admittedly, I suffered with a fleeting panic, praying I understood the questions correctly, but our collaboration worked well in the end. The entire event was slated to last thirty-five minutes, but it ran nearly an hour. Norman, once revved up, was not easy to stop—even at eighty-four.

After we signed off and the technician had packed up and left, Norman and I sat at the table like we did **every morning**.

"That went well," I said.

"Yes," he said. "That was a good interview. I've never signed books that way before."

"Norman," I said. "*No one* has. You're the first author in history to sign books with an ocean between you and the book." He'd either forgotten what I'd told him the day before about the distinctiveness of the event, or he didn't care and had tossed the detail aside.

"Is that so?" he said, grabbing his cards to play solitaire.

"Yes. You've just made history."

"Well, in that case I'll have lunch."

TEN

Long Afternoons

Summer is, arguably, the best time to be in Province-town, and when the temperature rises, Brooklyn gets sticky. So, Norris spent much of the summer of 2007 at home with Norman. Her mother, Gaynell, was still at the assisted-living facility down in New York, so Norris made frequent trips back and forth to visit her. Nonetheless, she was around as much as possible. Clearly, Norman loved it when Norris was home. We all did.

My belief that I was adequate assistance for Norman while Norris needed to be away was diminishing. In the beginning I tried to tell myself that Norman would regain his strength and our days would roll on easily again as they once had. Now all I could think when I left for the night when Norris was gone was that he might plunge over that stair rail and I would find him in serious trouble the next day. I knew he was still tough enough probably to beat a tumble down carpeted stairs, but I also knew that if it did happen he would get seriously banged up. I lived with that dread for a couple of months.

He was visiting the attic less frequently, because it was simply too difficult: too many steps. Norman rarely complained about his stolen breath or that his eyes blurred within an hour of starting to read, but the afflictions did bother him and he was unable to fully mask his irritation at his betraying body. This powerful man who had been in control of his every cell was now becoming a casualty to time, and frankly, it quietly angered him. Christina arrived late in the summer to help out and offered, as is her way, levity to all our days. Norman and she would have lively talks about books and food and relationships that were valuable to both of them. Christina was in a deadlock with both her novel and a love affair. Norman proffered advice about both, and she paid him back with good sweets she baked.

"How are *you* doing?" she asked me in the car on our way to the market to buy dinner groceries and chocolate for one of her velvety cakes. I was planning a large meal for the family that evening and wanted it to be special. Several of the kids were in town, as were Norris and Norman's sister, Barbara.

"I'm okay most of the time," I told her. "But some days . . . not so much."

"Norman?"

"Yes," I said. "Obviously. For the first time I absolutely hate the concept of time. I feel like we're all going broke."

I did feel that way. The valuable times with Norman were dwindling. I felt like I was watching a bag of paper money blowing away, bill by bill, in a windstorm. All I could do was watch it happen, powerless.

"Is Thomas there for you?" she asked.

Christina was aware of the ups and downs of my relationship with Thomas, and she and I had both suffered in matters of the heart. Naturally, we commiserated about those issues and helped each other survive personal catastrophes as best we could. However, she did not know about the most recent development in my relationship with Thomas. It was time to tell her.

Thomas was indeed dealing with conflicts that, as Norman had astutely observed, men like he and I could never comprehend. Thomas's bewilderment about his life was rooted in the unique, excruciating truth that he was transsexual. It was a situation not unlike the one Gregory Hemingway had suffered, except in this case Thomas was in accepting company who cared. After years of professional therapy, Thomas had finally realized he'd been born in the wrong body. The label *gay* has nothing to do with gender identity or its inherent confusion, I came to understand. As a boy, he'd suppressed his feelings, violently at times, and that repression reverberated throughout much of his adult life. Hence, Thomas had used booze and drugs as walls and faced bottomless depression and scores of emotional failures while trying to exist in his own skin. His quandary finally came to a head in the early months of 2007. He knew he had to accept himself or die, simple as that. So, he made the brave, if intricate, decision to pursue life from then on as female, while immersing himself in hormone therapy, embracing his inevitable transition properly and responsibly. He, *she*, was headed toward full transsexualism, and I was left with unimaginable ambiguity. I felt abandoned by everything I knew us to be as two men who cared for each other. This strong man, this carpenter, the love of my life, was, beneath it all, female. It was a shock and a relief to finally know the truth, because, while wholly unexpected, it answered the avalanche of questions as to why our life had been riddled with difficulty and obscure despair. It explained his disconnect, his inability to face life with personal honesty. For years I had tried everything to make our relationship good, to nurture it toward a healthy center, but in the end I necessarily confronted his truth. There was nothing I could do to alter what God or the cosmos or fate had instilled in him, in *her*. Emotions cannot adjust fortune, no matter how vigilantly we tend to hope. Thomas was not a male in the precise sense of the word, and never had been; he'd simply *appeared* to be a perfect example of one. His was a startling revelation for me to absorb. After I learned about it I discussed the situation with Norman briefly, and he did not seem overly surprised.

"Keep your head together and know what's valuable," Norman told me.

I took away from that comment the notion that mine and

Thomas's friendship should not be sacrificed to troubling social abstracts. My goal, in part to Norman's council, was to never obliterate the optimistic strength that endured between Thomas and me, even while the structure of our relationship settled into only profound friendship and, ultimately, trust. I would not lend credence to a world that often dictated sorrowful ends, like the one that befell Gloria Hemingway, who had died mired in torment, gloom, and fractured hope. My Thomas has been strong and smart and lives now with dignity as Sarah these years later—and as my dear friend.

"Norman knows this about Thomas?" Christina asked that day I told her the story in the car. Thomas had yet to fully transition and still appeared, more or less, the same as he always had. But the changes were coming.

"Yes. He knows about what's happening. What's great is that Norman never bats an eye or shows any sort of reservation when Thomas comes to visit or work. He still depends on Thomas's input when it comes to fixing things in the house, just like always. It's *me* who has the problem sometimes; me who can't let go of who Thomas was. Norman regards Thomas's situation with no fanfare at all. The man is so much more advanced than anyone I know."

"He does have a way with human nature," she said.

"I'm ashamed. This thing with Thomas was in my face the entire time and I never saw it."

"Or you couldn't," she said. "You shouldn't feel ashamed. You didn't do anything wrong, and neither did Thomas."

Christina was, of course, right. I'd come to understand,

through so many talks with Norman about human complexity, that we tend to examine dilemmas in a flimsy mirror of ourselves. In doing that, we don't realize that what we see is wafer thin, prone to shattering at the slightest tap. I kept Thomas close, mindful of what was most important. Norman had instructed me that I must do that, and the advice was accurate. Over the months I did manage to hold onto the best of what we had, even while embroiled in complicated circumstances in other areas, specifically watching Norman become fragile. Always, I had battled anxiety that the treasure of Norman's companionship could also slip away, but he was stronger than most men I knew, and I optimistically always put my money on that.

The film script for *The Deer Park* was now with Michael, and we awaited the go-ahead for a November filming date in Provincetown. *The God Book* was at the publisher by the middle of the summer, and *The Quote Book* that few knew about was finished also, but put away for later. Norman busied himself by reading further for the second Hitler book. I continued my trips to the copy store, destroying more volumes in order to blow up the pages so he could see them better. I didn't argue with him much about ruining books anymore. What was the point? He needed to work, and I was there to help him with what he needed to do. So my petty irritation took a backseat.

In the last few months he was in Provincetown, I began to regard our ways toward each other with more tenderness than I had before. I knew he more or less felt the same, because there was a sweetness to his voice that was more prevalent, easier to discern. He was not the kind of man to show outward affection often, but he was the type to let you know, loud and clear, how important you were to him. You felt it like a bear hug when he looked at you with his dazzling blue eyes or bid you good morning with a smile. Although Norman's taste for food was still vanishing by the hour, meals remained the center of his day, our day.

Whenever I brought his lunch to him he would push aside everything he was reading to dig into it, even though his appetite was less voracious than it had been. What hadn't faded was his love for chocolate. He liked a small treat of it each afternoon after his lunch. Sometimes, I thought, lunch was just a stepping stone to the Hershey's Bar.

"Do me a favor, pal, break me off three squares," he'd say.

Half of the time, I'd look down and see that his tuna sandwich and halved grape tomatoes sprinkled with balsamic were not yet finished when he asked me this. I buried my urge to point this out and got him his chocolate. He'd earned the right to eat whatever he wanted, whenever he wanted. He rarely overdid his chocolate consumption, employing balance to it as he did most everything. He'd break three small squares from a Hershey's Bar and place them evenly on a napkin in front of himself and then savor each one slowly. Always three squares— no more, no less. In addition to the candy, however, there were Dove Bars, the chocolate-covered vanilla ice cream on a stick, which he adored.

"It's the perfect dessert," Norman said often. "Too bad

good restaurants don't see that." Grandiose desserts were as silly as unnecessary adjectives to him.

Grapefruit was in favor for lunch through August and September. Most people eat it for breakfast, but Norman preferred it as a midday meal. I didn't approve of it as a main course, because it did nothing to improve the numbers on his bathroom scale.

"It must be cut in half, sliced carefully into nine or ten sections, which should then be loosened from the rind like this, so they float in the juice." He showed me the process one day as we stood together at the black granite kitchen island. "This nasty core should be discarded." He flung the pulpy center string on the stone.

"Float in the juice . . ." I said.

"Yes. It makes for a satisfying drink in the end," he said smiling, then meandering to the table to allow me to carve the second half exactly as he'd done the first. By day two, I was a pro.

"Ahh . . . good, very good," he said when I put the two halves of the pink fruit in front of him. "You clearly appreciate the art of the grapefruit as much as I do." He was being droll, of course, as he always was when commenting on my mastering of the mundane.

The art of the grapefruit. Only Norman could get away with saying this, only Norman would consider slicing fruit precisely as going steps beyond basic culinary skill. He consistently looked at the world in an unusual light. Even fruit, for Norman, was an object to be studied, to be considered. I thought about the night we'd met in the grocery store four years before and how he'd pondered the bananas. Soon after coming into his life I learned that he'd been looking for a perfect cluster that day, midway between green and ripe. He would then rush their ripeness by putting them in the lowest, coldest part of the refrigerator, where they turned black in a day. Their sweetness doubled, but their flesh remained firm against a slicing knife. Even the lowly banana had never been merely breakfast to him.

I urged Norman, as often as I could without sounding harpish, to indulge in something different than only a grapefruit for lunch.

"Nothing sounds good to me," he said leaning back while his hand reached down to rub his troublesome knees.

"What about going back to the oats and greens?" I asked. "You love eating that."

"What?"

"The teriyaki oatmeal with broccoli, green beans, and peas," I said. "You ate it for lunch all the time a while back."

"I did?" he asked.

He evidently had no recollection of the dish he'd created. In the year and a half since the ritual had stopped, the memory of it had run away completely.

"Norman, you ate it every day for months to get your cholesterol down," I said. "Come on, you loved it."

"I hate broccoli, always have. There's only one way it should be prepared. Did I ever tell you how?"

"Yes," I said, "quick-seared with Asian sauce in a hot wok

and served immediately. But you ate broccoli with teriyaki oats for months."

"Oh man. Sorry, pal, I guess I just put it out of my head."

I found the discussion hard because the mingling of oats and greens had been his idea and his alone. In fact, he'd been so proud of concocting the dish that I think he ate it for so long out of pure satisfaction that he'd invented the formula. Now he had no memory of his lunch. I felt a pang of sadness and decided the best thing I could do was go to the kitchen and make a batch. I did and let it ferment overnight, which made it even better.

The next day I offered him a bowl.

"It doesn't look too good," he said.

"It never did," I said, "but you like it."

"Well, I'm thinking tuna today," he said, "but thanks." So, he sat down and waited for a sandwich. I made the sandwich and then joined him at the table with my own bowl of oats.

"It's that good, huh?" he asked, watching me munch away at his creation.

"Yup," I said.

"Well, then, maybe tomorrow."

But tomorrow never came. He went back to grapefruit for lunch the following day, claiming the tuna had toyed with his constitution. So grapefruit was the name of lunch for the weeks to come, rarely with deviation.

"I'm worried about Norman losing so much weight," Norris said to me one day on the phone. "Get him to try one of my weight-gain shakes." She was down in Brooklyn for the week, tending to her mother again and dealing with her own doctor's visits.

"He'll claim it tastes like plastic," I said. I knew him well enough to know that if he even suspected food came from a powder, ingesting it would be out of the question.

"Well, he has to eat *something* besides oysters," she said. She was right. Norman was ostensibly living on oysters and only tolerating most other foods, except omelets and grapefruit. Yes, I made salmon and other fish for dinner, and the occasional meatloaf or German meatballs, but he seldom finished his plate anymore.

"I know, Barb, but I don't know what to do," I said to Norris. His once-splendid love of food had become like the fond memory of an object he'd put into a cabinet and now thought about only rarely.

Norman spent his evenings alone, a preference he held onto not out of defiance but common sense. He was still capable of managing the majority of his personal needs unaided if Norris happened not to be around, able to haul a small meal from the warming oven to the table and pour a glass of wine if he chose. More and more he went out with Mike and Donna Lennon for dinner, and bagged their oyster shells as well as his own to cart home.

The number of poker games increased to four or five times a month. It was easy to round up his poker pals that year. I'd cook a meal and leave it for whoever showed up to serve before the game. The next day Norman would detail what had gone on and who had won.

"I lost my shirt. Twenty-five bucks," he'd say. "Busa won, the sonofabitch." He let out a chuckle at his rebuke of his friend Chris Busa, the publisher of *Provincetown Arts Magazine* and a man Norman had known since Chris was a boy. The downside was that Chris had a habit of talking through each hand, much to the irritation of the other players. Norman liked him a great deal and had even recently financed a photography book Chris was publishing through his small press. Norman wrote the foreword for the collection, which featured images of Provincetown at night. Business and friendship aside, Norman's affection didn't extend to times when Chris subjected the table to chatter during Texas Hold 'em.

"Why don't you tell him to shut up," I said.

"I did. *I have*," Norman said. "It won't take."

In the years I knew Norman, I never saw him duck a friendship, but he could be irascible in his analysis of someone he cared for. He could also be merciless when it came to their writing (if they were daft enough to ask his opinion), and short with them if they questioned his health. He did not like cheats and liars, and that was reflected in his choice of friends. Norman had no patience for—or as he said, no *time* to indulge—fools. What was appropriately assumed about him was that he was strict about always doing what was right *publicly*. Privately, however, at home, he could occasionally be petulant, with a need to get his way, and would sometimes use irrational means to get it.

The older he got the more I think he believed he had earned the right to be difficult. He had no real outlet for things that bothered him or, perhaps, privately terrified him. He could be a perplexing mix of gentle and coarse, but was usually fair to those of us around him, but not always. Norman was a fine teacher of learning how to get what you feel you deserve, and also about what methods *not to use* to get those things. I learned from his example.

In the middle of that last summer, as I left for the evening, I told him I would not see him the next day until sometime after noon. I needed to help my dear friend Astrid, a restaurateur and poker pal of Norman's, with an errand. Norman knew Astrid well, and when they played poker together he affectionately chided her about never being able to remember the correct worth of her chips. She brought fresh oysters to him once, however, and that sealed their friendship—above and beyond the silly chip confusion.

"I won't be back until around twelve or twelve thirty," I said, my hand still resting on his shoulder as it always did briefly while I said good night.

"Oh fine, fine," he told me as I left. We'd enjoyed a fine day of me typing and him reediting parts of the filmscript and telling me stories about when the play version first premiered on the stage in New York. In the afternoon we'd sat in the sun talking about nothing more unusual than the ocean and the habits of gulls. We liked to watch them drop their valuable clams from high up, aiming at large rocks on the beach below, which would crack them open to expose their meat.

The next day I drove Astrid's expensive Audi to her mechanic in Orleans, who was to replace the tires. She was wildly busy with her summer restaurant and unable to get away, so I'd volunteered my early morning. The tires cost five hundred dollars apiece and she'd given me cash to pay for them. When the job was done, I headed the thirty miles back to Provincetown just before noon. It was a hot Friday, and the traffic was unforgiving, as anyone who lives near a summer resort can imagine. Compound that with an accident on the only road leading to town, and you have a situation that can only be waited out. The clock ticked on, and at twelve thirty my cell phone rang.

"Where *are* you? You said you'd be here by noon," Norman said. His voice was stern, unnecessarily so.

"Stuck in traffic. There's been a car accident up ahead."

"Well, I've got work to do today and now I won't get to it!" he bellowed.

I was immediately flustered by this unexpected outburst. Plus, his strange need to suddenly "get to work" was a flimsy excuse. Something else was bugging him. If anyone knew what work needed to be done it was me—I was the guy who scheduled it, typed it, and sent it out. This wasn't really about work.

"Well," I said, trying to remain calm, "I'll be there in less than an hour." Traffic wasn't moving.

"Well, I don't understand why you said you'd be here by now and you're not," Norman said.

In all of our years together we'd both rejected, more or less, silly absolutes when it came to the time of my arrival or departure. Neither of us liked that kind of structure, unless we were on deadline. Then, of course, there was necessity: media days were structured; travel days, even more. That was all well and good. I never scoffed about sacrificing my time on weekends if I was needed; he knew that. So this sudden bark at me while I was helping a friend with a task that "cut into his time" made no sense and, frankly, made me mad.

"Norman, I've got a car accident in front of me and a line of traffic that would make you go through the roof if you were here. I'll be there as soon as I can." I hung up the phone.

Forty-five minutes later I walked into the house to find him at the table playing solitaire, the "work" he needed to do, the foreword to the Provincetown photo book, was lying next to him untouched and in exactly the same spot it had been the night before.

"Ah, there you are," he said in a fake, measured calm when I sat down.

"So what's the rush today?" I said.

"You said you'd be here by noon," he started again. "Now it's one. The whole day is shot."

"I said twelve or twelve thirty. There was a car accident, man. Come on! I don't control the goddamn road!"

"What the hell were you doing anyway?"

"I went to buy tires for Astrid," I said.

"Well, why couldn't she get her own tires? I needed you here today!"

"For what?"

"I want to get to work. Couldn't one of her waiters have done it for her? Tires!"

"She's not comfortable handing two thousand bucks in cash to some waiter," I said. "What the hell is the problem? I'm here now; let's work. What do you want to do?" I knew he had nothing. I knew his plate was empty except for the foreword, which was only a thousand words, and it had no definite deadline.

"Is this the latest draft?" he asked, reaching for the papers that were the latest copy of the piece. They remained unmarked as far as I could see. If Norman had needed to get to work so badly he could easily have edited without my being there. He'd done it a thousand times.

"Yes," I said. He was questioning my doing a favor for someone else that was important to her and not *him*.

He yanked the papers close, pulled his pen from his shirt pocket, and began to edit. I got up and left the table. I remember secretly hoping that his pen would burst between his fingers and soil the pages. My anger was, I knew, silly—he was elderly and he felt he needed me, but I couldn't think in such immediate, clear terms.

From my office near the living room I could hear him whispering as he edited, tapping out his words on the dining table. With every tap of his hand in the other room my resentment grew. I was not mad at him for any other reason than that he thought he'd been mildly betrayed because I'd helped someone else.

I went back into the dining room and sat at the table. He stopped editing and we stared at each for a second.

"You can't do that to me," I said. "I never shirk from any request from you about anything, and you should respect that."

"You said you'd be here by noon!" he shouted.

"You make me feel like a fucking idiot," I said.

"Don't be ridiculous."

"Then why the hell were you so mad that I was late because of traffic?"

"Listen, the point is you weren't here when you said you'd be here. Now, I don't want to talk about this anymore." His voice had calmed and he looked down at his pages.

"Well, the whole thing makes no damn sense," I said.

"Let's move on."

That was Norman's way. He'd say "let's move on" as if everyone around him could magically do that when he decided it was time. He'd leave your anger dangling.

"No, I did something for Astrid today, and you're mad about it."

"Well, you weren't here when you said you would be."

It was like hitting a brick wall; there was absolutely nothing I could say. He was being utterly absurd. I knew my own anger was overblown and also knew, logically, that he was full of rancor about his increasing requirement for consistent assistance. Nonetheless, he'd never admit fault or to being reactionary about issues that were deeply personal. I'd seen him behave in this inflexible manner toward Norris, and now that same rigid stance was manifesting itself toward me. That's what this small problem had evolved into.

I knew there was no way out of the situation except to allow for the umpire of time. So I got up and left him to his editing. I went into the kitchen to cut a grapefruit for his lunch, without saying anything. He had not asked me to do this, but I knew from the clock that he'd want to eat soon. It was just as well he didn't ask me, because the less I heard his voice at that moment the better. I plopped the food down near him and left without saying, "here you are, pal," or getting a "thank you," as would have been normal. I went outside to grab a cigarette from my car and lay low for a while, fuming.

When I returned to the kitchen he was standing at the island breaking hunks of Hershey's Bar for himself. I didn't offer help.

"What do you want for dinner tonight?" I said as measured as I could.

"Whatever you want to make," he said rather calmly. This was out of character, because he usually had something to say about dinner. What I had hoped to hear was, "I leave the decision to you, because I have been atrocious." Of course, he didn't say that. He just shuffled back to his chair to read the *New York Times*.

Norman finally did stumble upon the obvious: that he'd pressed me too far, been too quick to jump when jumping wasn't necessary. He actually looked moderately remorseful when I glanced through the doorway as he munched on his Hershey's chocolate.

"I'll bake fish," I finally said, joining him at the table. He put his chocolate down on the napkin and leaned back in his chair, looking me directly in the eye.

"I may have overreacted," he said. "I'm sorry."

Of all the people I'd ever been angry at in my years, Norman was the only one who had the ability to feather it away with one statement. I realized then that the intensity of fondness I held for him, the height of the pedestal he'd perched himself on in my soul, was towering. Logically I was still bothered, still angry at him for being ridiculous. But when he admitted that he'd overstated the issue and apologized for doing it, everything in me fell away to what was most relevant: maintaining the balance.

"I guess I should have called you to tell you I would be late before you called me," I said, trying to meet him halfway. "I just didn't think it would cause such a stir."

"Well. We've got the doctor tomorrow," he said, his voice suddenly spry again, relieved to discuss another topic. "What time are we due?"

"I think two," I said. "Let me check so we can plan it right."

I made him fish that night: salmon with scallions and Asian sauce, green beans, and mashed potatoes. When I left for the day and told him it was in the oven for whenever he wanted to eat, he looked up with those blue eyes as he settled onto his couch for a short, late-afternoon nap and thanked me.

"Try to eat it all," I said. "Norris says you need to get a little weight back."

"Okay, man," he said. "She's the boss. See you tomorrow."

"Yes," I said.

The next morning I came over around the usual time and nothing else was ever mentioned again about timing or tires or traffic trouble. Nothing needed to be said. We were good, and there was a whole new day before us.

· · ·

The fallout had faded away into so much nothing in the matter of a few hours, but the unexpected neediness embedded in his initial phone call still bothered me. Such a sharp, quick display of indignation wasn't ordinary for him. In my years with him he'd never been so swift to tell me the "what for" over such silly stuff—important deadlines and decisions about work, yes, but not being a little late arriving. This biting manner, which was clearly a thunderous yell that he desired to have me around as much as possible, was vaguely unsettling. His nature was by and large unvarying, but in the days following our run-in, I noticed he had developed a tendency to drift in and out, lost in his thoughts one minute and then turning to me with a wish to know exactly what time it was the next, his voice speedy and inquisitive. I knew I could never understand all he must be mulling, so I'd tell him the time and go back to my work. His movements around the house became overtly cautious also: he gripped hold of every surface available as he passed through a room. I was more alert when he stood up to head for the Second Office or moved toward the phone to make a call. He spent less and less time each morning on the phone in the bar, with its broad windows overlooking the beach and bay. He'd always preferred talking in that room while looking outside. There, he could watch the birds, occasional beachcombers, and the tide edging up or pulling out. Lately he'd taken to remaining in his chair at the table, asking me to dial the number and bring the cordless handset to him instead. The several steps involved to perch himself on a stool in the bar to talk and watch the water had become, nearly overnight, too taxing.

On a day in late summer he climbed to the attic to work. He hadn't been up there for days, perhaps weeks.

"I'll be up today," he announced as I served his breakfast and sat down with my own cup of coffee.

An hour later he ascended to his study. We had nothing pressing slated to be done that I could think of, so I assumed he was just going up there to read. As he managed the stairs I hung back a bit, not too far behind, paying attention on his clump, clump, clump. He made it to the third floor. I waited before going up to see what he was working on, and sure enough he was reading one of the books I'd enlarged, its pages cluttering the desk.

"Norman, do you want some tea?" He had come to like a cup now and then as he read in the afternoons.

"No. Perhaps after lunch. I'm fine now. Sit down."

I pulled a chair over and sat near him.

"Do you have the Iraq piece handy?" he asked me. He was referring to an essay he'd begun in April and never finished. It was, more or less, the last piece of any size he'd written, except for the foreword to the photo book. I told him I would run down to the dining room to get it from the window ledge.

"We don't have a copy up here?"

"No, we don't," I said. "You wrote it downstairs, and that's where I left it."

"I did? Oh fine, fine," he said.

The climb had worn him out, and his once rapid-fire hands

were moving to search his desk for something unhurriedly. His squint was pronounced also as he studied the papers in front of him.

"Norris will be back tomorrow," he said. "We should have a good meal."

"Of course."

"Any ideas?"

"Pot roast and mushroom polenta? With green beans."

"Sounds good."

I knew it didn't sound all that great to him; he was just being polite. He had little excitement left in him about food, even my shitake polenta. What really saddened me was that his old verve about menu decisions was gone. There was no more sport to our talk of food.

"Well, that's settled then," he said. He looked around on the desktop. "Oh, the Iraq piece?"

"Coming right up," I said. I dashed downstairs and got it.

"I'll come down in a while for a grapefruit," he said when I came back and handed it to him. "I'll just read a little longer and work on this. But do me a favor, pal. Organize the files for everything after 1906. I'd like to have all the files in one spot on my desk for '06 to 1914."

He was gearing up for serious preparation for the sequel again. He hadn't mentioned the book for a few weeks, other than in passing, but I knew it was constantly in his mind. Now, apparently, he was ready to take action.

The files he was referring to concerned the eight years following the conclusion of *The Castle in the Forest*, which ended in

1906. Adolf Hitler moved to Vienna in those years and lived with another poor art student named Auguste Kubizek, in a small room—with one bed. The two boys shared every waking hour together for several months, painting pictures, discussing opera. Then, after a mysterious and swift end to the boys' seemingly intimate companionship, Adolf moved into a homeless men's shelter on the outskirts of town. The files full of details about that period, the ones Norman wanted, were on the other side of the attic, already stacked and waiting for him. All I would have to do was move them to his desk.

"And bring me the script," he said, talking about *The Deer Park*. "We should have a copy of that up here, too."

"Sure thing," I said. I grabbed an orange Post-it note to write the dates to place with the files he wanted and stuck it on the stack for later.

He suddenly had three projects he wanted to tackle. He'd not done much of anything serious for a few weeks, as far as writing was concerned, and now he wanted to devote attention to a filmscript, a complex political essay, and a novel. It was setting up to be a potentially long afternoon. I was happy to be rushed to gather material for him again. For too long there had been no hurry, no deadlines except the contrived one the day I came over late. And that had only to do with abstracts of attention in the end.

He didn't stay in the attic office for very long that afternoon. He came down after an hour or two, to have lunch and read the rest of the paper. I went up to the attic to move the wooden paper tray full of Hitler files to his desk, just to the left of his chair. On the front of it I tacked the orange Post-it note so he would be sure to see it. The pages he'd been reading needed straightening up; they were spread over the desktop. I grabbed the Iraq essay to take back downstairs, because I figured he would want to work on it after lunch. It hadn't been edited or expanded yet.

The Iraq piece was intriguing because it had little to do with anything inherently political at first. Rather, it dealt with defining the most difficult tasks every man has to face. The initial theme was honor, ostensibly its place among troops, and in it Norman addressed undefined ideas about one's order of personal decency and where that fits into the ugliness of war. The piece was pure Mailer. He began by examining his own stint in the military during World War II; however I couldn't help but wonder if the piece had evolved from what he was battling internally at the time he wrote it.

> What was damnable about service is that it was almost impossible to be any kind of half-way decent soldier without finding that one had to call on one's honor, the honor to persist under the most disagreeable circumstances, the honor to live with the constants of fear, the honor to rise above the emotional misery of being a relatively untutored draft soldier in a profession one had not chosen.

I put the essay back on the ledge of the bay window in the dining room, for when he decided to work on it again. He never did alter it, but it lingers as one of the more self-exposing pieces he wrote during my time with him. In it, he revealed what I knew the center of him to be as a man and as my friend, which was, above all, remain upright in the face of whatever came his way.

ELEVEN

Keeping November Open

I enter muddled territory when I think about the last month Norman spent in Provincetown before traveling to Brooklyn that final time. So much about that period was delicate, so much indistinct. In August of 2007 it was decided he would finally go be with Norris and closer to good doctors. The tip of Cape Cod is not the place to be if one's health and mobility are at issue. I thought it was the best idea, and he, although not happy with the prospect of spending too much time away from his home by the ocean, had finally agreed. In his optimistic style, he downplayed leaving Provincetown.

"A couple of weeks down there will be good," he told me. "Then I'll come back here."

I didn't respond, because I knew it would be more than a couple of weeks. Norris and the children had decided the time had arrived where Norman could not be alone in the house anymore, even for short periods. Yes, I was there every day; yes, the basics were provided, but the truth was that Norman was not fully able to manage in the large house alone any longer. The stairs up to his bed on the second floor were enough of a drain on his energy. Somewhere along the line, and I don't know when exactly, it became clear to him that his physical instability demanded that a choice be made.

All of us who were around him then saw what was burdening the man we loved so much. As the one who was with Norman so often in those days and living nearly every hour of my life with his well-being in mind, I was trapped between thinking I would have liked to see him stay and knowing he could not.

Norris traveled back and forth between Provincetown and Brooklyn a few times to prepare for Norman's eventual arrival there in the later part of September. She was only as far away as a phone call or email from everything that went on in the house as the days wound down to when he would leave. I know it killed her to have their life together splintered yet again in that last month, but it was necessary. Norman and Norris spoke on the phone often when she happened to be gone, so no more than a few hours passed without communication. It was clear his breathing was becoming worse and worse. The doctors continued to insist the cause was asthma, but I had doubts about the diagnosis. Norman put a lot of faith in his various inhalers, yet none seemed to do any good. A walk of twenty feet could beat him down to the point where he had to stop to sit, and his breaths after were labored and long. It killed me to watch, but I said nothing and did nothing, except lend a hand or sit for a moment beside him. He would look at me, shaking his head. Norman rarely admitted to any serious pain in his lungs, and I don't believe there was any. It was just difficult and frustrating for him to get air. His discomfort, when he did show it, was from being damn angry that his lungs weren't doing their job correctly, and sometimes, it seemed to me, neither were the doctors. Once, when he was aggravated by yet another suggestion that he try new a medication, Norman called them "mechanics who fuck with fate." He utilized the new inhaler, suffered through its dreadful taste and odor, and declared it just as ineffective as the "purple one was." That's how he kept them straight: by color.

Kids came and went, Christina showed up again, Norris was arranging for everything as only she could, and the house was a flurry of activity. Day after day Norman and I tried to stick to our routine, figuring out ways to further his writing work. There was always, always talk about upcoming projects. He continued unflinchingly to think about getting his pen going again on part two of *Castle*. He wanted to read as much as possible to prepare, but the reading was tough on his declining eyesight. One thing that was not hindered was his thoughts about where the book would begin.

One morning he asked me to gather research about shopping malls. I had no idea why, and he didn't initially tell me, other than to say, "I think D.T. would be there." Later he mentioned that he thought he would resurrect his devil, D.T., in America, to begin telling part two of Hitler's tale. Since D.T. was a phantom and could travel in time as a spirit, he could narrate his version while anonymously entrenched in the bowels of what Norman believed was America's supreme illustration of bad taste: the shopping mall. The idea was outlandish, but I believed it was brilliant. Perhaps I'd been with him long enough that my mind easily slipped into his rationale when commenting on America's distortions of itself. The idea was both whimsical and socially funereal, and above all, ingenious. I spent a day compiling files of statistics, which Norman pored over: pages relating to size, square footage, and traffic through the largest shopping centers. The more he read, the more he was sure he'd landed on a fine idea. He now had a foundation for his plan, backed up with eighty-four years of authority from which to comment. Part two wouldn't only tell about Hitler; it would also enlighten readers about what Norman believed was fractured in his country.

In August a unique request came to us from *Esquire* magazine. They wanted Norman to go on the road with Barack Obama. The press and public didn't know how well or unwell Norman was at the time, so various requests for appearances and interviews kept coming. Clearly, *Esquire* saw the enormous value of having the writer who'd profiled JFK in the famous 1960 piece "Superman Comes to the Supermarket" now examine a new political phenomenon, who seemed to dwell in similar glorified light. Obama was being virtually ordained across the country as *the* exceptional voice, inspiring and youthful. Norman saw this, too, although he was personally leaning toward Hillary Clinton as the Democratic Party's best bet. I said I thought Obama might have the same juice as JFK, enough of it at least to make it farther than the lackluster others who also were running. Norman agreed, but said we don't live in a smart world, so he was skeptical about America electing a black president just yet. As Norman said, "We have an inclination toward racial terror, which is symptomatic of America's disfigurement." Obama was going to be a force, but Norman was unsure that his spark and its corresponding blaze could overcome America's cultural cancer. Nonetheless, he was intrigued by Obama and knew the junior senator had slipped into the niche all politicians crave but few ever imbibe.

For a day Norman considered saying yes. Why wouldn't he? His pen had taken unprecedented measures of presidential candidates for over forty years. The offer presented an opportunity for him to inimitably dissect a candidate, his chief objective in any political writing. No one made a mark like Norman did when it came to character analysis, and he knew it. Norman's observations would have been atypical not only because Obama was a powerhouse force but also because Norman embraced the fact that Barack Obama was an exceptional writer. In Norman's mind, a fine man who is also a good writer made for a man of high value. Doubtless, readers would have been awed by Norman's evaluation and how Obama rattled ranks and, ultimately, thrashed Norman's diagnosis of what plagues the country. Had he done it, the Obama piece, too, might be resurrected in forty-eight years when another political beacon begins to glow and we need to look again at what once was.

Norman told me to decline the request. This was not easy for me to hear, because I wanted desperately to see what he would write about the man who did, in the end, become our forty-fourth president. When Obama was about to win the election, newspapers and magazines across America and around the world could not resist quoting passages from "Superman." Perhaps they were accurate to cull heavily from it, because the general glow around the two men was comparable. But had he written the piece, Norman would have been innovative and not reached to the past, even into his own works, to examine Obama. He detested looking backward and knew that although both men were shining inspirations, their polish came from vastly dissimilar cloths.

Maggie, Norman's youngest daughter from his brief fifth marriage to Carol Stevens, was married in early September, and the entire family and eighty friends gathered in Provincetown to celebrate. Maggie, petite, dark-haired, and always full of spirit, looked exceptionally beautiful that day, and Norman was, naturally, thrilled to be able to give her away. The wedding ceremony was to be held on the flats of the beach at low tide, fifty yards from the deck, with a reception afterward in the house. The home bustled as it had so many times and in so many celebrations before, but this happening was about family and new beginnings. Good people from town came as both friends and caterers to ensure the feast and festivities went perfectly.

In late August, Norman had been admitted to the hospital for five days, during which time doctors again tried to alleviate his bronchial irregularities. Unfortunately, the visit did little to make breathing less irksome for him. His lungs and the muscles around them were simply losing a battle to gathering fluid and time. There was some question as to whether he would be able to attend the wedding of his daughter, but he insisted, and so, two days before the event, he came back home.

The first time I saw him the day of the wedding he was descending the stairs in a fine dark blue suit that had once fit better. His charisma, however, was, as always, at a high level, and he smiled as I came to assist him. As he sat in the living room in a wicker chair waiting for his sons to escort him out onto the beach, he mentally geared up for the trek. I sat down with him for a time, but we didn't discuss anything of importance. Then, after a few moments, I went over to the umbrella stand by the front door to get him a second cane.

"Ah yes, that one," he said, pointing when I offered up a choice of two from across the room.

Then I left him alone, and soon his boys walked him out onto the wide beach, where he gave Maggie away as the sun slipped down to accommodate evening.

Norman had stated that he did not want to stay in Brook-lyn for more than a week or two, but he did not set a firm return date. Some days before he left, he handed me one of the small notebooks he carried in his shirt pocket. In it he'd made a list of books and files and other materials he wanted me to gather for him to take along.

"I must have work down there with me," he said. "It's all here, so we need to figure out what I should take."

I looked through the notebook but couldn't make out much of what he'd written, so we went over the list together.

"I can't read my own damn handwriting," he said with a wry, low laugh. "I bet that makes you feel pretty good, doesn't it?"

It didn't. Norman's writing had always been, since I came on the scene at least, difficult to decipher, but I knew that before my time it had been easier to read, full of swirl and swagger and precise line and loop.

I gathered the papers and books he wanted to take and put them in a pile on the table for him to go through to make a final decision. He wanted to bring a fair amount with him, so I also filled a box that contained less urgent works than the serious material, which I deposited into his black leather carry bag.

Shortly after the wedding he had mysteriously stopped playing solitaire every morning. I don't know why, and I never asked, but Norris noticed it too, and I think we both knew that his overall vivacity was dimming. He loved his game each day or, as is he put it, his brain-combing. Now the cards stayed untouched in the middle of the table and he devoted all of his morning to only reading the papers and mail and minding the hours with one eye on the clock. Norman, it was clear, was tired in ways he'd never been before. He napped twice a day in the TV room off the kitchen now and rarely brought up potential projects.

Two days before he left for Brooklyn, his old friend Bill came to visit. Norman had known Bill since the Jack Henry Abbott days, and their friendship was one that Norman respected more than most. Often when people would call to chat, he declined to speak, quietly urging me to tell them he was working and couldn't be disturbed. It simply took too much out of him to talk for long stretches on the phone, even with the added pleasure of seeing the beach out the window as he talked in the bar. When Bill rang, however, Norman always ambled over to the bar phone and sprang easily into conversation with his friend. Bill was an ex-detective turned private eye, and Norman loved the Dashiell Hammett–like grit about him. When Bill came for his visit that last time, they drove over to Wellfleet for lunch. They shared a leisurely afternoon at the Bookstore Café, eating oysters and talking about the future. When they first arrived at the restaurant, however, Norman, in his gentlemanly way, declined to be dropped off at the front door and insisted on staying in the car and walking from wherever Bill parked. Bill put the car as close to the café as he could, fifty feet away. Norman tried to make it across the parking lot, but Bill told me later that he had to dash to get a chair when Norman became winded halfway to the door. Norman sat for a spell, mustered his strength, and finally made it inside for their lunch. He may have needed to take a break, but there was no keeping him from the oysters or Bill's fine conversation.

Bill left the following day, soon after Norman's daughter Danielle and her husband, Peter, arrived. It had been decided by Norris and all the children that Norman would ride with the two of them down to Brooklyn. The three of us knew it was going to be a hard trip for Norman, so we prepared well for it. The next morning, September 22, I arrived to the house early. Peter had packed the car to the hilt, with personal items Norman had come to need in the past months, along with a smattering of his favorite clothes. He insisted with an upbeat voice that I pack two extra dress shirts because, as he said, "I may decide to take Norris out on the town."

"I'm making you an omelet," I said that final morning as he appeared at the bottom of the stairs. I didn't even give him the option of having something different. I knew it was the last time for a while that he'd get to enjoy one of his favorite meals.

"With cream cheese today?" he asked.

As the clock neared noon we knew the three of them needed to get on the road. Summer had just left Provincetown, along with most of the tourists, and it had begun to get dark noticeably earlier. None of us wanted them to be stuck driving through night.

Danielle was nervous about making the trip all the way to New York with her father. Norman was not one to rattle on with small talk on a road trip, so filling the coming long hours of travel worried her slightly.

"He won't read in the car," I said. "He just won't do it. But don't worry, everything will be fine. You'll have plenty to talk about. We drive up Cape together all the time, and he fills the hours with stories. Just be prepared to stop a lot along the way."

"You know, I told him that we'd make a place for him at our home in Connecticut," Danielle said. "He didn't shoot it down *too* quickly. I'm so worried about dad."

"He loves you so much, Danni," I said. "Every time he talks about you he beams. Remember how he wanted your input on *Modest Gifts*? It was hugely important to him that you have a say in that manuscript." Danielle is a superb artist with precise taste and mind-boggling ability.

We were on the steps outside where we'd sat the day I first met her, when she told me how much Norman appreciated my cooking. This time we talked about when her father might return to Provincetown. Neither of us said to the other that we thought it might never happen, but we could hear the echo of that all around us.

I heard Norman call out my name as we went inside. I knew he had not put his hearing aids in yet, because of the volume of his voice. I'd come to know exactly when he was wired for sound and when he wasn't.

"Yes, Norman?" I hollered back. He was in the small room off the kitchen, the one with the red leather chair, red couch he napped on, and the old twenty-six-inch television he preferred. He had more or less ignored the fifty-four-inch giant TV on the second floor of the house during our years together. Its remote control was too complicated, and none of us, except Norris, ever completely figured it out. The only time I ever watched it with Norman was when we looked at the boxing films together, its expansiveness serving us as well as a movie screen.

"Sit down a minute, pal," he said. I did, and waited for him to speak. "I wanted to know if you'd help me with these." He indicated his Ugg boots. He wore them constantly because they were comfortable and sensible, like slippers on steroids.

"Of course," I said, pulling the ottoman nearer to assist. I helped him guide his foot into one black boot and then the other. I stayed with him for a moment while he inserted his hearing aids, or "plugs," as he sometimes called them. As he popped them in they let out a high-pitched whistle, a sound he never seemed to hear but one that always made me wince.

"Ahh, there. Now I can hear you better," he said.

"Everything's packed," I told him. "Danielle is ready whenever you are."

"You have my papers in the bag, right?"

"Yes, Norman."

"And a copy of the script. I'll need that, too."

"Sure."

"Tell anyone who calls that I'll be at the Brooklyn number," he said.

"I'll pass on the message, yes," I said.

"And one more thing," Norman said. He put his strong, old hand on my forearm. "Whatever comes up, make sure to keep November open."

"I will, buddy." November would be for filming his movie *The Deer Park*. Nothing was going to detour him from directing again, from bringing to life, finally, the vision he'd first created half a century before.

I could hear Peter and Danielle in the living room, talking quietly. I knew it was time to go, so we walked out to them. Norman had wanted his "smoked glasses" for the ride, and he slipped them on as we stepped out the front door. When he put those square sunglasses on his face, four decades of time faded away and I could clearly see how he once wooed the world.

As I assisted him into the backseat, he finagled his two canes to be near, careful to place them so he could rest his hands on them. He always preferred to have them close, even while in the car, just in case.

"I'll see you soon," he said, and reached out to shake my hand. His grip was strong and full of intention. It was a fine so long.

"We'll talk tonight," I said. "Bye, Norman."

"See ya, pal," he said. I shut the door and leaned in the front passenger window to kiss Danielle.

I stepped away, back to the brick walkway to watch him leave. As Peter turned onto Allerton Street, the first road that would take them out of town, Norman turned and gave me a salute of a wave: hand to forehead and down, with a slight smile and strong nod. I raised my arm to wave back, but I don't know if he saw me. In the brightness of the Provincetown sun he cut a striking image as the car moved out and away: that shock of white hair, the powerful profile, and those sunglasses! Norman, at that moment, appeared to me to be the coolest man on the planet.

Norman settled into Brooklyn, but it took a few days. The apartment there—two floors with a third "crow's nest" level for writing, nautical in design and beautifully appointed with old wood, fine books, and family pictures on every wall—was his New York base, but it was not his beloved Provincetown. In the earlier years of his writing life it had been his showcase home, the setting for countless literary parties bursting with famous guests and his brood of children. He'd designed the main room to resemble the hold of a ship—right down to a shiny wooden living room ceiling that gently bowed. The landing to their main entrance was three long flights of stairs up from the street, Columbia Heights, and even a sturdy visitor can become winded by the ascent. Norman made the climb the night he returned. It took some time, but he did it.

"He wants to go home already," Norris told me on the phone two days later. "I bought him a new bed before he got here, but he says he can't sleep. I was up and down adjusting the air in the room and his covers every half hour. We're going to have to get some help down here, because I don't know if I can handle it alone."

"I'll come down."

"No," Norris said. "Not yet. You're going to Vermont with Thomas. Take your time. You deserve it and you need it. We'll talk when you get back."

"Are you sure?"

"The kids and I will handle it," she said. "It's just going to take time."

I did travel to Vermont for several days with Thomas—

who had yet to begin calling himself Sarah. I had not gone on vacation for years, and our trip was a needed getaway and an important period for reconstruction. We spent time on Lake Willoughby, with its high twin mountains that appear, from a distance, as one sliced in half with a blue, bottomless lake through its middle. While there, we redefined promises to stay honest from then on. What was, to outsiders, an admittedly odd and impossible impediment to a relationship instead became a solidifying component for our *friendship*. As Norman had said, keep the important elements alive. Thomas's transsexualism was his, hers, to manage alone, but unwavering support was mine to give.

Norris and I emailed every day while I was gone, so I was never far removed from what was happening in Brooklyn. When I returned to Provincetown, the entire village seemed strangely empty to me. The life I'd grown accustomed to over the years with Norman had altered. I'd always been of the mind that I could be of use, but during the month after Norman left, I felt only a hollowness that extended out and away from me and permeated every cranny of town. I missed my dear friend; I missed our easy mornings.

Norman's days in Brooklyn were difficult at first, but after a time routines settled in for him. The kids came all the time to visit their father, and from what Norris told me, Norman was rediscovering degrees of happiness about being in the old apartment whose construction he'd overseen forty years before. John brought the actor Sean Penn to visit one afternoon in early October, and Norman, who admired Penn's work immensely, took a liking to him immediately. Norris said they spent an hour discussing projects, politics, and film. Nothing elevated Norman's mood more than an hour of good talk full of substance.

The doctors in New York decided Norman should be admitted to the hospital for another procedure to alleviate the fluid buildup in his lungs. Upon hearing the news, I didn't like the sound of it. While the experts said it would be the best move, all I could hear was the booming of Norman's voice drowning them out in my head: "Experts are only right fifty percent of the time!"

Close friends whom Norman cared for deeply came to visit him in the hospital. This made him an epicenter again, and funneled life into the disagreeable surroundings that was his sterile room. He was, at his root, a profoundly social man. Yes, he'd lived a mostly private life for the years I knew him, but his nature was one that required effervescence. The outpouring of friendship that greeted him during his stay at Mount Sinai in Manhattan was robust, to say the least. Of course, every so often the press would print an update about his condition. After one tenacious photographer tried to sneak in to get a photo of him, Norris hired a guard to stand outside the room, supplying the sentry with a list of who could and could not enter. When I heard about the guard situation, I became irritated. Couldn't the press, who'd reported on his every move for fifty-five years, now just leave him alone? Of course, later I realized that while Norman's condition was not terribly sensational or newsworthy unto itself, his decades as a public person *were*, and so I calmed myself about the issue after giving it some thought. Norman had, undisputedly, courted the press and the world with his talent, provocations, and personality, and done a fine job of it—naturally the world was still curious about him.

The surgical procedure went as expected, and his doctors said he could well be on the road to recovery and back in his apartment in Brooklyn soon. Hearing the news, I remained on in Provincetown to mind the house so that when Norman came back eventually, it would appear exactly as he'd left it. I didn't even move his playing cards or pens on the table. I knew there is no better boost for someone who has been away from home than to return to find it ready, warm, and the small details unchanged.

On the twelfth and thirteenth of October the annual meeting of the Norman Mailer Society assembled in Provincetown once again. It was confusing for me to have a gathering at the house without Norman or Norris there. Mike and Donna Lennon and I ran the party as usual, but there seemed to be a pall lingering over the evening for me. I had never truly enjoyed the party in the past, and certainly didn't this year. I knew it was important for the members, who held Norman in such high regard, but for me it celebrated only a fraction of the man I knew. As the hours dragged on, my face began to ache from my forcing myself to smile when all I truly wanted to do was hide in the quiet of the attic.

When November came, I knew it was nearing time for me to get my ducks in order and travel to New York. I hadn't seen Norman for well over a month, and unfortunately, after the operation to clear his lungs, he was forced to remain in the hospital. The procedure's initial success had soured after a few days, and Norman's condition worsened. Norris explained developing details each day to me in calls and letters. By the middle of the first week of November, the news was not encouraging. His doctors still insisted Norman could regain strength, but if he did, it would take a long time.

"Sweetie, you might want to think about coming down soon," Norris said to me on the seventh. "He wants to see you. He asks about you every day."

Norman wasn't able to speak, of course. The physicians had put a breathing tube into him, to assist his exhausted lungs, and with such a device, the patient can't talk. That alone, I thought, must be making him mad as hell. If there was one thing Norman liked to do besides write, it was talk. He was able to write notes, but that presented another problem, because many of them were illegible. If his handwriting had been difficult before, I could only imagine what it must be like now.

"I'm coming down tomorrow," I said to Christina. She had gone to New York and was there in the hospital room with Norman as I sat at his desk in the attic. I'd taken down the curtains that had been up for years blocking the view, so I could see the sun sink behind our town and the ever-towering monument. The spectacular sunset bathed everything in orange and purple and crimson, more abstractly and vividly than any impressionist could ever put to canvas.

"I'll tell him," she said.

"Tell him I took the curtains down in the attic, too," I told her. "Let him know I'm sitting at his desk minding the sky for him."

She did, and later told me Norman had nodded his head and smiled approvingly.

Norman knew I didn't particularly like to drive and that I rarely found any substantial need to leave Cape Cod. So when I walked into his hospital room in New York City, he turned to look at me with a wide grin. He still couldn't speak because of the breathing tube, but his sharp blue eyes were noisy with words. I clutched his hand, which he had immediately extended toward me, and held it for a few moments. There was still plumpness to his fingers, which curled with surprising reserves of strength around mine. We enjoyed a little time catching up, silently and differently, yet in much the same way we'd done every morning for a thousand days.

"Well, buddy, you got me to cross the bridge," I said, referring to the old bridge that spans Cape Cod Canal. Norman squinted his eyes and nodded in hearty, noiseless laughter.

Susan, Danielle, Betsy, Kate, Michael, Matt, Maggie, and John Buffalo were all in or just outside of the room, as were their spouses and several of Norman's closest friends; his sister Barbara and nephew Peter were there also. Stephen, Norman's second eldest son, had not arrived yet. Word had gone out to summon all the children, but he was farthest away—out west on an acting job. His plane hadn't landed in New York, and it was near to four in the afternoon. Christina had needed to fly home, as she'd been visiting Norman for several days. All those present, however, were family—those by marriage and those by friendship. What Norman had created in his life was robust. The walls of old Mount Sinai could barely contain what he brought to the floor.

Norris gave me a hug that made my insides melt, because she and I had been through much together that had led to this day, to this sterile-smelling room. In all deference to the family connection that I could never share, she and I knew what we'd managed in quiet talks we'd had about the best way to ease Norman's situation. Norris was Norman's life; I was his right-hand man. She was my rock, and we were each other's good pearl of trust.

Everyone wanted me to read the notes Norman had written on a large tablet. Unfortunately, I couldn't make out most of his words any better than the rest of them, and so it became, for a while, a happy group effort.

"Come on, Dwayne, you've been reading his handwriting for years," someone said to me jokingly. It was true, I had. What they did not know was that the process had always been difficult, and now it was nearly impossible. All I could think was that Norman could hear the exchange and that I was failing him. Was this my final offering to a man whom I loved as I might a grandfather? Moments later I necessarily excused myself to gather my senses. That Norman's ability to communicate was fading was devastating, and symbolic of all I feared we might lose. It was no one's fault, including mine, that his words were impossible to read.

When I returned to his room Norman was in the midst of

indicating that he wanted a drink. He was holding court, not unlike the one he'd held during countless parties and dinners and family gatherings in better days. Now, at this juncture, he wanted a cocktail. I stood to the side of his bed, near the door, while Michael mixed orange juice with a shot of smuggled-in rum. Everyone in the room was at ease; there was not an ounce of outward unhappiness or lament to be found at that moment. We all moved closer as Michael gave the drink to Norman, who held it up in a toast to us all. Because he could not swallow due to the breathing apparatus, Michael dabbed his father's mouth with a long blue swab designed for moistening a dry mouth, similar to a large Q-Tip. Michael soaked it with booze and juice and gave his dad a drink with it. Norman smiled and then turned to his son and furrowed his brow with a mock fatherly scold. Not enough rum, damn it! Michael poured another stream of Bacardi into the glass, mixed it, and dabbed Norman's mouth again. Pure satisfaction spread across Norman's face, and his still-sturdy arm pulled at his son's, saying, "More, more!" To explain who exactly was host, Norman began pointing at all of us around him one by one, and then he raised his drink. "Pass it around," he said, "pass it around." We did.

Each of us tipped his glass to our lips to toast the man who'd brought us all together: sons and daughters and their mates; his wife, sister, nephew; his friends; and at least one who was also close, devoted, and indebted. It was my first taste of alcohol in nearly eighteen months, and fitting that it came at the urging of the one who'd taught me to start discovering personal order.

We were told the doctors wished to move Norman to a higher floor for the night, floor eleven. After seeing it, I thought it looked more like a five-star hotel than a hospital room. Just before they wheeled him to the elevator for the trip up to his suite, he reached for my hand and pulled me toward him. I leaned down and his eyes repeated again all he wanted to say to me. His words were plain, and in his deep, still-vibrant blue pools I could almost see my reflection floating. He said thank you and that, yes, we'd shared some good days, fine mornings bursting with nothing and everything. A thousand really good mornings . . .

"Thank you," I said, tightening my grip. I was worried he'd hear a crack in my voice, so I said it low and close and steady. "Thank *you*, Norman."

TWELVE

The Red Dory

The call came to me at quarter to six that Saturday morning, November 10, 2007. Norman had died, while Stephen sat near him, at four thirty. Stephen had arrived to the hospital late, and as the others left one by one for the night, he stayed on with his dad. It was fitting that those two were together as Norman drifted off, because they were both passionate artists who'd experienced strains with each other. Now they were just dad and son sharing a long night.

I had slept at the apartment in Brooklyn. After the phone call, I went to the living room to be with Norris. She'd made coffee and was surprisingly calm. We had hoped and believed that Norman would still be with us today, but he wasn't. Norris said he was off pestering God for answers about everything. She was, of course, devastated, but she had somehow found a concrete resolve whose pedestal was relief. We both had. There were things to attend to, but nothing seemed to merit rush, and so we sat quietly for a while speaking little. Surprisingly, there was not much to say—so much had already been said and written—and so I looked out at the city across the East River as I sipped my coffee. The sprawl of Lower Manhattan, which dominated the view from the living room, seemed like a painting on glass, one so large you had to turn your head to take it all in.

The phone rang and plans started to formulate. Norman would be transported to Campbell's funeral home, on Eighty-first and Madison, for attendance and then up to Provincetown the next morning for interment two days after that. Norris and I began to gather items to take to the funeral home and when she held up his vest, sweats, and Uggs as she stood in the door to his bedroom, our thoughts immediately synched. There was no question Norman would prefer his usual outfit for this trip, just as he had for all the others. It was a weirdly funny moment, because we knew we were going against the grain of what was probably expected. Nonetheless, the country's greatest author would not like to endure eternity dressed in designer duds. Hell, he could barely endure two hours in them any other time, so why change the program now?

When we went downstairs that morning a photographer was

lurking on the opposite side of the street behind a tree. Norris was still inside the foyer, speaking to a neighbor, so I went over to the man and said I knew I couldn't stop him from taking a picture, but if he came close to, or bothered Mrs. Mailer in any way, I'd hit him. My behavior was alien and inappropriate, and what I said shocked even me as it came out of my mouth. He assured me he had no intention of bothering Norris. Then, he told me, and rightfully so, to chill out. Finally, he promised to stay far away—a promise he kept. I would have kept mine, too, if he hadn't.

As the car snaked across the Brooklyn Bridge toward Manhattan, it struck me that my idiotic threat of violence would likely have made Norman happy. He enjoyed it when I got my anger up—even when that anger was aimed in his direction. So often he accused me of needing to insist everything go smoothly, without any bumps or rough spots. He knew I tried endlessly to avoid trouble or embarrassment or awkward situations. "You're a spoiled darling," he'd say to me, laughing. "I know that because I'm one too. All writers are spoiled darlings!"

Newspapers all over the world put notice of Norman's passing on their front pages. The Sunday *New York Times* began their five-thousand-word coverage not only on the cover but above the fold. Norman was a son of New York, and a man who was admired throughout the world, so the treatment was well deserved. And, frankly, he would have liked that his last hurrah appeared above the fold in the Sunday *Times*. "They got it right!" I can hear him say, hitting the table with thumping triumph. "Ha!"

A friend who flew in from France two days later brought me the November 11 edition of the newspaper *La Liberation*. On the cover was a full-page photograph of Norman with only these words *Un Américain,* and the date. An American. That pretty much summed it up.

Campbell's brought Norman back to Provincetown the day after he passed away. After the outpouring of reverence and gratitude paid by people at the wake in Ptown the following evening, Norris asked everyone who had come to offer their respects to join us at the interment the next day. The burial had initially been scheduled as a strictly private family affair, but Norris changed her mind.

"Pass the word," she told me, the kids, and Mike Lennon. "Everyone should come tomorrow if they want. Norman would want it that way." The next day more than a hundred people gathered at the top of the hill in the Provincetown cemetery. The service was, for the most part, restrained, simple, and uncomplicated—everything Norman was not.

It began shortly after noon when fifty cars streamed from one end of Ptown to the other, slowly and with their lights on. Norris directed that we drag the town a final time, with Norman leading the way. At the circle by the old Provincetown Inn motel, in the West End, each car took turns navigating the rotary. I thought of Norman's assessment of the place he'd written twenty years before—"and the only homage to the Pilgrims is that it is called an inn"—and smiled.

Then it was up to the hill for the last stop of what had been a long, good ride. As I climbed out of my old car and into the sunlight, along with Norman's editor, who rode with me, I thought that the imposing Pilgrim Monument, which dominates our skyline, looked just as commanding as ever. Didn't that looming tower of granite know what had happened? Must it remain as an unsympathetic, enduring spike skewering a bright sky that had also not dimmed for the occasion?

More Provincetowners also walked in clusters up the hill past the hundreds of aged stones—many leaning and battered by centuries of weather—to say farewell to Norman. As we gathered in groups around the spot where Norman would remain, Thomas, now Sarah, came to me and took hold of my hand. She'd made it a point to come bid goodbye along with me, remaining faithful to our partnership and to show her deep reverence for Norman. As we stood together I noticed a woman across the way and to the side of the mourners who was no longer young enough to be wearing the bright, short dress she wore flitted about with peculiar playfulness among us who were dressed in darker clothes. Others noticed her as well, and it was clear from their expressions that no one seemed to know where she was from or who had brought her—but there she was, full of silliness. At first I panicked, praying that Norris, who was seated at the front, wouldn't see the woman's twitching dance. Luckily Norris never did, and only learned about her after the service.

The eccentric woman seemed giddy about attending the service of a celebrity. Considering the celebrity, I found whimsical irony in her unforeseen appearance. She was blond and clearly nuts, and Norman would likely have found something fitting about her presence. Had it been a less solemn kind of gathering, an altogether different occasion, he would have either tossed her out on her insane ear or asked her to co-host. That was the thing about Norman: you never could predict exactly which avenue he'd take when he bumped into crazy. A minute or two into the service, Michael Mailer went to her, escorted her far off to the side, and sat her down on the grass. For me, she haunted the service like someone's leftover drug flashback.

Of those who spoke that day, none broke up the crowd quite like Doris Kearns-Goodwin. In her resonating, reverent voice, she told a story about the last visit Norman made to her home, north of Boston. They'd shared dinner and a fine night of conversation, and in the morning, at breakfast, Norman told Doris she should look into getting a new commode for the guest bathroom. The one in there was old and the water level was too damn high.

"Why?" Doris had asked him.

"My balls got wet when I sat down," he told her.

The crowd roared with laughter.

What a few of us did know was that Norman was knowledgeable about an agreeable lavatory and believed he spoke with utmost authority when he encountered one not up to standard. Whether it was a curse of his ageing body or simply that he liked a quiet room to repair to, he once said about his tendency to linger there, "I *do* get a lot of reading done."

Indeed he did. Poetry, baseball statistics, the *New York Post*,

the *Times* and *Boston Globe*, crossword puzzle books, exposés
on Iraq, the Koran, Nietzsche, Kierkegaard, Goethe, Homer,
Proust, *Mein Kampf*, *The New Testament*, and De Tocqueville's *Democracy in America* were just some of the materials he'd squirreled
away to peruse in his Second Office. I know this because a few
days after he left us I went in there to take inventory. Every
book and paper had been read and reread and scribbled on,
many with pages mercilessly, carelessly folded in half length-
wise to mark his place.

In April 2008, a larger, more public memorial was held for
Norman at Carnegie Hall in Manhattan. That gathering was
attended by thousands, and for two hours people ranging from
Charlie Rose to Joan Didion, Don DeLillo and Tina Brown to
Sean Penn, spoke about the famous Norman Mailer as well as
the private man. Observations flew, one after the other, through
the venerated auditorium about the man who had altered the
literature of our times and taught a new way for Americans to
write and think about politics. Norman had also set the bar
for how we write about boxers in a ring, a great movie star, an
artist, a murderer, Hitler, war, love, women, wives, and even
Christ. Mike Lennon talked about his best friend, and all nine
of Norman's children took Carnegie Hall's stage to tell us what
kind of father Norman had been, how thankful they were that
he was their dad.

When Stephen approached the dais, he assumed the ghostly
guise of his father. He morphed into character, channeling
Norman impeccably. With the imposing, gravelly voice that everyone in attendance recognized, he looked out onto the crowd

in the hallowed hall and declared, after a long, deliberate pause, "Carnegie Hall, huh? Well . . . why the fuck not?"

Some weeks later, sitting at my desk in Provincetown, I thumbed through one of the small notebooks Norman had used. In it he had scribbled, "Wherever my memorial service is held it better have good acoustics or I'm going to come back to haunt you."

Well, we got you Carnegie Hall, pal. Why the fuck not, indeed. . . .

Five days after the party we held after his Provincetown funeral, an event he would have loved to have hosted, no doubt, I came back to the house that was now empty and quiet. Everyone had gone, left to return to their lives. As I sat in the wicker chair in the living room where I'd first chatted with Norris the day I came over to meet with Norman years before, I was overrun by emotional leftovers from the previous five years. They lurked all around me in the form of low sounds and faint smells, books lying on tables and photographs and paintings hanging on walls, artwork that Norman's children and Norris had created. As my eyes drifted over each piece, I was greeted by fine memories of Norman scrutinizing each of them periodically, wholly appreciative that he'd been the primary source of their inspiration.

It was getting chilly on the Cape. Fall was in the deep end of its swing, and the bay looked gray all through the day now. The exception, of course, was the fleeting stretch of evening, when the water and sky glowed sapphire and burgundy, just before the sun dipped down. Norris had dubbed that period the Blue Hour over the years, and during that glimmering period of twilight, one can often see groups of seagulls making their way out toward the open ocean, to rendezvous with incoming fishing boats. I moved into the bar and listened for familiar noises as I looked out across the bay, but I didn't hear any except the clank of the boiler in the basement switching on. The wind sometimes made a reassuring racket as it assaulted the house, but it was not a remarkable sound nor was it one that offered comfort to my ears now, which were straining for echoes of a particular voice, glaringly absent.

Outside on the water I noticed that the red boat the birds visited every year was no longer playing stand-in as a roost. The family of herons had been there only two weeks before, dawdling and at rest in their migration. It seemed to me that their timing had been off this year—but what did I know of birds? I simply missed seeing them now, and wished they were still around. The afternoon before I drove to New York to see Norman they'd been on the boat. I was sorry I didn't take longer that day to watch them, maybe even call to let him know they were there. This was the fourth year we would have spent time in front of the window considering the birds. Norman loved to watch them preen, stretch, and dip now and again into the water for food.

Two weeks later, in early December, we suffered a small Nor'easter. It was not an extraordinary storm, and no trees came down or sea walls ruined, but small changes did occur. The day after it blew over I returned to the house to stand on

Norman's deck to watch the beach, as he often did, and I noticed that something was not quite right. It took me a moment to put my finger on what had changed, but when I finally did, I made a mental note.

For at least five years the small red dory out on the water had held its own through squalls and mean waves that I know humbled more rigid vessels. Now, it was nowhere to be seen. All I could conclude was that it had finally been bested by what amounted to little more than a few angry whips of wind. I was sorry that the herons would have to find another boat on which to rest during their next journey. The red dory had, at last, blown away.

I must remember to tell Norman.

ACKNOWLEDGMENTS

Foremost, I thank Norris Mailer for her love and encouragement over the past many years. Beyond allowing the use of several unpublished passages of Norman's work, she's given me immeasurable support, and that is no small thing. The Mailer children are also in my thoughts as I write this; Susan Mailer, Danielle Mailer, Betsy Mailer, Kate Mailer, Michael Mailer, Stephen Mailer, Matthew Mailer, Maggie Mailer, and John Buffalo Mailer. I am honored to call them friends and respect and value each of them.

I had many around me who were exceptionally helpful during the writing of this book. Astrid Berg supported me in ways I am unable to explain properly. Suffice it to say that without her this book would have taken much longer to come to light—if at all. Sarah Kallisto, my dear friend, often listened to my worries, and I am deeply beholden to her for that. Teddy and Marilyn Rodes exhibited extraordinary patience and faith in me. Those who read various early drafts of the manuscript and gave me serious, fine criticisms, and whom I cannot thank enough, include Rose Kennedy, Michael Tonello, Chip Hamlen, Christina Pabst, Andrew O'Hagan, Chris Busa, Marcene Marcoux, Clarence Walker, Bill and Joann LaVallee, Jim Roby, Eric Mitkus, Suzanne Long, Peggy Phillip, Sue Fox, Alisyn Camerota, Dennis Rhodes, Tony Jacket, Virginia McKenna, Deb Elam, Jonathan Bovee, Marc Lovely, Tom Junod, and Pat Doyle. My editor, Kate Hamill, did a remarkable job keeping me in check, and I thank her profusely for her keen insights and direction. My agent, John W. Wright, is a man whom I admire greatly, and I am proud that he represents me.

And lastly I'd like to thank the countless fans of Norman Mailer and the fine people of Provincetown who, I hope, will appreciate this book.